FLEMISH CITIES EXPLORED

Cover illustration
The palace of the dukes of Brabant in Brussels, destroyed by a fire in 1731. On the brow of the hill to the right is the Nassau Palace, which was demolished in the eighteenth century. The tilting yard in the foreground was redesigned as the Parc de Bruxelles in 1787. Anonymous artist, sixteenth century, Musée Communal, Brussels.

FLEMISH CITIES EXPLORED

BRUGES, GHENT, ANTWERP, MECHELEN AND BRUSSELS

DEREK BLYTH

THE BODLEY HEAD
LONDON

ACKNOWLEDGEMENTS

I would like to thank the following people who offered information, advice, or other kinds of support: Helen Bannatyne, Jill Black, John Chalker, Corinne Hall, Jane Hedley-Prole, Andrew Johnstone, Mary Maclure, C. M. Maclure, Menno Spiering, Guido Waldman and Deborah Whitworth.

A CIP catalogue record for this book is available from
the British Library

ISBN 0 370 31229 5

Printed in Great Britain for
The Bodley Head Ltd
20 Vauxhall Bridge Road
London SW1V 2SA
by Butler & Tanner Ltd,
Frome and London

First published in Great Britain in 1990.

CONTENTS

LIST OF PLATES

LIST OF CREDITS

Plates 1 and *14:* Reproduced by courtesy of College van Burgemeester en Schepenen, Antwerp; copyright Stedelijk Prentenkabinet.

Plate 2: Reproduced by courtesy of the Bildarchiv Preussischer Kulturbesitz, Berlin.

Plates 3, 4, 5, 6, 7 and *9:* Reproduced by courtesy of the College van Burgemeester en Schepenen, Bruges.

Plates 8, 15, 24, 26 and *35:* Taken by the author.

Plate 10: Reproduced by courtesy of the Conservator of the Institut Royal du Patrimoine Artistique; copyright A. C. L. Bruxelles.

Plates 11, 12, and *13:* Reproduced by courtesy of the Stadsarchivaris, Ghent.

Plates 16, 18 and *19:* Reproduced by courtesy of the Burgomeester en Schepenen, Antwerp; copyright Rubenshuis.

Plates 17 and *23:* Reproduced by courtesy of the Director of the Alte Pinakothek, Munich.

Plate 20: Reproduced by courtesy of the Burgomeester en Schepenen, Antwerp; copyright Museum Plantin-Moretus.

Plate 21: Reproduced by courtesy of the Instituto Centrale per il Catalogo e la Documentazione, Rome.

Plate 22: Reproduced by courtesy of the Director of the Koninklijk Museum voor Schone Kunsten, Antwerp.

Plates 25, 27 and 28: Reproduced by courtesy of the Stadsarchivaris, Mechelen.

Plates 29, 31, 32, 33, and *34:* Reproduced by courtesy of the Stadsarchivaris, Brussels. Photographs by Simon Grimberg.

Plate 30: Reproduced by courtesy of The Metropolitan Museum of Art, New York (Robert Lehman Collection), 1975.

LIST OF MAPS

FLANDRIA
MARIS GERMANICI PARS
Milliaria Flandrica parva mediocria & magna
Petrus Kærius cælavit
66

INTRODUCTION

Bruges, Ghent, Antwerp, Mechelen and Brussels are cities that we sometimes glimpse in the background of Flemish paintings. Through an open window behind a Virgin and Child we may see a street of Flemish houses, as in Dirk Bouts' demure *Madonna* in London's National Gallery. At other times we gain only a tantalising glimpse of a city, such as the street that is reflected in a tiny convex mirror in the foreground of Quinten Metsys' *The Money Changer and his Wife* in the Louvre. Or it may be a distant view of spires and gables that we see, as in Roger van der Weyden's *Bladelin Altarpiece* (pl. 2) in Berlin's Dahlem Museum. These paintings may tempt us to visit the Flemish cities, just as Van Gogh's landscapes draw us to Provence, or Canalettos take us to Venice.

We may be disappointed, on arrival, to find that the cities have aged and weathered since they were proudly built of brick and stone many centuries ago. Only in Bruges, and parts of Mechelen and Ghent, do we still find scenes reminiscent of mediaeval Flemish paintings. The cities of Flanders are still beautiful, yet they seem somehow tinged with sadness. They seem to look back wistfully upon the distant golden age when great fortunes were amassed within their walls, and majestic spires and belfries soared above the flat countryside. Bruges, it seems to me, dwells on its

Plate 1 Map of Flanders in 1648

fifteenth-century glories, while Antwerp remembers its heyday in the nineteenth century. This romantic nostalgia gives the cities of Flanders a sad and mellow mood; they are particularly attractive, I think, on misty autumn days, or in winter when the streets are hushed by a blanket of snow. The bright sunshine of a summer's day tends to draw attention to their imperfections, like the wrinkles on the aged face of a once-beautiful film star.

Flanders has been a region of vague and shifting boundaries since it was first settled. It originally encompassed the area of northern Europe ruled by the counts of Flanders, whose power eventually extended over the territory covered by the sixteenth-century map published in Antwerp by the Plantin Press (pl. 2). On this map, Flanders extends from northern France to Zeeland, now part of the Netherlands. Ghent and Bruges are clearly Flemish, but Antwerp, Mechelen and Brussels seem not to be. However, it would be wrong to exclude them from this book, as the boundary of Flanders ceased to exist politically in 1384, and the term Flemish now refers to all the Dutch-speaking provinces of Belgium. Bruges in the province of West Flanders, Ghent in East Flanders, and Antwerp and Mechelen in the province of Antwerp are all Flemish cities by this definition. Brussels, however, is still a borderline case, as its 19 *communes* form a separate bilingual enclave within the province of Brabant. Though now predominantly French-speaking, Brussels has been included in this guide because of its Flemish past, and its museums and galleries filled with treasures of Flemish art.

According to one school of philology, Flanders (Vlaanderen in Dutch) means 'the flooded land'—an apt description for this low-lying area at the delta of the River Scheldt. Like neighbouring Holland, Flanders had to be drained and diked to make it habitable. Holland and Flanders are alike in certain other ways, too; for example, the architectural traditions in both regions are based on brick, as stone is so scarce. However, Flanders straddles the frontier between French and German civilisations, and so has endured a much more turbulent and tragic history than Holland. If Flemish culture sometimes seems to have an edginess and anxiety compared to that of Holland, it is perhaps because Flanders has been, as Collins English Dictionary puts it, the 'scene of many battles in many wars'.

As long ago as 1640, James Howell described Flanders as 'the cockpit of Europe'. Looking again at the sixteenth-century map (pl. 1), we see numerous place names evoking bleak images of war. Outside the walls of Kortrijk (spelt Cortrycke on this map), a Flemish army crushed the French at the Battle of the Golden Spurs in 1302. The *Chronicles of Froissart* tell of a battle 80 years later on a hill near Roosbeke, at which Charles VI of France defeated the Flemish weavers. Not far from Roosbeke, we see the names of many other small Flemish towns that were the scene of horrifying battles in World War I, such as Passendale, Diksmuide, Poperinge and Ypres (Ieper in Dutch and corrupted to Wipers by the British troops).

The tragic history of Flanders began during the waning years of the Roman Empire, when German tribes poured into the northern area of Gallia Belgica, but failed to penetrate the region to the south. This remained populated by the Romanised

Plate 2 Bladelin Altarpiece

Wala, who were protected by a vast forest, the Silva Carbonaria, which at that time extended from the Rhine to the North Sea. Although now much reduced in extent, the forest still extends to the south of Brussels, where it is known as the Forêt de Soignes in French and the Zonienwoud in Dutch. The invisible language frontier that divides present-day Belgium into French-speaking Wallonia and Dutch-speaking Flanders runs through the middle of this thick forest. Driving south of Brussels through the woods, you may notice that the names on signs change from Dutch to French: Brussel becomes Bruxelles, Leuven becomes Louvain. At that point you have crossed the frontier from Flemish Brabant to French Brabant, from German to French civilisation.

A new frontier was drawn across this region by the Treaty of Verdun in 843, under which the Empire of Charlemagne was divided into the Western, Middle and Eastern Kingdoms. The River Scheldt formed the boundary in northern Europe between the Western Kingdom and the Middle Kingdom. The nascent cities of Bruges and Ghent lay to the west of the Scheldt, in the Middle Kingdom, and so became subject to the French king, whereas the cities of Antwerp, Brussels and Mechelen lay to the east, and so were subject to the German king.

In the Early Middle Ages the counts of Flanders gave a distinctive identity to the area of French civilisation west of the Scheldt. To defend the land against the Vikings, Baldwin of the Iron Arm, the first Count of Flanders, built a castle at Bruges in 865 and at Ghent a few years later. His successor, Baldwin II, added to the defences by building city walls around Bruges and Ypres. In the eleventh century, the counts of Flanders gradually conquered the lands to the east of the Scheldt.

At the turn of the eleventh century, the Flemish rulers turned their energies to the Crusades. Count Robert II of Flanders earned himself the title of 'Lance and Sword of Christendom' in the Holy Land, while Count Baldwin IX of Flanders was appointed Emperor of Constantinople in 1204. By the thirteenth century the counts of Flanders had exhausted their military ambitions, and they then devoted their energies to a more peaceful struggle against the North Sea, building dikes to reclaim the marshes and bogs of their flooded land.

In the thirteenth century the Flemish cities of Ypres, Ghent and Bruges grew enormously wealthy from the production of cloth. It was then that the proud belfrys, cloth halls, meat markets and town halls were built. The Flemish cities at this time developed close ties with England, which supplied the high-quality wool demanded by the Flemish weavers. 'All the nations of the world are kept warm by the wool of England made into cloth by the men of Flanders,' wrote Matthew of Westminster. But the wool trade led to a conflict of loyalties during the Hundred Years War. The aristocracy of Flanders remained feudally bound to the French king, whereas the guilds pragmatically supported the English king to safeguard the wool supply. In the late thirteenth century, Edward I of England attempted to protect the Flemish trade by sending an army to repel Philip the Fair of France. But when Edward was forced to withdraw this army to deal with the Scots, the French promptly marched back to reclaim their territories. They were again driven out in 1302 by a Flemish uprising known as the Matins of Bruges. Attempting to regain Flanders soon afterwards, the French knights suffered a humiliating defeat in the Battle of the Golden Spurs.

Upon the death in 1384 of Count Louis de Male, Flanders passed to Philip the Bold, Duke of Burgundy, who married Margaret of Flanders, daughter of Louis de Male, in Ghent in 1369. The Duke of Burgundy thereby inherited the great cities of Flanders and Brabant, including Ghent, Bruges, Mechelen and Antwerp. This meant the end of Flanders as a political entity, and the beginning of the language problem, for the dukes of Burgundy and the nobles at the court spoke only French, whereas the craftsmen and shopkeepers of the Flemish cities spoke Dutch. Hence, in fifteenth-century Flemish portraits, the mottos of the nobles and clergymen are invariably in French.

The Burgundian period was a golden age for the cities of Bruges, Brussels and Ghent. The patronage of the highly cultured dukes and nobles of Burgundy led to an extraordinary blossoming of Flemish art and architecture, symbolised by the fifteenth-century altarpieces of the Flemish

Primitives and the soaring Late Gothic spires of the churches and cathedrals.

Duke Philip the Good, the grandson of Philip the Bold, skilfully expanded the territories of Burgundy during his reign. He did so by ceremonies, contracts and cunning, rather than by military conquest. Having succeeded to Flanders in 1419, he bought Namur in 1421, inherited Brabant, Limburg and Antwerp in 1430, and plotted the fall of Jacqueline of Hainaut in 1433 to acquire Hainaut, Holland and Zeeland. He then bought Luxembourg 10 years later, had his nephew elected Bishop of Liège and, finally, saw his son installed as Bishop of Utrecht. The prosperous feudal states, counties, duchies and lordships acquired by Philip the Good formed the Burgundian Netherlands, an area which corresponds roughly to the present-day states of Belgium, the Netherlands and Luxembourg.

Our knowledge of the Burgundian Netherlands is extremely vivid because the art of painting was then so precise and factual. Works were commissioned by cloth merchants, bankers, jewellers, mariners, butchers, fishmongers, burgomasters and judges. They were hard-headed practical people, interested in cloth, bills, nails, meat, iron, fruit, jewels, spices and shoes. The fifteenth-century Flemish Primitives produced paintings that were as satisfying and well-made as a dolls house. When we look at the works of Jan van Eyck, for example, we hardly notice their form, for we are captivated by the *things* they represent. We notice the grain of the wooden floorboards in the *Arnolfini Wedding Portrait* in London, the individual threads of a frayed carpet in the *Madonna with Canon Van der Paele* in Bruges, the hedgerows in the *Adoration of the Mystic Lamb* in Ghent. We are enthralled by the Flemish Primitives' child-like delight in illusion, deception, ceremonies and hidden secrets.

The death in 1477 of Charles the Bold, the son of Philip the Good, brought an end to the brief and brilliant period of Burgundian rule in the Netherlands. His daughter, Mary of Burgundy, married Maximilian of Austria, later Emperor of Germany. Maximilian's grandson, Charles V, became Emperor of Germany through his father, Philip the Fair, and King of Spain through his mother, Joanna the Mad. The Flemish cities were favourably placed to benefit from the vast wealth generated by the Empire of Charles V. But there was a nagging doubt, a rumour of dissent, at the heart of sixteenth-century Flanders. We see it in the paintings of Hieronymus Bosch, in the crowded Renaissance studies of the Antwerp Mannerists, and even in some of Pieter Bruegel the Elder's works. These artists were no longer at ease with the world; their paintings were a protest, a prophecy of doom, anticipating the religious torments of the sixteenth century. Under Charles V a few unfortunate heretics were burnt; under his son Philip II entire cities were set alight.

The Dutch Revolt against Philip II of Spain split the Burgundian Netherlands in two. The two halves became as irreconcilable as the two Germanies today. The Southern Netherlands (now Belgium) remained staunchly Catholic, whereas the Northern Netherlands (now the Netherlands) turned vehemently Protestant. We may nowadays scarcely be aware of this difference as we travel between Belgium and the Netherlands, for the boundary does not correspond to any natural division. Like the frontier that runs through Germany, it was purely a military demarcation, following the front in 1648, when the Dutch and Spanish signed the Treaty of Münster. The boundary cut indiscriminately across provinces, dividing Brabant and Limburg in two.

There may be no visible frontier between Belgium and the Netherlands, but there are still fundamental cultural differences. From 1579 (when the northern provinces banded themselves together to resist Spanish oppression) until 1713, the Spanish Netherlands was a remote territory of the Spanish Hapsburgs. The great cloth cities and trading ports of Flanders declined into provincial backwaters. Cities that had once astonished travellers such as John Evelyn and Albrecht Dürer with their wealth and their art were now depopulated, aging and enervated. The Protestant weavers, diamond cutters, merchants, bankers and printers had almost all fled to Holland or to England.

The role of the Spanish Netherlands in the seventeenth century was as a bulwark of Catholicism. In the former Northern Netherlands, the

Dutch were rapidly establishing a maritime empire, constructing ships, warehouses, banks, exchanges, weigh houses and arsenals. But in the Spanish Netherlands whatever money was available was devoted to constructing Baroque churches and filling them with paintings, statues, confessionals and pulpits.

In 1713 the Spanish Netherlands passed into the hands of the Austrian Hapsburgs; a remote government in Madrid was replaced by a remote government in Vienna. Initially the Austrians were indifferent to the Netherlands, provoking riots in Brussels, but under the Empress Maria Theresa the economy of the Austrian Netherlands gradually improved.

In 1795 Napoleon's army invaded; a remote government in Vienna was then replaced by a somewhat less remote government in Paris. In the 19 years of French administration that followed, the churches and monasteries of Flanders were again sacked, and art treasures carried off to Paris. French became the official language of the administration, and the population of Flanders became more strongly divided than ever into a French-speaking upper class, and a Dutch-speaking lower class.

After the final defeat of Napoleon at Waterloo in 1815, the Treaty of Vienna created the new state of the United Kingdom of the Netherlands, which briefly reunited the northern and southern Netherlands. This was something of a marriage of convenience, intended to create a strong state to the north-east of France. But the allies had not realised just how incompatible these two countries had become after 236 years of separation. The southern part of the new kingdom was now Catholic and predominantly French-speaking, whereas the northern part was Protestant and Dutch-speaking. Fifteen years later the inevitable split occurred. The south rebelled against the north and, after a brief and rather unspectacular revolution, the state of Belgium was born. In 1831 Prince Léopold of Saxe-Coburg, a favourite uncle of Queen Victoria's, was invited to be King.

The reign of Léopold II, his son, was a period of extraordinary growth and prosperity, fuelled by industrialisation and rampant colonialism. The difference between Belgium and the Netherlands

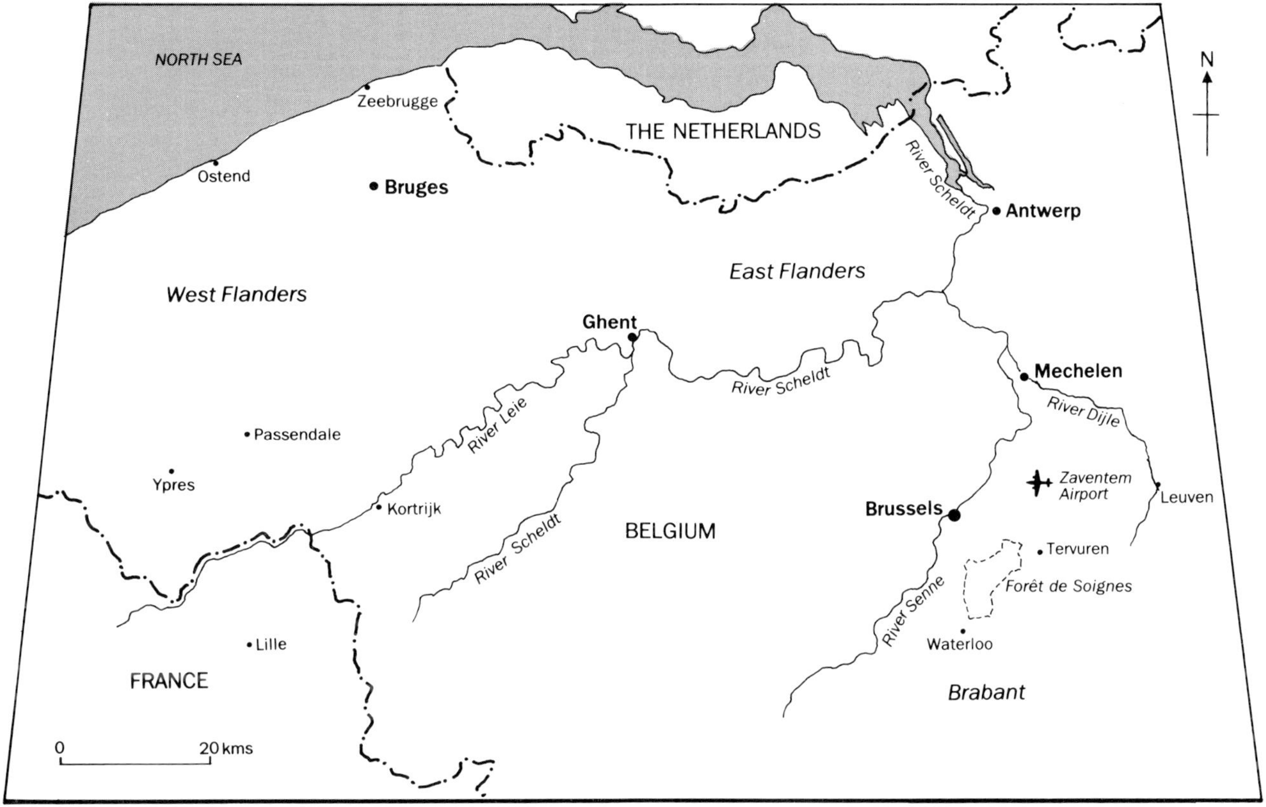
NORTH SEA
Zeebrugge
Ostend
Bruges
THE NETHERLANDS
River Scheldt
Antwerp
N
East Flanders
West Flanders
Ghent
Mechelen
River Scheldt
River Dijle
River Leie
Passendale
Ypres
Zaventem
Airport
Leuven
Kortrijk
Brussels
BELGIUM
River Scheldt
Tervuren
Forêt de Soignes
River Senne
Waterloo
Lille
FRANCE
Brabant
0
20 kms

became even more pronounced in this period. Whereas the cities of Holland even today possess a modest quality, with their neat little houses and precise details, the cities of Belgium, particularly Brussels and Antwerp, were rebuilt on a colossal scale, with echoes of nineteenth-century Paris or even ancient Egypt. If you take a coach tour in Brussels, you will probably be shown one of the largest buildings in the world, the Palais de Justice, whereas on a tour of Amsterdam you are more likely to be shown the smallest house in the city.

World War I marked the end of a golden age in Belgium, as it did in Britain. In 1914 the German army swept through Belgium from the Ardennes. Liège fell six days after the invasion, soon followed by Charleroi, where the French army was defeated, and Mons, where the British army fell back. A few days later Leuven and Brussels were taken, and the government fled to Antwerp. The Belgian army made a final stand behind Antwerp's massive ramparts and advanced forts, supported by a detachment of British troops commanded by Winston Churchill, who had gallantly rushed to the aid of 'plucky little Belgium'. But after 12 days of bombardment Antwerp fell, and the Belgian army retreated to defend a last tiny corner in the north-west of the country, beyond the River Ijzer. The opposing armies then dug a line of trenches across Flanders and, in the years of heavy shelling that followed, many of the mediaeval dikes built by the Counts of Flanders were destroyed, turning Flanders once again into 'the flooded land'.

Because of this war, the names of many Flemish towns such as Passendale and Ypres are laden with sadness, and to talk of Flanders today is to evoke images of war and misery, rather than beautiful Gothic paintings or soaring mediaeval spires. It is unlikely that these painful associations will ever be erased, for the landscape of Flanders is too crowded with regimented military cemeteries. There is even an American military cemetery with the name 'Flanders Field'; it is at Waregem, not far from the site of the Battle of the Golden Spurs, and is commemorated in John McCrae's elegiac poem that begins, 'In Flanders Field the poppies blow,/Between the crosses, row on row'.

The war may be over, but Belgium is still plagued by the old conflict between German and French civilisations. Its population is divided into Flemings, Walloons and a tiny, almost forgotten, enclave of German speakers in the eastern Ardennes. The Flemings, concentrated on the plain of the River Scheldt in the north of the country, are Dutch speaking, although the language they speak is rather old-fashioned compared to the Dutch spoken in the Netherlands. The Walloons, who inhabit the valley of the Meuse to the south, speak French, although it too is rather archaic and quaint. Whether travelling in Flanders, the Dutch-speaking area of Belgium, or in Wallonia, the French-speaking area, it is probably advisable to speak English, which serves as a neutral language throughout the country.

Many of the institutions of the European Communities are now based in Belgium. The significance of a united Europe can best be appreciated in Brussels by visiting the Musée de l'Armée, a vast hall which is filled with the relics of World War I. A five-minute walk through the Parc du Cinquantenaire then brings you to the Berlaymont building, where the 12 states of the European Communities now work together in a sort of harmony which would have seemed unimaginable to a soldier in World War I. The country once described as the cockpit might now be said to be the crucible of Europe.

Bruges

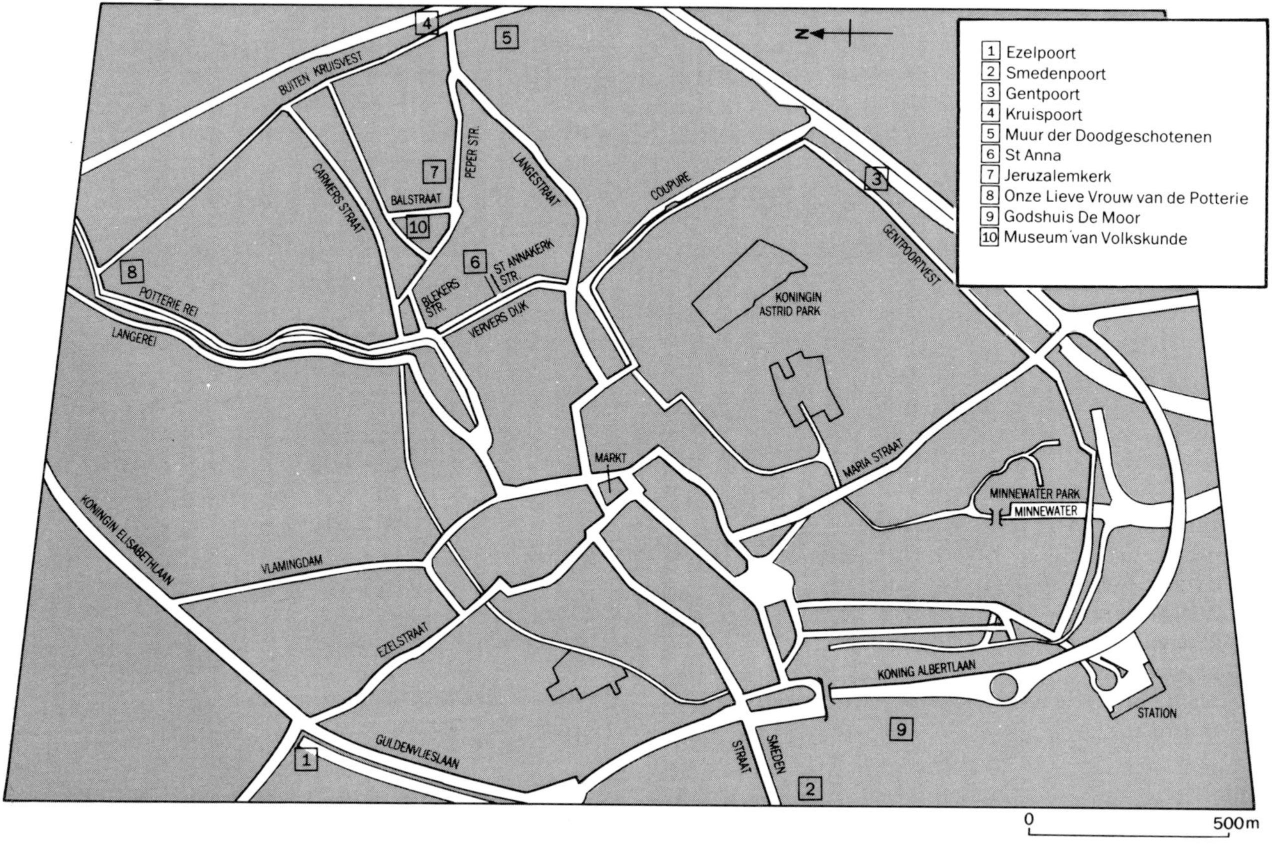

1 Ezelpoort
2 Smedenpoort
3 Gentpoort
4 Kruispoort
5 Muur der Doodgeschotenen
6 St Anna
7 Jeruzalemkerk
8 Onze Lieve Vrouw van de Potterie
9 Godshuis De Moor
10 Museum van Volkskunde
N
BUITEN KRUISVEST
CARMERS STRAAT
PEPER STR.
LANGESTRAAT
BALSTRAAT
COUPURE
GENTPOORTVEST
ST ANNAKERK STR.
BLEKERS STR.
VERVERS DIJK
POTTERIE REI
LANGEREI
KONINGIN ASTRID PARK
MARKT
MARIA STRAAT
MINNEWATER PARK
MINNEWATER
KONINGIN ELISABETHLAAN
VLAMINGDAM
EZELSTRAAT
KONING ALBERTLAAN
STATION
GULDENVLIESLAAN
SMEDEN STRAAT
0
500m

CHAPTER 1: BRUGES

The beautiful old town of Bruges is the ideal starting point for a tour of Flemish cities. Almost nothing disturbs the mediaeval atmosphere of this decayed maritime city, where crumbling brick houses are mirrored in placid canals, and cobbled lanes gently meander past old almshouses. Exploring Bruges we come upon many picturesque spots reminiscent of old Flemish paintings, such as the marvellous view of distant spires from the eastern ramparts above Kruisvest. Bruges is a profoundly mediaeval city, even down to tiny details such as the Gothic letter *b*, the symbol of the city, which appears on everything from museum guard uniforms to the carpets in the town hall. Many of the street corners are watched over by a statue of the Virgin and Child, of which there are about 500 in the old city. Some are very elaborate indeed, such as the wonderful eighteenth-century wooden calvary at the corner of Carmerstraat and Korte Speelmansstraat.

This compact town of some 118,000 inhabitants has a charm that is almost impossible to resist. Even in the sixteenth century, when Bruges had passed its prime, Hadrianus Borlandus, Professor of Rhetoric at Leuven University, wrote: 'The cities of Ghent, Antwerp, Brussels, Leuven and Mechelen are beautiful, but they are nothing in comparison to Bruges.' Disillusioned by the 'air-conditioned nightmare' of American life, Henry Miller was delighted, on a visit to Bruges in 1953, 'to see the world afresh with the eyes of a child'. Much of the joy in visiting Bruges is indeed to rediscover forgotten pleasures, such as meandering down a cobbled lane, listening to the tinkling of a distant carillon, or watching the abstract reflection of a swan on the ruffled surface of a canal.

But a word of warning: not every visitor has been captivated by Bruges. In 1896 Arnold Bennett complained: 'The difference between Bruges and other cities is that in the latter you look about for the picturesque, while in Bruges, assailed on every side by the picturesque, you look curiously for the unpicturesque, and don't find it easily.' Having seen so many of our cities ruined by the 'unpicturesque', we are unlikely to be as pernickety as Bennett, but we may well find that the narrow streets of Bruges are rather too crowded in the summer months. It is advisable to avoid this season if possible, and to visit Bruges in the spring, when the precincts of the Begijnhof are carpeted with daffodils. Better still, visit in the autumn, for the mellow browns and golds of the autumnal trees lining the canals are perfectly in keeping with the sad crumbling beauty of the town.

A settlement existed at Bruges as early as the seventh century, and in 865 Baldwin of the Iron Arm, the first Count of Flanders, built a castle here as protection against Viking raids from the coast. The prosperity of Bruges was founded upon commerce, and from the thirteenth to the fifteenth century it was the principal trading city of northern Europe. Merchants from 17 different European countries settled here, conducting their business in splendid trading houses in the northern quarter of the city.

Wool was the chief commodity traded at Bruges. This formed the basis of the Flemish cloth industry, upon which the prosperity of the region depended. Cloth-making had been important in Flanders since Roman times, when flocks of sheep were introduced to the Scheldt and Leie valleys, and Flemish weavers became renowned throughout Europe for the exceptionally fine quality of their cloth. As demand increased in the eleventh century, wool was imported from England, Scotland and Ireland. The lime soils of the Cotswolds and Yorkshire produced a particularly high-quality wool with long silky fibres ideally suited for weaving the luxury cloth of Flanders. A regulation introduced in Bruges in 1282 stipulated that only cloth made from English wool could be stamped as first class. Scottish wool was stamped second class, while Flemish wool was deemed third class. For many years Bruges was the exclusive market on the Continent for the export of English and Scottish wool, and the merchants who traded here took home Flemish pantiles to roof their houses and Flemish paintings to hang in their chapels. That is why buildings in the Cotswolds and the east coast of Scotland often have such a strong Flemish character.

Bruges also had a large community of Italian merchants from Venice, Lombardy and Tuscany, who shipped fruit, spices and silks. These commodities gave the burghers of this damp northern city a dazzling splendour, causing a French queen visiting Bruges in 1302 to exclaim: 'I imagined myself alone to be queen, but I see hundreds of persons here whose attire vies with my own.'

In the fifteenth century Bruges became an important artistic centre, to which Flemish painters and sculptors flocked in search of commissions. Jan van Eyck settled in Bruges in about 1425, and was later appointed by Philip the Good as court painter, which entitled him to a regular salary. His work for the Duke included several diplomatic missions, as well as two secret assignments whose purpose remains an intriguing mystery. In 1428 Philip the Good commissioned Van Eyck to paint a portrait of Isabella, the daughter of the King of Portugal, whom he intended to marry provided that her looks were satisfactory. They apparently were, and in 1430 Philip married Isabella in a ceremony of unprecedented Burgundian splendour. Fourteen ships brought the Portuguese guests to the port of Sluis and a gargantuan feast was held in the Prinsenhof in Bruges. As part of the wedding celebrations Philip the Good founded the Order of the Golden Fleece. The collar worn by members of this chivalric order was decorated with a sheep pendant, symbolising the vital importance of the wool trade to Flanders. This chain appears frequently in fifteenth-century portraits, on memorial tablets in churches and even on the façade of a building on Jan van Eyckplein.

The last Burgundian festivity in Bruges was the marriage in 1468 of Duke Charles the Bold, son of Philip the Good, to his third wife Margaret of York, sister of Edward IV of England. The fountains of Bruges ran with Burgundian wine shipped north in massive barrels for the occasion, and the streets were decked with decorations designed by the great Flemish artists of the day, including Hans Memling and Hugo van der Goes. After the procession had passed through the streets of Bruges, a banquet was held in the Prinsenhof, at which entertainments were staged, including a motet of singing goats and a model whale which opened to reveal some 40 performers within.

One of the guests in 1468 was William Caxton, who had been a member of the English Nation in Bruges since about 1441. At the time of the wedding he was Governor of the English Merchant Adventurers in the Burgundian Netherlands. Caxton resigned in 1470 to enter the service of Margaret of York, and was sent to Cologne, where he learned the art of printing. On his return to Bruges, he set up a printing press with the help of a local manuscript illuminator named Collaert Mansion. Using type founts probably obtained from a printer in Leuven, Caxton printed *The Recuyell of the Historyes of Troye* at Bruges in 1475, the first printed book in the English language. Caxton produced several other English books in Bruges before returning to London to set up the first printing press there in 1476.

Towards the end of the fifteenth century, Bruges slowly began to decline. The main cause was the silting of the River Zwin, which led to Bruges being cut off from the sea. The city failed to respond to this catastrophe, and in 1505 the Fuggers of Augsburg, the important German banking family, prudently moved their business to Antwerp.

Most of the other trading nations followed the Fuggers and Bruges eventually became a moribund city, so dead indeed that Baedeker's 1905 guide has nothing to say about its history after the sixteenth century. But a curious episode in the seventeenth century suggests that Bruges cannot have been entirely dead; for here the young Charles II of Great Britain spent three years of exile during the rule of Cromwell and the Commonwealth. Together with his brothers Henry and James, and some 200 loyal followers, Charles II lived in Bruges from 1656-9. An entire block of houses on the Hoogstraat was put at the disposal of the exiled king and his retinue. Charles II spent much of his time in the company of the military guilds, and it was at Bruges that he founded the Grenadier Guards.

The rot does seem to have set in by 1786, however, when the British traveller Philip Thicknesse wrote of Bruges: 'When you have seen what this town offers to the notice of a stranger, you will be, as I was, glad to quit it, for the inhabitants (quite the reverse of their neighbours the French) are all shut up within their houses, and a stranger is apt at Bruges, to think himself in a city just depopulated by the plague.'

Frozen in the Middle Ages, Bruges was rediscovered in the nineteenth century by British travellers on their way to view the battlefield of Waterloo. In his *Memorials of a Tour on the Continent* William Wordsworth found in Bruges 'a deeper peace than in deserts found'. Accompanying her brother on this tour in 1820, Dorothy Wordsworth noted in her journal that at Bruges: 'The race of the Great and Powerful by whom the noble public edifices were raised has passed away, yet the attire, the staid motions and the demeanour of the present inhabitants are accordant with the stateliness of former ages.'

The Victorians admired Bruges, as they admired Venice, because of its mediaeval architecture. The High Victorian architect A.W.N. Pugin even sent his son to Bruges to study its Burgundian Gothic architecture. Gradually, a curious colony of British expatriates formed in Bruges; they had their own school in the Engelse Klooster (a convent founded by several British nuns in 1629), they attended services in the Anglican church on Ezelstraat, and could even peruse English newspapers in a reading room established in the former trading house of the Genoese merchants on Vlamingstraat. With typical Victorian zeal, the British expatriates set about rescuing Gothic Bruges from centuries of neglect. When the cathedral tower burned down in 1839, a British resident even provided the necessary funds to construct a new one. Encouraged by the British, local architects in Bruges studiously began to design every new building in Neo-Gothic style. Numerous statues were also erected on the main squares celebrating illustrious citizens, such as Jan Breydel and Pieter de Coninck, who led the successful uprising against the French in 1302, and are commemorated by a statue on Markt.

The publication in 1892 of Georges Rodenbach's novel *Bruges-la-Morte* brought a new type of visitor to Bruges, quite different from the Gothic-minded High Victorians. Set in the silent and deserted streets of Bruges in the dead of winter, this elegiac novel describes the melancholy wanderings of Hughes, a British exile who had come here not to admire the Gothic, but to recover from the untimely death of his wife Ophelia. 'In the silent setting of the water and the deserted streets, the suffering of his heart weighed less heavily on Hughes, the thought of death became more endurable.' The idea of a dead city had an immense appeal to world-weary Europeans, and travellers flocked here from the fashionable coastal resorts of Ostend and Blankenberge to savour its mood of languid decay. The strange and symbolic paintings of Bruges by Fernand Khnopff also capture its melancholy atmosphere. There is even a hint of this in Pamela Hansford Johnson's novel *The Unspeakable Skipton*, recounting the adventures of a languid British exile in Bruges in the 1950s.

Finally the authorities of Bruges decided that the epithet *la-Morte* had to go and they embarked on various imaginative schemes to revitalise the city. In 1958, for example, the city inaugurated a procession to commemorate the marriage of Charles the Bold to Margaret of York. This event, which takes place every five years in August, features processions in splendid Burgundian costumes, although sadly the fountains do not gush Burgundian wine as they did for the wedding in 1468.

The canals of Bruges have also been purged of weeds, an operation that was concluded by the Burgomaster drinking a glass of canal water. As a result of this municipal élan, Bruges is now a booming tourist centre, with numerous new hotels situated in beautiful historic buildings, an abundance of good restaurants, elegant boutiques along Steenstraat, and lively cafés on many of the squares. Since 1949 Bruges has also been home to the College of Europe, which has helped to restore the cosmopolitan atmosphere of the fifteenth century. Nevertheless, if you visit Bruges in the autumn or winter, when most of the tourists have gone home, and many of the hotels and restaurants are closed, you can still savour something of the atmosphere of Bruges-la-Morte, the town which reminded Hughes of Ophelia, 'it, too, being entombed by its stone quays, with the arteries of its canals turned cold when they ceased to beat with the sea's strong pulse.'

Walk 1: The Buildings on Markt and Burg

On this walk we will look at the two great squares of Bruges. We begin on **Markt**, the great market square overlooked by the belfry. It is probably unnecessary to provide directions for getting to Markt, for we are ineluctably drawn towards it by the white stone lantern of the belfry rising above the mossy brick walls and red roofs of Bruges.

Of the many cafés where we might read our way through this walk before setting off, my favourite is **Craenenburg** at Markt 16, a pleasant old-fashioned place with Neo-Gothic stained-glass windows and gleaming brass chandeliers. It stands on the site of a mediaeval house called Craenenburg where in 1488 the citizens of Bruges imprisoned the Archduke Maximilian for four months. To console the Archduke, the captors commissioned the painter Gerard David to paint scenes on the window shutters of the prison. Finally,

Maximilian was released, having promised to respect the rights of the Netherlands Estates, but a few weeks later his father, the Emperor Frederick III, marched into Ghent to wreak vengeance on the rebellious Flemings.

'In the market place of Bruges,' begins Longfellow's poem *The Belfry of Bruges*, 'Stands the Belfry old and brown/Thrice consumed and thrice rebuilt/Still it watches o'er the town.' Begun in the thirteenth century as part of the cloth hall, the **Belfry** rises from the flat, featureless polders of West Flanders as a potent and omnipresent symbol of mediaeval civic pride. Soaring to a height of 83 metres, it is still the first building we see when approaching Bruges by road or rail. Its impact on mediaeval travellers must have been even greater, and its graceful octagonal lantern inspired architects throughout Europe.

But was the belfry perhaps also a symbol of human arrogance and folly? G.K. Chesterton was not enthralled with the edifice, which he described as 'an unnaturally long-necked animal, like a giraffe', built 'in defiance of all decencies of architecture'. This sounds rather like the familiar sour tone of the irascible Englishman abroad, yet perhaps Chesterton was right, for, as Longfellow's poem recalls, the belfry has burned down three times in its history. The original wooden edifice was destroyed after being struck by lightning in 1280 and a new belfry, built of stone, was erected in 1282-96. This is the building we see in the background of paintings by the Master of the Legend of St Lucy in the Groeningemuseum and the St Jacobskerk. In 1483-7 it was crowned with a tall octagonal lantern in Brabant Late Gothic style, which in turn was surmounted by an ornate wooden spire. Six years later, however, the wooden spire burned down after being struck by lightning. It was rebuilt soon afterwards, but was also consumed by fire in 1741, and never rebuilt. The belfry remained flat-topped, and in 1822 was surmounted by the present stone parapet, like a trimming of Bruges lace.

When we climb the 366 steps of the belfry—ideally at the end of our time in Bruges, as then many of the buildings will be recognisable—we will see a room within the tower known as the *secreet comptoir* where the privileges of the city

Bruges

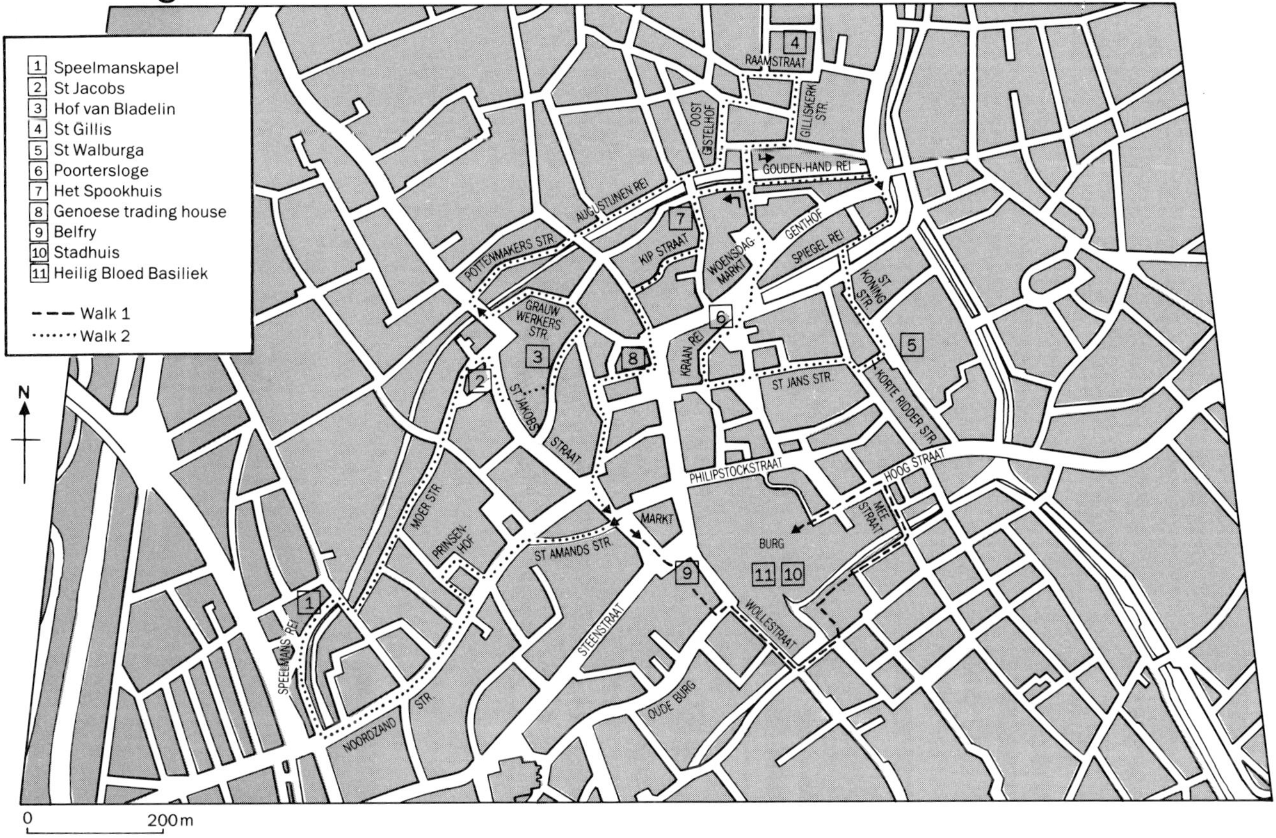

1 Speelmanskapel
2 St Jacobs
3 Hof van Bladelin
4 St Gillis
5 St Walburga
6 Poortersloge
7 Het Spookhuis
8 Genoese trading house
9 Belfry
10 Stadhuis
11 Heilig Bloed Basiliek
Walk 1
Walk 2
N
0
200m
RAAMSTRAAT
GILLISKERK STR.
OOST GISTELHOF
GOUDEN-HAND REI
AUGUSTIJNEN REI
POTTENMAKERS STR.
KIP STRAAT
WOENSDAG-MARKT
GENTHOF
SPIEGEL REI
ST KONING STR
GRAUW WERKERS STR.
KRAAN REI
ST JANS STR.
KORTE RIDDER STR.
ST JAKOBS STRAAT
PHILIPSTOCKSTRAAT
HOOG STRAAT
MEE STRAAT
MARKT
BURG
MOER STR.
PRINSEN-HOF
ST AMANDS STR.
STEENSTRAAT
WOLLESTRAAT
SPEELMANS REI
NOORDZAND STR.
OUDE BURG

were kept. These documents, in which the Counts of Flanders granted certain rights to the city, were so precious that they were kept in a sturdy chest fitted with seven locks. The chest—now displayed in the Stadhuis—was originally kept in the belfry behind an ornate double iron grille made in 1290-2. This was secured by an elaborate lock that could only be opened using nine separate keys, each key held by a different official.

The thirteenth-century **Halle** (Cloth Hall) at the foot of the belfry was modelled on the great cloth hall at Ypres. The wing facing Markt was built first in an Early Gothic style, the long side wings were then added in 1363-5, and finally the rear wing on Oude Burg was built in 1561-6. This last wing has an arcade on the street side that recreates the atmosphere of an Italian Renaissance city, as do the two Renaissance galleries overlooking the courtyard. In the Middle Ages the cloth hall was occupied by stalls piled high with lengths of vivid red and blue cloth, and the courtyard was filled with the smells of exotic spices sold here by Venetian merchants.

The row of buildings opposite Craenenburg stands on the site of a second cloth hall, the Waterhalle, built in the thirteenth century on a bridge over the River Reie to permit boats to unload bales of wool directly into the hall. It was demolished in 1786, and all that now remains are two stone columns standing in the Arentspark. The three public buildings erected on the site of the Waterhalle are interesting examples of Neo-Gothic architectural design. The dazzling white stone edifice in the centre was designed by Louis Delacenserie for the Provincial Government of West Flanders. Delacenserie borrowed several motifs from the fifteenth-century Gruuthuse mansion, such as the parapet and the dormer windows, and modelled the four slender turrets on those of the town hall on Burg. The building to the left was added in the 1920s in the delicate style of Burgundian Gothic. We may nowadays tend to disapprove of architects who slavishly imitate historic styles, but in Bruges (as in Venice) the Neo-Gothic style has played an essential role in preserving the impression of a mediaeval city.

Let us now leave Markt and look at Burg, the other large square in Bruges. On leaving

Craenenburg, we turn right past a curious old dwelling house on the corner of St Amandsstraat. Dating from 1480, it has an octagonal compass which was once attached to a weathervane on the roof. This curiosity was added by the city fathers in 1682 to provide the merchants of Bruges with a convenient method of ascertaining the wind direction. Like many mediaeval buildings in Bruges, the house has a crenellated curtain wall at the top, which is purely decorative, as you can clearly see when you look down from the top of the belfry. This feature was added—in defiance of all decencies of architecture—to give a common dwelling house the appearance of a lofty castellated mansion.

Some rather unusual buildings are to be found in the quiet streets behind the cloth hall. At Oude Burg 7-9 (which can be reached through the courtyard of the cloth hall) there are two curious wooden façades decorated with numerous carved figures. Although they may look mediaeval, these two frontages were erected here by a furniture shop as recently as 1955 and 1961. The decoration of Oude Burg 7, the older building, is a whimsical play on the shop owner's name, De Jonckheere (literally, 'the young man'). Numerous carved wooden figures depict aspects of manhood, and an elaborate frieze illustrates woman's relationship to man, with scenes such as Eve tempting Adam, Delilah cutting Samson's hair, and a wedding feast. The adjoining frontage is decorated in a like manner to illustrate certain aspects of womanhood.

Turning left along Oude Burg and then right down Wollestraat, we come upon two other delightful curiosities. First, at **Wollestraat 9**, a Neo-Gothic building now occupied by a lace shop. The ornate loggia has been decorated in the style of an old Bruges house, and there is a marvellous mechanical model of an aged lace-maker at work. Further down the street, at **Wollestraat 28**, is an interesting house dating from 1634 with three polychrome reliefs, illustrating the siege of Bruges in 1631 by the Protestant army of Frederick Henry of Nassau. A little lane on the opposite side of the street, at Wollestraat 35, leads into a small square with a beautiful view across an old canal to the historic buildings on Burg.

VISCHHANDEL
H MESTDACH DE BAC

Then we cross a bridge with a statue of St John of Nepomuk, the patron saint of bridges, and turn left along Rozenhoedkaai (pl. 3). In the novel *Bruges-la-Morte*, Hughes rented a room overlooking this quay after the death of his young wife. We turn left from here into an intimate square, Huidenvettersplein, once an enclosed courtyard where the guild of tanners carried on their messy trade. Just beyond the square, a little bridge crosses the Reie, to the right of which we see the curious Gothic gables of the fifteenth-century **Brugse Vrije**, designed by Jan van den Poele in 1520-32. A lane, Blinde Ezelstraat, leads directly to Burg from here, passing beneath an attractive Renaissance archway (pl. 4). Tempting though it is to walk down the lane, I propose that we take a slightly longer route to Burg, continuing along Steenhouwersdijk, an attractive canal, then turning left to stand on an old stone bridge dating from

Plate 3 Rozenhoedkaai

Plate 4 Blinde Ezelstraat

1392. Few people ever cross this bridge, yet it offers one of the most enticing views in Bruges. We now continue straight ahead down Meestraat and left on Hoogstraat past the mouldering vestiges of the **Huis de Zeven Torens** (House of the Seven Towers) at number 7, built in 1320 for Wouter Bonin van den Gapere, an official at the court of the Count of Flanders. The house now looks somewhat forlorn, its seven towers having been lopped off in the eighteenth century.

Burg is the site of a castle built in the ninth century by Baldwin of the Iron Arm. All evidence of this fortress has vanished, apart from the plaques marking the sites of its former gates, and the square is now a harmonious ensemble of buildings in Romanesque, Gothic, Renaissance, Baroque and Neo-Gothic styles.

A small park on the north side of Burg contains a few benches where, if the weather is fine, we can sit beneath the chestnut trees to read about the buildings before us. This little park was once the site of the great Carolingian cathedral of St Donaas, which was demolished in 1799 by the French Republicans, leaving in its wake a sad empty space. All that now remains of St Donaaskathedraal is a fragment of the choir, apparently marking the spot where in 1127 Count Charles the Good was murdered. A nineteenth-century statue of Jan van Eyck erected nearby recalls that this artist was buried in the cathedral in 1441.

The oldest building on Burg is the **Heilig Bloed Basiliek** (Basilica of the Holy Blood). Tucked away in a corner on the right of the square, the basilica comprises a lower and upper chapel, both originally Romanesque buildings erected in 1139-49, although the upper chapel was totally rebuilt in Late Gothic style in about 1480. The two curious oriental towers that rise above the chapel are also Late Gothic details. The basilica is entered by a curious bluestone portal designed in 1529-34 by Willem Aerts, which looks Late Gothic from afar, but incorporates some Renaissance details.

Entering the lower chapel, we are plunged unexpectedly into a sombre and austere Romanesque building with massive columns supporting a low vaulted roof, and thick walls pierced by tiny windows. The only decoration in the chapel is a twelfth-century baptism scene on the tympanum of the former entrance. The lower chapel was founded to house a relic of St Basil, the patron saint of masons, seized in the Holy Land during the First Crusade by Count Robert II of Flanders.

A beautiful Late Gothic staircase built in 1523 ascends to the upper chapel. Its interior is a riot of Neo-Gothic murals, which contrast strikingly with the sobriety of the lower chapel. The curious pulpit, carved in the form of a globe, dates from 1728.

A phial said to contain some drops of the blood of Christ is housed behind the altar in this chapel. This relic was presented in 1150 by the King of Jerusalem to Dirk of Alsace, Count of Flanders, as a reward for his bravery during the ill-fated Second Crusade. Every year on the first Monday after the second of May, this holy relic is paraded through the streets of Bruges.

The **Stadhuis** (Town Hall) stands to the left of the Basilica. This dazzling white sandstone building constructed in 1376-1420 inspired many other Flemish Gothic town halls, including those of Ghent, Brussels and Leuven. Among its novel features, the most striking is the display of statues on the façade. Representing Biblical figures, counts, countesses and dukes, the statues were originally gilded and polychromed. A few may even have been coloured by Jan van Eyck. Disapproving of such symbols of aristocratic and religious authority, the French Republicans destroyed all 40 statues in 1792. The lost works were replaced in the nineteenth century, but the stone employed weathered so rapidly that a new set had to be carved in the 1960s. A plan to insert modern sculptures was proposed, but the prototypes provoked such a deluge of complaints that the idea was quickly abandoned.

A bluestone staircase ascends to the magnificent Gothic hall on the first floor of the Stadhuis. This was the setting of many spectacular Burgundian ceremonies, including the first meeting of the States General of the Netherlands in 1464. The hall retains a magnificent timber roof with a curious double vault. The outer ribs of the two vaults spring from corbels decorated with figures representing the twelve months and the four seasons, while the inner ribs meet in a row of pendants bearing bosses decorated with scenes from the Old Testament. The frescoes in this hall are romantic nineteenth-century representations of episodes in the mediaeval history of Bruges.

An adjoining room contains some interesting historical relics including some of the original fourteenth-century consoles carved by Jean de Valenciennes for the façade of the Stadhuis. We also see the original copper plates engraved by Marcus Gerards for the beautiful 1562 plan of Bruges. A fascinating view of Burg painted by Jan Baptist van Meunincxhove shows the scene in the seventeenth century, when several bookshops stood against the wall of the cathedral, and an iron cage on the corner of the Stadhuis protected the curious statue of *Our Lady of the Inkwell*, the patron saint of clerks.

The Stadhuis is linked by a bridge to the delightful **Oude Griffie**. Designed by Jean Wallot in 1535-7 to house the municipal records office, the Oude Griffie is like a chrysalis struggling to shed the old Gothic style and become a truly Renaissance building. There are vestiges of the Gothic style such as the gables and the vertical lines of the building, together with Renaissance elements such as Corinthian columns and friezes of arabesques. The gilded statues represent Justice, flanked by Moses and Aaron.

The final building before us is the **Gerechtshof** (Court of Justice), a stately Baroque edifice of weathered sandstone on the east side of Burg. It was built in the 1720s on the site of the fifteenth-century county hall of the Brugse Vrije (Liberty of Bruges), a body which exercised jurisdiction over an area of Flanders between the Rivers Ijzer and Scheldt, with the exception of Bruges itself.

A little doorway in the corner between the Gerechtshof and the Oude Griffie leads into the **Museum van het Brugse Vrije**. The three rooms of this elusive museum are all that remain of the fifteenth-century county hall of the Brugse Vrije. The former courtroom contains a magnificent chimneypiece carved from dark oak and black marble. Occupying almost the length of a wall, it was commissioned to celebrate the Battle of Pavia in 1525 and the Treaty of Cambrai in 1529, two events which together brought an end to French interference in Flanders.

Various sculptors and carpenters laboured on the work from 1529-31 under the supervision of the Bruges painter Lancelot Blondeel. Like the later Oude Griffie, it is executed in a tentative Renaissance style that retains some hints of the Gothic. The heavy sensuality and robust figures are very much in the spirit of the Flemish Renaissance, but the heraldic emblems are still rather mediaeval in style.

The five virtually life-size figures were carved from oak by Guyot de Beaugrant. The central figure in the composition is Charles V, whose robust policies finally persuaded François I of France to renounce his claims on Flanders. The two figures to the left of Charles V are his paternal grandparents, Maximilian of Austria (the Archduke imprisoned in Craenenburg), and Mary of Burgundy (who is buried in Onze-Lieve-Vrouwekerk in Bruges). To the right of Charles V are his maternal grandparents, Ferdinand of Aragon and Isabella of Castile. Partly concealed by Charles V's cloak are portrait medallions of his parents, Philip the Fair and Joanna the Mad. Above, but virtually invisible, are two other medallions. One honours Charles de Lannoy, the general who led Charles V's army to victory at the Battle of Pavia; the other contains a portrait of Margaret of Austria, Charles V's aunt, whose efforts led to the Treaty of Cambrai. A further two medallions, borne aloft by putti, contain portraits of François I of France and Eleonora of Austria, a sister of Charles V who married François under the terms of the Treaty of Cambrai.

The alabaster frieze on the mantelpiece is decorated with four scenes from the story of Susanna. While bathing in her garden, the naked Susanna (seen in the first scene) is surprised by two old men who threaten to bring a charge of adultery against her if she refuses their advances. Susanna does refuse and in the second scene we see her in the courtroom facing the false accusation. In the third scene, just before she is sentenced to death, the old men are cross-examined by Daniel, and proved to be lying. Susanna is acquitted and, in the final scene, the two old men are stoned to death.

Now that we know a little more about the buildings on Burg, let us explore some or all of them. Afterwards, we might stop in a café, such as

Garre, an attractive old Flemish tavern hidden down a narrow passage between two lace shops on Breidelstraat. For lunch or dinner in this neighbourhood, I recommend 't Dreveken at Huidenvettersplein 10, overlooking the canal. The restaurant occupies the former guild house of the tanners, which was rebuilt in Baroque style in 1680. The menu lists several tempting Flemish dishes, such as rabbit with plums, Flemish stew, and chicken in Rodenbach beer. In the afternoons 't Dreveken also serves coffee, home-made cakes, and excellent pancakes. Another reliable restaurant nearby is Malpertuus at Eiermarkt 9, a traditional Flemish restaurant with an attractive cellar that once belonged to a sixteenth-century monastery.

Walk 2: The Merchants' City

In the fourteenth and fifteenth centuries Bruges teemed with foreign merchants who congregated in the dense tangle of narrow streets and interconnected squares to the north of Markt. Some 17 different nations were once represented in Bruges, each with its own splendid trading house built in ornate Gothic style. Most traces of this early Common Market have vanished and often all that remains to remind us of a nation's presence in Bruges is the name of a street or a square. Engelsestraat, for example, was where the English Merchant Adventurers built a weigh house, while Biskajersplein recalls the Basque merchants' trading house which once stood here. Only a handful of mercantile buildings survive, such as the inn on Vlamingstraat where Spanish and Italian merchants met, the trading house of the Genoese merchants nearby, the Medici representative's house on Naaldenstraat, and the remnants of the trading houses of the Spanish merchants and the Hanseatic League. Although most of the buildings have disappeared, the street pattern is still much as it was when Caxton, Arnolfini and Portinari traded here in the fifteenth century. The warren of narrow, crooked lanes is strikingly similar to that of the City of London. However, the scale of London's mercantile quarter has changed utterly, whereas that of Bruges has remained constant, so that here we obtain a rare glimpse of the urban environment in which the modern European economy developed.

Our walk (*see page 21 for map*) in the mediaeval mercantile quarter of Bruges is not a lengthy one, and three hours should suffice to see all the sights. The irregular street plan of this quarter forces us to trace a somewhat winding peregrination, which may be rather difficult to follow, but to lose one's way in this area is not entirely undesirable, as almost every lane contains an interesting detail or an unexpected glimpse of a distant tower.

Let us begin by setting off down St Amandsstraat, where we pass several convivial bistros. In the fifteenth century, many splendid processions passed down this street, for it lay on the route between the Prinsenhof and the old cathedral on Burg. Turning left along Noordzandstraat, we soon pass on the right a street bearing the name Prinsenhof. The small and rather drab square to which this street leads was once the courtyard of the **Prinsenhof**, a magnificent palace begun by Philip the Good in 1429. The Prinsenhof was the scene of two extraordinary Burgundian banquets; the first at the wedding of Philip the Good and Isabella of Portugal in 1430, and the second 38 years later at the wedding of Charles the Bold and Margaret of York. It was also here that Philip the Fair was born to Mary of Burgundy in 1479. The age of the Burgundians came to a sad symbolic end in the Prinsenhof in 1482, when Mary died here after falling from her horse in the woods near Wijnendaele.

Thomas More twice lodged in the Prinsenhof while on diplomatic missions to the court of Charles V on behalf of Henry VIII. On his first visit here in 1515, he met his old friend Erasmus and took time off from his duties to travel with him to Antwerp. Inspired partly by conversations with Erasmus and other Flemish humanists, More then began writing *Utopia*. Six years later, he met Erasmus again in Bruges, where they parted for the last time.

Following Noordzandstraat, then turning right along Speelmansrei, we come upon a delightful little chapel, the **Speelmanskapel** (Minstrels' Chapel), founded in 1421 by the guild of minstrels, whose members enjoyed the exclusive right to play at weddings and feasts in the city.

Standing on the nearby bridge and looking northwards along the Reie, we see the squat tower of the **St Jacobskerk**, which can be reached by turning down Moerstraat. The St Jacobskerk was originally a simple thirteenth-century church. Serving as the parish church of the mercantile community, it expanded rapidly in the fifteenth century, when its two Late Gothic aisles were added.

So many paintings are hung on the walls of St Jacob's that it now looks more like an art gallery than a church. Look out in particular for the triptych of the *Legend of St Lucy*, painted in 1480 by the anonymous Bruges artist known as the Master of the Legend of St Lucy. We see Lucy in the left panel giving away her possessions to the poor, while a group of lean beggars look on. In the middle panel her fiancé, enraged at being cheated of Lucy's dowry, accuses her before the Roman magistrate of being a Christian. Lucy is sentenced to a life of prostitution, but divine intervention comes to her aid and in the final panel we see the brothel-keepers attempting unsuccessfully to drag her away using two oxen. In the background of this panel, we see the familiar spires of Bruges, including the belfry which at the date of this painting was still without its Late Gothic lantern.

The loveliest chapel in Bruges is found in St Jacob's, tucked into a corner to the right of the choir. It was built in 1516-18 by Ferry de Gros, Treasurer of the Order of the Golden Fleece. The polychrome mausoleum in this chapel was probably commissioned by Ferry de Gros after the death in 1521 of his first wife. Her recumbent effigy lies on the top tier next to Ferry de Gros. A difficult problem of etiquette was posed in 1530 when de Gros' second wife predeceased him. Simply to have forgotten her would have been unthinkably disloyal for a knight whose motto, repeated many times in the chapel, was '*Tout pour estre toujours lealle*'. The chivalrous de Gros therefore had a lower shelf added to the mausoleum, which bears the reclining figure of his second wife. What better demonstrations could there be of his pledge 'All to be always loyal'? The chapel also contains a small enamelled terracotta medallion of the Virgin and Child; this attractive Renaissance work attributed to the Della Robbia workshop was probably brought to Bruges in the fifteenth century by a Florentine banker.

The St Jacobskerk also contains mementoes of the Spanish mercantile community in Bruges. A chapel off the south aisle contains a brass memorial dated 1577 to the memory of Don Francisco de Lapuebla and his wife, while a chapel in the south aisle contains a memorial of 1616 to Don Pedro de Valencia and his wife, both looking rather stout and warmly wrapped in furs.

On leaving St Jacob's, we will find a lane on the north side of the church, at Moerstraat 6-16. At the foot of the lane is an unexpected little group of fifteenth-century almshouses overlooking the placid Reie. From this delightful spot, we now proceed into the heart of the old commercial quarter by turning right along St Jacobsstraat, and left down a lane called Botermarkt (Butter Market). It faces the Hotel Navarra, a handsome town house built in the seventeenth century by Juan de Peralta, consul of Navarre. The attractive round tower we glimpse as we walk down Botermarkt is a relic of the Hof van Gistel, a splendid town house built in 1444 by Antoine de Bourbon, Duke of Vendôme. It was later owned by Jean de Matance of Burgos, who headed the Spanish community in Bruges.

Our next destination is the **Hof van Bladelin**, a magnificent town house at Naaldenstraat 16, which we reach by turning left beyond the Gothic arch at the end of Botermarkt. The house was built in 1451 for Pieter Bladelin, who is portrayed kneeling before the Virgin in a striking Neo-Gothic polychrome sculpture above the entrance. This decoration, which relieves an otherwise blank wall, was the happy invention of Louis Delacenserie in 1892.

Pieter Bladelin was Philip the Good's Councillor and Treasurer of the Order of the Golden Fleece. Within the courtyard is an arcade with two interesting carved stone consoles on which the ribs rest. They are decorated with scenes alluding to Bladelin's duties: one has the figures of a woman and a dog, both conventional symbols of fidelity; the other illustrates the curious story of St Alphège of Canterbury. Kidnapped by the Danes in 1011, Alphège refused to pay the ransom demanded by his captors because it would have depleted funds set aside for the needy. He was finally killed by the Danes in 1012 during a drunken feast when they pelted him to death with animal bones.

Bladelin was one of the richest men in the Burgundian Netherlands, and in 1448 he and his wife, Margaret van Vagewiere, embarked on an ambitious project to establish a new town, Middelburg, on reclaimed land to the north-east of Bruges. The town, taking its name from the Cistercian abbey of Middelburg on whose lands it was built, is the only example in the Low Countries of a mediaeval town created by private wealth. A castle was built by Bladelin in 1448 and the town completed a mere six years later. Middelburg had its own walls and was even granted privileges, but today all that remains of it is the church. The silting of the River Zwin was as disastrous for Middelburg as for Bruges, and the site of Bladelin's vanished settlement is now occupied by a cluster of farmhouses.

The *Bladelin Altarpiece* in Berlin's Dahlem Museum (pl. 2) offers an intriguing glimpse of this vanished Flemish town. Pieter Bladelin commissioned this work from Roger van der Weyden to hang in the new church at Middelburg. Painted in 1452, it includes a distant view of Middelburg in the centre panel, and an attractive portrait of Pieter Bladelin at prayer.

Bladelin's house in Bruges was later owned by the Medicis, the powerful Florentine banking family. Cosimo the Elder sent a bank agent to Bruges in 1439, and in 1466 his son, the afflicted Piero the Gouty, bought the Hof van Bladelin to serve as a bank and residence for the Medicis' agent. Beneath the arcade on the street side of the courtyard are several tiny details added to the house while it was in the hands of the Medicis. The ribs spring from consoles bearing the symbol of three feathers passing through a ring—the emblem of Lorenzo the Magnificent, Piero's son. Following the ribs upwards, we come upon bosses decorated with seven red balls surrounded by a garland adorned with feathers and rings, another Medici device. But the most interesting features are the two Renaissance medallions attached to the wall facing into the courtyard. Decorated with the busts of Lorenzo the Magnificent and Clarice Orsini, they were probably carved to celebrate their marriage in 1469.

Tomaso Portinari represented the Medicis in Bruges from 1473-97, almost bankrupting his principals at one point by rashly lending money to Charles the Bold to finance his military adventures. True to the Medici spirit, Portinari was also a generous patron of the arts and in about 1474 he commissioned Hugo van der Goes to paint an altarpiece of the Nativity to hang in the Portinari family's chapel in the church of Santa Maria Novella in Florence. This extraordinary work is now in the Uffizi Gallery.

A remarkable swashbuckling adventure befell an altarpiece which a previous Medici agent, Angelo Tani, had commissioned from Hans Memling. In 1473 the altarpiece was taken to the port of Damme and loaded into the hold of a ship belonging to Portinari, and bound for Tuscany. But the ship was attacked and captured by the pirate Paul Benecke off the coast of England and taken to Benecke's home town of Danzig, where the booty of cloth, furs and spices was unloaded. Memling's painting—an uncharacteristically gloomy depiction of the Last Judgement—apparently caused quite a stir in the northern seaport because of its numerous naked figures. The altarpiece never did reach its destination, and it now hangs in a church in Gdansk.

If we now continue along Naaldenstraat and turn left up Grauwwerkersstraat, we come out again on the quayside. Crossing the bridge and turning right down Pottenmakersstraat we lose sight of the canal briefly, but meet it again at the

Vlamingbrug. Standing on this ancient bridge, we can see a delightful oriel window overlooking the canal, at Vlamingstraat 100. This ornate detail, an intricate example of Flemish Late Gothic brickwork, was commissioned in 1514 by the goldsmith Herman van Oudvelde. During a recent restoration, four tiny chimneys were discovered in the ceiling, suggesting that the goldsmith's workshop was located in this bay window.

Augustijnenrei, down which we now walk, is one of the most attractive quays in Bruges. On the far side of the canal are fragments of the first city wall, built in the twelfth century. Ahead of us lies the oldest bridge in Bruges, a handsome three-arched stone bridge known as the **Augustijnenbrug**, built in 1391 to provide the friars from a nearby Augustinian monastery with a convenient crossing into the city. It is one of several old bridges in Bruges with stone benches set into the parapet, where mediaeval merchants displayed their goods on fine days.

The quay we have been following comes to an end at the idyllically situated Hotel Ter Brughe and we have to head up Oost Gistelhof. A confusing tangle of quiet lanes leads us now to the **St Gilliskerk**. Turning right at the end of Oost Gistelhof along Sterstraat, left down Schottinnenstraat and then right along Lange Raamstraat is the simplest route to follow. The parish church of St Gillis has a similar history to St Jacob's. Begun in the thirteenth century as a simple aisleless church, it was converted in 1462-79 to a hall church by the addition of two aisles equal in height to the nave. This church is the only one in Bruges still roofed with a wooden barrel vault.

Several Flemish painters lived in the parish of St Gillis in the fifteenth and sixteenth centuries. Hans Memling, who owned three houses in the neighbourhood, and an atelier on Jan Miraelstraat, was buried in St Gillis in 1494. The Renaissance artist Lancelot Blondeel was also buried here in 1561, though the tombs of both artists have vanished.

If we now walk down Gilliskerkstraat we come to Gouden Handstraat, where Jan van Eyck lived with his wife Margaretha. Turning right here, then left down Torenbrug, we return to the canal we have been following since the Speelmanskapel.

Once over the bridge, we turn left and follow Gouden Handrei, a beautiful cobbled quay that leads to the broad main canal of Bruges. This canal once flowed from the Dampoort to Markt, but now disappears underground at Jan van Eyckplein.

Spiegelrei, which bends around to the right, brings us to the imposing fourteenth-century Koningsbrug. From this stone humpback bridge we obtain an impressive view down to Jan van Eyckplein. Perhaps we recognise there the **Poortersloge**, a Late Gothic building with a beautiful slender spire, which appears in the background of several paintings in the museums of Bruges, such as Gerard David's *Judgement of Cambyses* in the Groeninge. The Neoclassical school overlooking the bridge, at Spiegelrei 13, stands on the site of the trading house of the English Merchant Adventurers.

Let us now cross the bridge and venture down St Koningstraat to the **St Walburgakerk**. Begun in 1619, this is one of several Baroque churches in Flanders built by the Jesuit architect Peter Huyssens in the style of the Gesù church in Rome; there are others in Ghent and Antwerp. The interior of St Walburga illustrates the Jesuit fondness for opulent Baroque furnishings. The pulpit, designed by Artus Quellinus of Antwerp in 1667-9, is particularly spectacular.

By now following Korte Ridderstraat, then St Jansstraat, we come to St Jansplein, the first of a series of small squares which we will now explore. Dominating the square is the **Huis de Crone**, at Wijnzakstraat 2, a tall Late Gothic house built in the late fifteenth century. The four bays of the façade are defined by very tall Gothic niches which tend to create an exaggerated sense of height. The lofty and precarious chimney stacks continue this upward movement yet further.

A few steps further brings us to **Kraanplaats**, where a large municipal crane stood in the Middle Ages. This square appears in the background of Memling's *Altarpiece of St John the Baptist and St John the Evangelist* in the Memlingmuseum. Kraanrei, which we follow as it curves northwards, was once a canalside quay, and leads into Biskajersplein, where the trading house of the Basque merchants once stood.

At Jan van Eyckplein 1, just north of here, is the

Tolhuis, an impressive sandstone building erected in 1477 in Late Gothic style. Tolls were levied here on goods shipped inland from Bruges. Above the entrance, we see the splendid coat of arms of Peter of Luxembourg, who inherited the right to levy tolls, probably through marriage. Notice the chain of the Order of the Golden Fleece, which Peter of Luxembourg has proudly added to his coat of arms.

The very narrow Late Gothic building to the left of the toll house belonged to the guild of stevedores. Its ornate sandstone decoration is influenced by the Flamboyant Gothic architecture of Brabant.

Passing a statue of Jan van Eyck erected in 1879, we head right up Genthof and left into **Woensdagmarkt**, where a statue of Memling was placed in 1871. Crossing this quiet square and continuing north, we enter the small **Oosterlingenplein**. In 1478, the Hanseatic merchants commissioned Jan van der Poele to build a magnificent trading house

Plate 5 Oosterlingenhuis

on this square. A seventeenth-century engraving (pl. 5) shows the splendid Late Gothic building occupied by the energetic German merchants, who shipped fur and grain from the Baltic, beer from Bremen and Hamburg, and wines from the Rhineland. The crenellated main building is still standing, although it has been drastically altered over the centuries. The small building to the rear has also survived in a modified form. We may indeed be staying in this building, as German merchants once did, for it now houses the attractive Hotel Bryghia. Above the hotel entrance, we can still see a double-headed eagle, the sign under which the German merchants traded.

If we turn left along Spaanse Loskaai and left again down Spanjaardstraat, we come upon the last vestiges of the Spanish mercantile community. The main goods unloaded on **Spaanse Loskaai**, the Spanish Quay, were wool, hides and fruit. Spanish merchants remained in Bruges long after the Germans, English and Italians had resettled in Antwerp, which is why at Spanjaardstraat 16 we find a seventeenth-century Renaissance portal built for the Spanish merchant De la Torre. The house on the opposite side of the street at number 17 has two names: **Den Noodt Gods** (Divine Providence) and **Het Spookhuis** (The Haunted House). It was built in 1616 by the Spanish merchant Francisco de Peralta, who opted for a rather outmoded Late Gothic town house, albeit with a Renaissance portal.

The house at **Spanjaardstraat 9** was owned in the sixteenth century by Gonzalez d'Aguilera. Ignatius Loyola, the founder of the Jesuit order, spent his summer vacations here from 1528-30 while studying at the Sorbonne in Paris. On his visits to Bruges, Loyola befriended the Spanish humanist Juan Luis Vives, whose statue stands behind the Gruuthusemuseum.

Let us now walk down Kipstraat, an attractive lane below the walls of a Jesuit church built in the nineteenth century. As we near the end of the lane, we see the peculiar façade of a Late Gothic house at **Vlamingstraat 51**. It was built for the goldsmith Jacob Cnoop, whose daughter married Gerard David. Cnoop's house has perhaps the most eccentric top in Bruges, consisting of a bulbous protuberance decorated with eight crockets and a pinnacle, and flanked by two tiny triangular gables.

We now head left down Vlamingstraat towards Markt, crossing a square called Beursplein which once formed the heart of Bruges' mercantile quarter. If we stand roughly opposite the **Stadsschouwburg** (Municipal Theatre) and look north, we will see what remains of the square depicted in the seventeenth-century engraving by Sanderus (pl. 6). The square was named by Sanderus the Byrsa Brugensis, from which is derived *bourse* in French and *beurs* in Dutch as the name for a stock exchange. The usage, based on the Latin *bursa* (a purse), originated in Bruges in the thirteenth century, when Spanish and Italian merchants met to carry on business here at an inn with a sign showing three purses. The family that ran the inn later assumed the name Van den Beurse.

Nothing now remains of the original inn, but a later building, known as the **Huize ter Buerze**, built in 1453 as a bank and dwelling house, has been recently restored by the Bank van Roeselare en West Vlaanderen. We see it on the engraving (pl. 6), to the left of the house with the step gable.

The mediaeval Italian merchants conducted much of their business on this square. Venetian merchants were the first to establish a trading house here, buying a house named Ten Ouder Beurse in 1379, where they dealt in exotic and costly goods such as silk, velvet, spices and fruit. Their trading house—the building with the step gable in the engraving—was demolished in 1965 when Vlamingstraat was widened.

The merchants of Florence later erected a splendid turreted trading house next to the Venetians. This building, identified on the engraving as the Domus Florentinorum (House of the Florentines), has also vanished, and all there is to remind us of the Florentine merchants is a plaque on the side wall of Academiestraat 1, which quotes a verse from Dante's *Inferno* comparing a topographical detail of Hell to the dike erected by the Flemings between Bruges and Wissant (a town to the west of Calais). Dante probably heard about

Plate 6 Beursplein

Domus Genue nsium
Domus Florentin orum
BYRSA BRUGENSIS

this impressive fourteenth-century dike from Italian mariners who had visited Bruges or Wissant.

A third trading house was built on this square in 1399 by the merchants of Genoa, who shipped fruit, spices, silver, gold, gems, furs and alum to Bruges. Alum was an important compound used in Flanders to dye cloth and dress leather. The Genoese house is the only mediaeval trading house in Bruges to have survived intact, although it has been somewhat modified over the centuries, as we can see if we compare the crenellated building labelled Domus Genuensium (House of the Genoese) on the engraving, with the façade at Vlamingstraat 33. The **Genoese trading house** is, as we can see, a most extraordinary building, faced with a beautiful and costly honey-coloured sandstone from the Balegem quarries near Ghent. The house is entered by an ornate Late Gothic portal with a relief above depicting St George, the patron saint of Genoa, slaying the dragon. The first floor had pointed Gothic windows rather like a chapel, while the upper floor was originally a crenellated curtain wall.

After the Genoese merchants moved their business to Antwerp in 1516, the building was used as the cloth hall of the serge weavers. The iron sign we see bearing the name 'Saaihalle' (Serge Hall) is a reminder of this. In 1720 the Genoese trading house assumed a rather bizarre appearance when its crenellated curtain wall was replaced by a bell gable, proving how inessential the former decoration had been. To add to the strangeness of this building, the bell gable was pierced by a pointed Gothic window.

In the early twentieth century, the Genoese trading house attained a zenith of eccentricity (pl. 7). The building, now with a door and window added at street level, was occupied by a café and hotel. The walls are plastered with miscellaneous advertisements offering 'Rooms', 'Steaks at all Hours' and 'Fish and Herring Stew'. When Baedeker's 1905 guide was published, the English Reading Room was here, and in the early days of silent films a cinema was located in the building. Now it has been fastidiously restored, and all traces of these former uses have, alas, been completely erased.

We now turn right down Adriaan Willaertstraat, then left into Kuipersstraat, there coming upon another Gothic curiosity. Number 23, known as the **Zwart Huis** (Black House), is a tall, blackened Gothic gable built at the end of the fifteenth century. It now houses a three-screen cinema complex named Gulden Vlies (Golden Fleece).

Plate 7 Genoese trading house

Walk 3: The Groeninge and Memling Museums

The object of this walk is to explore the two magnificent collections of paintings at the Groeningemuseum and the Memlingmuseum. These museums contain splendid mediaeval works by Flemish Primitives such as Jan van Eyck, Hans Memling, Petrus Christus and Gerard David. These artists worked in mediaeval Bruges for wealthy patrons such as city officials, hospice governors and foreign merchants, and their works depict in astonishing detail the magnificent buildings and sumptuous costumes of the Burgundian age. As each of the collections is worth at least two hours of our time, an entire day should be set aside for the walk.

Try to be at the Groeningemuseum when it opens in the morning, for only then is it possible to enjoy the extraordinary impact of the *Madonna with Canon Van der Paele* by Jan van Eyck, which catches our eye immediately we enter room 1. Although painted some five centuries ago, it is still a fascinating and exciting work. We may have seen reproductions before coming to Bruges, but no photograph can ever convey the remarkable depth and texture of objects in the painting. Van Eyck achieved this result by a painstaking technique of painting with oil and varnish in multiple layers.

The altarpiece was commissioned in about 1436 by Canon Van der Paele and originally hung in Van der Paele's chapel in the old cathedral on Burg. It is now displayed against a wall of white Flemish stone to recreate as far as possible its original setting. The painting depicts the Virgin and Child in the choir of an unidentified Romanesque church. They are flanked by Canon Van der Paele with his patron, St George, to the right, and St Donatian, the patron saint of the old cathedral, to the left. The composition is rather conventional and the Madonna not particularly beautiful, but the truly thrilling quality of this work is the

Bruges

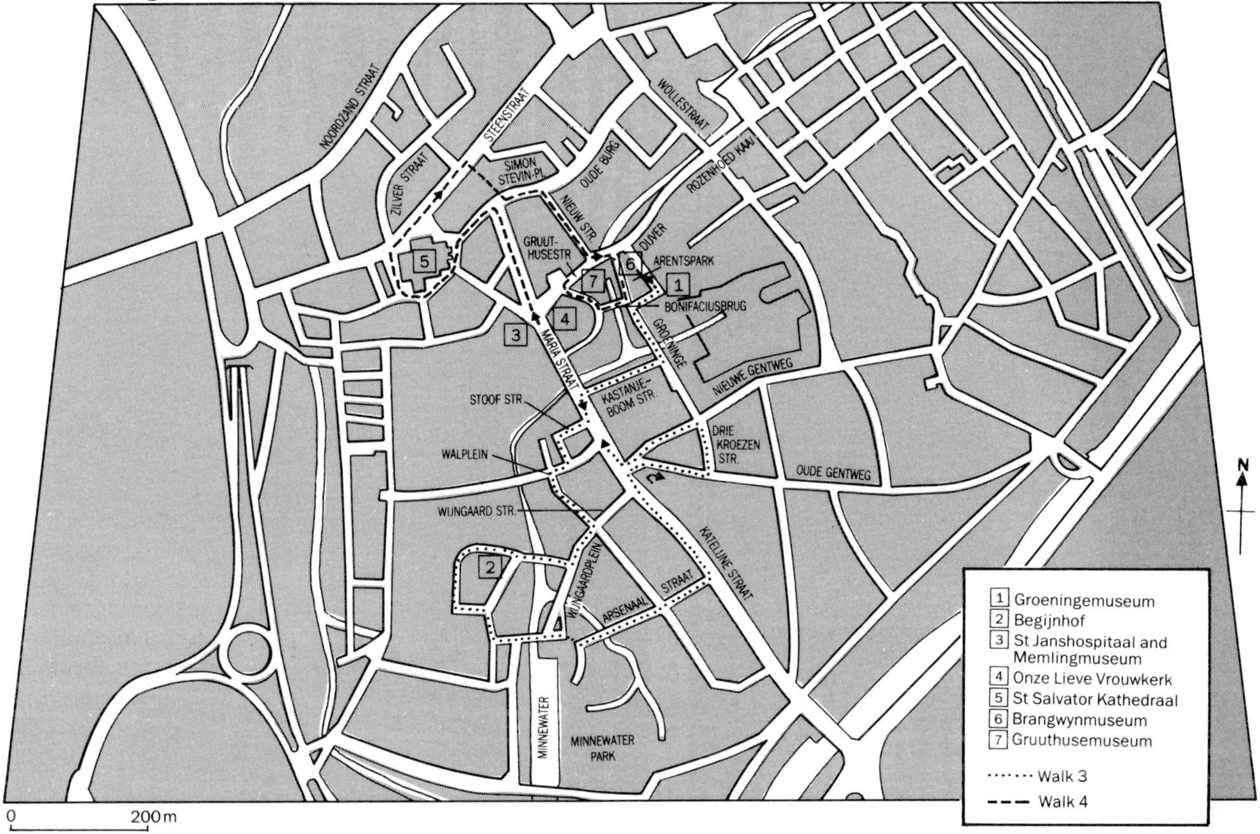

NOORDZAND STRAAT
STEENSTRAAT
WOLLESTRAAT
ZILVER STRAAT
SIMON STEVIN-PL
OUDE BURG
ROZENHOED KAAI
NIEUW STR.
DIJVER
GRUUT-HUSESTR
ARENTSPARK
BONIFACIUSBRUG
GROENINGE
MARIA STRAAT
NIEUWE GENTWEG
STOOF STR.
KASTANJE-BOOM STR.
DRIE KROEZEN STR.
WALPLEIN
OUDE GENTWEG
WIJNGAARD STR.
WIJNGAARDPLEIN
KATELIJNE STRAAT
ARSENAAL STRAAT
MINNEWATER
MINNEWATER PARK
N
0 200 m
1 Groeningemuseum
2 Begijnhof
3 St Janshospitaal and Memlingmuseum
4 Onze Lieve Vrouwkerk
5 St Salvator Kathedraal
6 Brangwynmuseum
7 Gruuthusemuseum
Walk 3
Walk 4

flawless realism of details such as the tiled floor of the church, the folds of the Madonna's vivid red cloak, and the slightly frayed edge of the thick carpet in the foreground. The portrait of the aged Canon Van der Paele is so realistic that doctors, dermatologists and dentists have diagnosed the various ailments afflicting the canon, who was then in his sixties.

Jan van Eyck was one of the first painters to sign his works and sometimes he would even include a hidden self-portrait, as in the *Arnolfini Wedding Portrait* in London's National Gallery, where his blurred reflection can be seen in a convex mirror. In the Van der Paele altarpiece a mysterious figure, perhaps the artist, is reflected in the shield strapped to St George's back. This detail is so well concealed that it was only recently discovered by an attentive critic.

Two years before his death, van Eyck painted a portrait of his wife, Margaretha, which is also hanging in room 1. The Dutch inscriptions on the frame relate: 'My husband Jan completed me on 17 June in the year 1439' and 'My age was 33 years.' The artist's ambiguous device *'Als ik kan'* ('As I am able') also appears on the frame. Van Eyck was one of the first artists to paint a portrait of his wife, and he depicted Margaretha with such a masterly and uncompromising realism that we feel almost in the presence of this rather severe woman.

Another fascinating portrait, by an anonymous master, is that of Lodewijk van Gruuthuse, whose splendid fifteenth-century mansion is still standing in Bruges. Van Gruuthuse was a fabulously wealthy Burgundian noble who belonged, as the chain around his neck reveals, to the Order of the Golden Fleece. As well as being a politician, diplomat and patron of the arts, van Gruuthuse was a military leader. Carved on the oak frame of the picture is his device, *'Plus est en vous'* ('There is more within you'), an allusion to the superior fire power of his artillery.

Petrus Christus was to some extent Jan van Eyck's successor in Bruges, softening the Eyckian style somewhat and introducing sweeping views of landscapes. Although he worked in Bruges, no complete work by Petrus Christus survives in this city. What we see at the Groeninge are mere fragments of larger works: the *Annunciation* and the *Nativity* are two panels from a lost triptych painted in 1452, and the *Portrait of a Donor with St Elizabeth* perhaps formed the left wing of a triptych. The kneeling woman attired in splendid Burgundian clothes in this lovely work may be Isabella of Portugal, the wife of Philip the Good.

Gerard David, another follower of Jan van Eyck, painted the marvellous *Baptism of Christ* in about 1508. It is set in a beautiful landscape with lovingly rendered details such as flowers and rippling water. The left wing has a portrait of the donor, Jan des Trompes, with his patron saint John the Baptist, while the right wing shows his first wife, Elisabeth van der Meersch, under the protection of her patron saint Elizabeth of Hungary. Gerard David's *Judgement of Cambyses* is a work which no visitor to the Groeninge ever forgets. It is a diptych commissioned in 1498 to hang in the Stadhuis on Burg and illustrates the story of a corrupt judge put to death by Cambyses, King of the Persians. The left panel shows the arrest of the judge, while the right panel depicts him being flayed alive. Although illustrating a sixth-century legend, the setting is unmistakably fifteenth-century Bruges, for the left panel includes a view of the Poortersloge on Jan van Eyckplein and the trading house of the Florentine merchants. The judge is apparently modelled upon Pieter Lanchals who, 10 years before, had been beheaded during the uprising against Maximilian of Austria.

A painting of *St Nicholas* by the Master of the Legend of St Lucy shows us this popular Christmas saint attired in luxurious bishop's vestments. Through the windows we see familiar features of Bruges, including the Minnewater, the belfry, the Poortersloge, the spire of Onze-Lieve-Vrouwekerk and, on the far right, the strange tower of the Jeruzalemkerk. The belfry at the time of this painting was still without its octagonal lantern.

Stepping into room 6, we enter the rather different world of the sixteenth-century Flemish Mannerists. Many of the works by these artists are Last Judgements, an indication of their melancholy world view. Jan Provoost's *Last Judgement* was painted in 1525 to hang in the Aldermen's Room of the Stadhuis. This room was already rather gloomy, for it was here that the *Judgement of Cambyses* hung, to remind the aldermen of the consequences of corruption. The scene of Hell in the lower corner of Provoost's work, in which several church officials appear among the damned, was overpainted in the mid-sixteenth century after Charles V issued a decree banning defamatory representations of the clergy. Another *Last Judgement* in the Groeninge is by Hieronymus Bosch, whose vision of burning cities and warring armies was eerily prophetic of Philip II's reign of terror.

The rooms that follow contain some likeable eighteenth-century works, such as *Afternoon Tea*, painted by Jan Garemyn in 1778, which reveals the thoroughly English tenor of life in eighteenth-century Bruges. *The Invention of Drawing* is a striking Neoclassical work by Jozef Suvée in the style of Jacques Louis David. Fernand Khnopff's *Secret-reflet*, an ambiguous work of 1902, depicts the side wall of the St Janshospitaal and its reflection in the waters of the Reie, while a panel above shows a mysterious woman gazing at a mask.

The last room of the Groeninge is devoted to Belgian Surrealism. Paul Delvaux's *Serenity*, painted in 1970, illustrates the mystical peace of his later works. There is also a cabinet of curiosities filled with works by Marcel Broodthaers, whose quirky Surrealism dwells on typical Belgian themes such as overflowing pots of mussels.

On leaving the museum, we might pause for coffee in the Taverne Groeninge at Dyver 13, an attractive café decorated with gritty expressionist works by Frank Brangwyn. From here we head back down Groeninge, right along Kastanjeboomstraat, left on Mariastraat and then right into Stoofstraat, a narrow, rather secret lane. It emerges on Walplein, one of many lovely squares in Bruges. Crossing it, we pass the Henri Maes brewery discreetly concealed behind a nineteenth-century dwelling house at Walplein 23. The brewery was established in 1564 in a house named 'The Half Moon', from which it derived its trade mark.

We then turn right at a corner overlooked by a statue of St Roch, the patron saint of plague victims. He wears the shell sported by pilgrims and is accompanied by his dog, carrying a loaf of bread in its mouth to feed its plague-stricken master. On the corner of the house opposite is a curious Virgin in a grotto. Wijngaardstraat leads into a quaint little square where carriages congregate and horses snort and stamp their hooves impatiently on the grey cobblestones.

A Neoclassical portal dated 1776 leads us into the precincts of the **Begijnhof** convent, a delightful experience rather like entering a secret garden. All that can be seen from the outside is a brick wall with a few red tiled roofs poking above, but on pushing open the door we enter an enchanting little community of whitewashed houses, each with its own gate and wrought iron bell-pull (pl. 8). The houses are grouped around a broad green which is particularly attractive in spring when it is carpeted with daffodils.

A priest in Liège named Lambert le Bègue is credited with establishing the order of Beguines in about 1189. Its aim was to provide a semi-religious retreat for the widows of Crusaders, or women who had no prospect of finding a husband due to the carnage of the Crusades.

Inspired by the Béguinage at Liège, of which no trace remains, the daughters of Baldwin the First of Constantinople, Margaret and Joanna, founded a number of similar institutions in Flemish cities in the thirteenth century. Presumably the crusading zeal of the Flemings had left numerous widows and spinsters in Flanders. The movement spread throughout the Low Countries and up the Rhine, though the only Begijnhofs to survive are in Holland and Flanders. There are beautiful examples of intact Begijnhofs in quiet corners of Ghent, Antwerp, Leuven, Kortrijk, Lier and Amsterdam. Sometimes the houses overlook a courtyard or green, as in Bruges, Ghent and Amsterdam; elsewhere they are reached by a warren of narrow cobbled lanes, as in Antwerp, Leuven and Kortrijk. These villages of women, as they essentially were, usually contained a church and infirmary. The Beguines lived and dressed like nuns, although they took no formal vows and continued to live in separate dwelling houses. They devoted themselves to caring for the sick, or lace-making. The Begijnhofs in Holland were disbanded by the Protestants, and in Flanders the order has almost died out, though we will still occasionally see sisters in the precincts of the Begijnhof in Bruges.

Bruges' Begijnhof was founded in about 1245 by

C
13

Margaret of Constantinople, Countess of Flanders. Although most of the houses now standing date from the seventeenth and eighteenth centuries, they still cling tightly to the conventions of mediaeval architecture. Number 4, for example, was built in the seventeenth century, but it still has mediaeval trefoils and pointed arches. The eighteenth-century houses at numbers 8 and 28 betray the relatively late date of their construction only by the ornate Baroque doors and fanlights.

We leave the Begijnhof, perhaps with a pang of regret, by its southern entrance, emerging on the water's edge of the picturesque **Minnewater**. The boatmen who ferry you to this corner of Bruges by motor launch claim that Minnewater means 'Lake of Love'; on seeing the stately swans gliding on the placid stretch of water, you may well consider the name apt, and imagine romantic trysts by moonlight on its shore. But the etymological truth is that Minnewater means simply 'inner harbour', though I doubt whether this scholarly quibble will persuade the boatmen and coachmen of Bruges to alter their recital. This inlet of water was created in the thirteenth century as a small harbour for boats bound for Ghent along the Lieve canal. Two tall round towers that once defended the harbour mouth were built by Jan van Oudenaerde at the same time as the Kruispoort and Gentpoort. The Poertoren on the west side of the Minnewater is still standing, but its counterpart has been demolished.

Plate 8 Doorway in Begijnhof

Kasteel Minnewater, a nineteenth-century mock castle, stands in a small park on the far side of the water. It contains a pleasant café and restaurant, where we might pause for coffee or lunch, either on the quayside terrace if the weather is good, or within its opulent Victorian interior.

We then leave the park and turn right along Arsenaalstraat, past a curious sixteenth-century chimney, now incorporated into the nineteenth-century Academy of Fine Arts and supported by a twentieth-century buttress. Turning left along Katelijnestraat we pass the **Godshuis de Generaliteit**, at numbers 79-83, founded, according to the numerals on the wrought-iron wall braces, in 1572. The attractive **Godshuis Onze-Lieve-Vrouw der Zeven Weeën** (Almshouse of the Virgin of the Seven Sorrows) can be found by turning right down Oude Gentweg, then left into Drie Kroezenstraat. A foundation stone on the Baroque portal reveals that this almshouse was established in 1654. It originally comprised seven tiny dwelling houses, which explains its curious name. Turning left on Nieuwe Gentweg takes us past the Late Gothic portal of the **Godshuis St Jozef**, at number 24-32, founded in 1634, and the Baroque portal of the **Godshuis de Meulenare**, at number 8-22, founded in 1613.

If we now turn right up Mariastraat, we come to the **St Janshospitaal**. This magnificent mediaeval hospice now houses the **Memlingmuseum**, a small, but exceptional collection of fifteenth-century paintings by Hans Memling. The hospice, built of weathered dark brown brick, is one of the oldest in Europe, and served as a model for similar institutions in Ghent, Ypres and Lübeck. The Heiligen Geist Hospital in Lübeck, which is still standing, is designed in a style strikingly similar to the St Janshospitaal.

Entering the hospice beneath a squat Romanesque tower, we reach a quiet courtyard down a narrow cobbled lane flanked by dusky brick walls. If the weather is mild, we might sit on a bench here to read about the hospital.

Dedicated to St John the Evangelist and St John the Baptist, the St Janshospitaal was founded in about 1150 on the north bank of the River Reie, which then marked the city boundary. Of the original hospice only a few fragments remain. The present building comprises three immense Gothic wards built in the thirteenth and fourteenth centuries. The middle ward, the oldest of the three, was erected in the early thirteenth century in a sober Romanesque style. It looks very like the nave of a church, and even has a splendid west portal in northern French Gothic style. The west portal's tympanum is decorated with scenes of the Death of the Virgin, and the Last Judgement. A second ward, parallel to the first, was added on the north side in about 1290, and a third to the south in 1310-15. To make the hospice more church-like still, the side walls of the middle ward were subsequently pierced with large Romanesque arches. The three vast and chilly wards were used for some seven centuries, up until the early twentieth century. A fascinating painting by Jan Beerblock hanging in one of the old wards shows the hospital in about 1778, the sick arriving in sedan chairs and the beds arranged into separated rows for men, women, surgery cases and the terminally ill.

Situated in a partitioned corner of the north wing, the former hospital chapel is decorated with handsome Renaissance carvings and a large Baroque altar. It is here that the six paintings by Hans Memling are hung. Of these works four were commissioned for the St Janshospitaal, while the other two, displayed in a room off the chapel, were brought here from a hospice dedicated to St Julian when it closed in 1815.

Memling was born in a village near Frankfurt in about 1435 and, after spending some years working in Roger van der Weyden's atelier in Brussels, he moved to Bruges in about 1465. Memling eventually became one of the richest men in the city, owning three houses on the St Jorisstraat. His clients were often foreign merchants or diplomats, so that many of his works are now located in far-flung places; there is a *Last Judgement* by him in Gdansk that was seized by pirates as it was being shipped to Tuscany, and an altarpiece in London's National Gallery commissioned by Sir John Donne of Kidwelly when he visited Bruges in 1468 for the wedding of Margaret of York.

The most remarkable work in the museum is the *St Ursula Shrine*. Two sisters who worked in the hospice commissioned this work in about 1480 to hold certain relics of St Ursula. The shrine is made of gilded wood and decorated with pinnacles and finials so that it looks rather like a little Gothic chapel. The sloping roofs, as it were, are decorated with six miniature medallions, while the figures at the four corners represent St John the Evangelist bearing a chalice, St Agnes with a lamb at her feet, St Elizabeth wearing a crown, and St James with a pilgrim's staff. A small painting at one end shows the two sisters who donated the shrine kneeling before the Virgin, while at the other end St Ursula is depicted sheltering 10 maidens with her cloak.

The two long sides of the shrine are decorated with six small panels depicting the legend of St Ursula. The panels are separated by arches so that we have the impression of looking out of a window as the scenes unfold from left to right. The story of Ursula is rarely depicted in paintings, and it may therefore be worth recounting this curious Rhineland legend based on a thirteenth-century manuscript by Jacob van Voragine. The story tells of a princess born in a hairy coat, and so named Ursula, the little bear. She was the daughter of a Christian king, and lived 'in partibus Britanniae'. This might mean either Britain or Brittany. If Britain, then the episode must have taken place after A.D. 600, when Britain was converted to Christianity. But other aspects in the narrative suggest that the events described took place at a much earlier date, and so it seems more likely that Ursula was a princess of Brittany. She was renowned for her beauty and a pagan king wished her to marry his son. Ursula said that she would give her consent on two conditions. Firstly, her suitor had to convert to Christianity and, secondly, he must send 11,000 virgins to accompany Ursula on a pilgrimage to Rome—or was it merely 11 virgins? The thirteenth-century manuscript used the Latin shorthand *XI.M.V*, which mediaeval readers took to mean eleven (*XI*) thousand (*M*) virgins (*V*). But punctilious critics have pointed out that the cryptic description might equally be decoded as 11 martyred virgins, which would make the tale more plausible, if less moving.

After receiving the Pope's blessing in Rome, Ursula and her 11,000 (or merely 11) companions returned home to Brittany (or Britain), accompanied by the Pope. After crossing the Alps, they sailed up the Rhine to Cologne, which during their absence had fallen to the Huns (suggesting that the story took place long before the Conversion of Britain). The maidens were captured and, after refusing to renounce Christianity, martyred outside the city walls. The son of the king of the Huns, we are told, was saddened to see Ursula put to death, having fallen in love with her.

Memling illustrates the later episodes of this legend, beginning with the virgins arriving in Cologne bound for Rome. We see Ursula, who is identified throughout the narrative by her blue robe and white cloak, inside a house, where an angel forewarns her of her death. Memling had spent some time in Cologne before moving to Brussels, and the view of the city is topographically accurate. Several of the buildings are still standing, such as the Romanesque tower of Gross St Martin and the Gothic cathedral. At the time Memling saw the cathedral, the unfinished south tower was surmounted by a crane. Work on it had come to a standstill in 1437 and in fact was not resumed until the nineteenth century.

The other scenes on this side show the arrival of the fleet of ships in Basel and the blessing of the virgins in Rome. These two episodes are linked together by a long procession of pilgrims, seen setting off for the Alps in one panel and entering the gates of Rome in the next.

The first scene on the opposite side depicts the pilgrims' return to Basel, while the two final scenes show their massacre in Cologne. There is another panoramic view of the city, including two other churches and the Bayenturm, a mediaeval tower still standing on the waterfront. The final scene shows Ursula about to be shot by an arrow, a dog at her feet to symbolise her fidelity. If we examine this scene closely, we will see that Ursula and the king are reflected in the breastplate of the love-stricken prince, while a soldier is likewise mirrored in the king's back-plate.

Another work by Memling in the hospice chapel is the large *Altarpiece of St John the Baptist and St John the Evangelist*, painted in 1479 for the high altar of the chapel. The work is sometimes referred to as *The Mystic Marriage of St Catherine* because of the scene in the middle panel showing the Christ Child giving a ring to St Catherine, who is identified by the broken wheel on which she was bound, and the sword with which she was executed. The beautiful St Catherine is possibly a likeness of Mary of Burgundy, while St Barbara (identified by a miniature tower) may, according to some critics, be modelled on her mother, Margaret of York.

The other principal figures in the middle panel are the patron saints of the hospice, St John the Baptist (identified by a lamb) and St John the Evangelist (identified by a chalice). The wings are decorated with scenes from the lives of these two saints. The left wing, depicting the life of John the Baptist, contains a beautiful landscape with the Baptism of Christ, Salome dancing rather stiffly before Herod in a Burgundian interior and, to the fore, Salome averting her eyes coyly as the head of John the Baptist is delivered to her on a plate. The right panel, devoted to John the Evangelist, shows his vision of the Apocalypse, including the four horsemen, the seven-headed dragons and several fiery rocks tumbling from the heavens. But Memling's vision of the Apocalypse is somehow unconvincing when compared with, say, Bosch's *Last Judgement* in the Groeningemuseum. His sky seems too blue, his sea is too placid, and even his monsters look rather tame.

Beyond the columns in the centre panel are yet more miniature episodes from the lives of the two saints. Behind John the Baptist are scenes depicting him preaching in the desert, his arrest, and the burning of his body. The tiny scenes behind the figure of John the Evangelist show him being plunged in boiling oil, and his departure for the island of Patmos. The latter episodes are set on the Kraanplaats in Bruges, where a great wooden crane once stood. The figure in the foreground wearing a black gown was probably the person employed by the St Janshospitaal to gauge imported wine here. In the fourteenth century the St Janshospitaal was granted the privilege of testing and taxing wine as a means of raising revenue.

On the backs of the wings we see the two brothers and two sisters who jointly donated this altarpiece to the hospice. Following Gothic convention, the donors are shown kneeling before their patron saints: St James of Compostela, Abbot Anthony (identified by a pig with a long snout), St Agnes with her lamb, and St Clara.

Memling adopted a rather subtler method of portraying the donor's patron saint in the exquisite *Diptych with the Virgin and Martin van Nieuwenhove*, painted in 1487 when Martin van Nieuwenhove was 23. If we look at the top left-hand corner of the panel with Martin van Nieuwenhove, we will see a stained-glass window with a tiny figure of St Martin, the donor's patron saint, cutting off a length of his cloak to clothe a beggar.

This work is a rare example of a complete

Flemish diptych with both wings still joined together. Most diptychs have been divided and the wings have ended up in different collections, as in the case of the twin portraits of Erasmus and Gilles (pls. 21 and 22). The Van Nieuwenhove diptych contains an intriguing detail which might never have been noticed had the two panels parted company. Behind the Virgin is a convex mirror in which appears both her reflection and that of Martin van Nieuwenhove. By this variation on an Eyckian technique, Memling reveals that the two figures are seated in the corner of a room. The two panels are bound together further by the ornately patterned carpet covering the table in both scenes, and the length of the Virgin's scarlet cloak that appears beneath the book that Martin van Nieuwenhove is reading.

This diptych, which was once owned by the St Julian's hospice, is one of Memling's most attractive works. He has copied Van Eyck's intense inner world of jewels, mirrors and symbols, but he has also learnt from Van der Weyden to throw open the window shutters and reveal beguiling landscapes with winding roads and pale blue distant hills. This felicitous style appealed immensely to the nineteenth-century German Romantics, who discovered in their fellow countryman's paintings an appealing world of innocent maidens and arcadian landscapes.

The other painting brought here from the St Julian's hospital is a portrait of a woman called the *Sibylla Sambetha*. This strange title comes from the inscription in the top left-hand corner, which must have been added by a later hand, as it is set in a Renaissance frame. The inscription on the flowing banderole at the bottom of the frame, quoting the Persian Sibyl's prophecy of Christ's coming, was probably added at the same time, presumably by a Renaissance artist who thought that the mysterious and pensive young woman resembled an Old Testament prophet. She may in fact have been a daughter of Willem Moreel, Burgomaster of Bruges.

In 1479, one year before the Sibylla Sambetha, Memling was commissioned by Jan Floreins, another brother at the hospice, to paint the small *Triptych of the Adoration of the Magi*. The donor of this altarpiece is seen kneeling on the far left of the middle panel. He was 36 at the time, as we discover from tiny numerals that look as if they have been chiselled in the wall alongside. The king kneeling to the left of the Virgin may be a likeness of Charles the Bold, who fell at the siege of Nancy in 1477. It has also been suggested that the figure peering through the window to the right is Memling himself, wearing the yellow cap of convalescents at the hospice. According to an old legend, the artist was admitted to the hospice on returning wounded and exhausted from the Battle of Nancy, where he had fought on the side of Charles the Bold.

Another small triptych, the *Lamentation over Christ*, was commissioned one year after Jan Floreins' by brother Adriaan Reins. Based on a painting by Van der Weyden now in the Mauritshuis in The Hague, it is a somewhat unsatisfactory work, revealing Memling's inability to deal with tragedy and suffering. The left panel has a portrait of the donor with his saint, the right panel an attractive St Barbara.

Before leaving the St Janshospitaal, we should glance into the seventeenth-century dispensary, which contains several magnificent oak chests, one with a bas relief of a hospital ward, revealing that patients more often than not slept two to a bed. It also boasts a magnificent collection of Delftware dispensers' jars. A series of portraits of hospital governors hanging in the dispensary provides an interesting insight into the development of dress, beards and and hairstyles in Bruges from the seventeenth to the twentieth century.

Walk 4: Onze-Lieve-Vrouwekerk, St Salvatorskathedraal and the Gruuthusemuseum

This is a short walk (*see page 45 for map*) easily accomplished in an afternoon, taking in the two great Gothic churches of Bruges and a museum of decorative arts situated in the splendid Burgundian mansion of Lodewijk van Gruuthuse.

We begin in **Onze-Lieve-Vrouwekerk** (Church of Our Lady), which stands opposite the Memling-museum. Begun in the thirteenth century on a site previously occupied by two successive Romanesque churches, Onze-Lieve-Vrouwekerk has an impressive west front, flanked by two round towers, a typical feature of the austere Early Gothic style known as Tournai Gothic. The spire, a thrilling structure soaring to a height of 122 metres, is constructed entirely of brick, the natural building material of West Flanders. The base dates from the thirteenth century, while the top was added in the fifteenth century. It remained the tallest building in the Burgundian Netherlands until the completion, in 1518, of the north spire of Antwerp Cathedral, a mere one metre higher, and it is still, I believe, the tallest brick tower in the world.

Onze-Lieve-Vrouwekerk contains several major works of art, including a *Virgin and Child* by Michelangelo. It is easy to overlook this small statue, which is displayed in a black marble niche set in a rather overbearing altar at the end of the south aisle. Carved soon after the famous *Pietà* in Rome, this work illustrates Michelangelo's soft and serene early style. It was bought in 1506 and brought back to Bruges by Jan Mouscron, a merchant of Italian descent. Dürer was one of the first to admire this statue when he visited Bruges in 1521.

The choir of Onze-Lieve-Vrouwekerk was the scene in 1468 of a splendid chapter of the Order of the Golden Fleece, convened to celebrate the marriage of Charles the Bold to his third wife Margaret of York. The coats of arms of the knights that attended this sumptuous wedding are still hanging in the choir.

The choir also contains the **mausoleums of Charles the Bold and Mary of Burgundy**. Both father and daughter died in tragic circumstances. Charles the Bold met his end while laying siege to Nancy in 1477. His mutilated body was discovered in a frozen pond a few days after the battle and buried at Nancy. Deciding that his great-grandfather deserved a more magnificent memorial, Charles V ordered the body to be exhumed and taken to Bruges. It was not entirely certain that the mutilated body found in the ice outside Nancy in 1477 had been that of the king, and by the time the skeleton was exhumed in 1550 it was of course impossible to identify. But the remains were sent back to Bruges anyway. The journey went very slowly, partly due to a three-year halt in Luxembourg and, by the time the shipment arrived in Bruges, Charles V had abdicated. It therefore fell to his son Philip II to build the mausoleum. Designed in 1559-62 by an Antwerp sculptor, Jacob Jonghelinck, it is inscribed with Charles the Bold's device, 'I have made the venture; may it prosper.'

The work was meant to imitate the beautiful mausoleum of Mary of Burgundy, who had died five years after her father, in 1482, after falling from her horse while hunting in the Wijnendaele woods. In 1495 her husband, Maximilian, commissioned the mausoleum in Onze-Lieve-Vrouwekerk. It is surmounted by a bronze recumbent figure of Mary cast by Renier van Thienen and gilded by Pieter de Beckere, a Brussels jeweller.

In a chapel off the choir we come upon another sad relic of the Late Middle Ages: Pieter Lanchals' ornate mausoleum. This is decorated with his emblem, a swan—alluding to his name, which in Dutch means 'long neck'. After the uprising against the Emperor Maximilian in 1488, Pieter Lanchals, a city official, was beheaded on Markt for allegedly betraying the interests of Bruges, that is, siding with Maximilian. The unjust judge in Gerard David's *Judgement of Cambyses* was apparently modelled on the unfortunate Lanchals.

The story has a curious, typically mediaeval ending, for the townspeople were later required to atone for the murder by introducing swans (Lanchals' emblem) to the canals of Bruges.

While in the choir, be sure not to miss the beautiful Late Gothic bay window set into the north wall of the ambulatory. It bears the device, *'Plus est en vous'*, which we may remember having seen on the frame of the portrait of Lodewijk van Gruuthuse at the Groeningemuseum. The mystery of this intriguing bay window will be revealed before the day is over.

After exploring Onze-Lieve-Vrouwekerk, we continue to **St Salvatorskathedraal**, which in 1834 became Bruges Cathedral. A striking way of approaching this church is to head up Mariastraat, then turn left into St Salvatorskoorstraat. This quiet lane is terminated by the choir of the church, which is surrounded by an attractive cluster of radiating chapels added in 1480 by Jan van den Poele. The tower at the west end rests on stone foundations dating back to the twelfth century. After a fire in 1853, the upper tier of the tower was rebuilt with British funding and by a British architect, Robert Chantrell, in a somewhat dull Neo-Romanesque style.

The Gothic choir, transepts and nave were built almost entirely of brick in the thirteenth century. The choir contains misericords carved to commemorate the foundation of the Order of the Golden Fleece in 1430, and hanging above them are the coats of arms of the knights that attended the chapter held here in 1478, including those of Edward IV of England.

The transepts and choir of the cathedral are particularly interesting to explore. Off the north transept is an interesting chapel built for the guild of shoemakers in 1372, and enlarged in 1424. An overbearing Baroque altar placed here in 1667 is decorated with the guild's emblem, a fashionable high-heeled leather boot surmounted by a crown. This motif also appears on the gable of the shoemakers' guild house built in 1527 at Steenstraat 40.

The radiating chapels in the ambulatory were built, as we have already noted, by Jan van der Poele in a beautiful Late Gothic style. The first chapel on the north side has a screen dated 1513 with a mysterious monogram, while the next chapel, commissioned by the guild of wheelwrights, is closed off by an attractive screen dating from 1517 with reliefs illustrating aspects of the wheelwright's trade.

St Salvatorskathedraal is now rather overcrowded with paintings, sculptures, reliquaries and relics, much of which once hung in the old cathedral on Burg. The most important works of art are now kept in the **Cathedral Museum**, situated in a Neo-Gothic cloister with an adjoining chapter house strangely lit by round neon lights in the shape of haloes. One of the highlights of the collection is the *Martyrdom of St Hippolytus*. The centre panel, painted by Dirk Bouts, shows the saint being torn apart by four wild horses after refusing to renounce his faith. The donors' portraits on the left wing were added later by Hugo van der Goes.

Six monumental brasses from the old cathedral are also displayed in the cloister, including that of Jacob Schille-Waert, who died in 1483; he taught theology at the Sorbonne, and is depicted in the midst of his students. Another charming work is a fifteenth-century wooden figure of a solemn-looking Daniel in the lions' den. There is also an unusual altarpiece with a hinged door, commissioned in the fourteenth century by the guild of tanners.

The Virgin between St Eloi and St Luke was painted in Bruges in 1545 by the eccentric Renaissance artist Lancelot Blondeel. St Eloi, a seventh-century Frankish metalworker who later became a missionary, is the patron saint of goldsmiths, silversmiths and blacksmiths. In the same room we see a silver reliquary of St Eloi made by Jan Crabbe in about 1616. But perhaps the most curious relic in this museum is a lead tablet with an inscription in Latin found in the grave of Gunhilde, sister of Harold, the last Anglo-Saxon king. After the Battle of Hastings, in which Harold was slain, Gunhilde fled to Bruges, where she died in 1087.

There are numerous attractive restaurants for lunch in the neighbourhood of the cathedral. The restaurant Vasquez is situated in a beautiful Late Gothic town house overgrown with ivy at Zilverstraat 38. It was built in 1468 for Juan

Vasquez, Isabella of Portugal's Spanish secretary, who accompanied her to Bruges in 1430 when she married Philip the Good. Another attractive restaurant in this street is the Zilveren Pauw at number 41. There are also restaurants and cafés grouped around the quiet courtyards of the Zilverpand, a shopping centre reached down a passage next to Vasquez.

After lunch we head down Steenstraat and then right on Simon Stevinplein, a square named after the Bruges mathematician who invented the decimal system. Straight ahead, the fifteenth-century **Hof van Watervliet**, at Oude Burg 27, was once the home of the unfortunate Pieter Lanchals. In 1567 it was bought by Marcus Laurinus, dean of the cathedral and a friend of many Flemish humanists. Erasmus, Pieter Gilles, Thomas More and Guy Morillon were all guests in this house.

Turning left on Oude Burg, then right down Nieuwstraat, we reach Dyver. The **Brangwynmuseum** at number 16 is a small museum situated in an eighteenth-century house, the Arentshuis, built astride the River Reie. It contains a collection of some 400 drawings and paintings by Frank Brangwyn, born in Bruges in 1867. His father, William Brangwyn, was a British Victorian architect who settled in Bruges; he campaigned vigorously for the restoration of Flemish Gothic architecture, and even designed a number of buildings in Flanders in Neo-Gothic style. Frank Brangwyn shared his father's enthusiasm for Bruges and in 1936 presented the city with a collection of his works 'as a memorial of my love for your great city'. Many of the works are sombre, such as *Last Boat from Antwerp*, an engraving sold during World War I to support Belgian refugees in Britain. The museum also has some views of Bruges by various artists, and a bizarre collection of objects made of mother-of-pearl.

A lane beside the museum leads into an attractive little park, the **Arentspark**, once the garden of the Gruuthuse mansion, and standing on the opposite side of the river to the house. Notice the two squat columns standing somewhat forlornly in this park. The little iron signs attached to them have become illegible with rust, giving them a delectable air of mystery; they are in fact the last vestiges of the Waterhalle that once stood on Markt.

Pausing for a moment by the water's edge, we can look across the Reie to a magnificent brick Gothic gable rising from the water. This is the oldest wing of the **Gruuthuse mansion**, built in 1425 by Jan van Gruuthuse, whose coat of arms, and that of his wife, appear on the gable. The design of the façade is based on twelve Gothic trefoils of different sizes, including one that ingeniously embraces all the others.

Let us now stroll to the attractive little hump-backed bridge called the **Bonifaciusbrug** that spans the River Reie at this point. This is one of the loveliest spots in Bruges, with the river gently lapping at the crumbling brick foundations of aged ivy-covered houses. It comes as a slight disappointment, however, to discover that the bridge was placed here only in 1910. Attached to a wall is a curious stone tablet decorated with a boat, which once served as a sign for a waterside inn at Nieuwpoort.

Thanks to the bridge, we obtain a magnificent view of the Early Gothic choir of Onze-Lieve-Vrouwekerk. The choir is modelled on that of Tournai Cathedral, which in turn was inspired by the great cathedrals of northern France. Rising dramatically to our right is the south wing of the Gruuthuse mansion, added by Lodewijk van Gruuthuse in 1465-70. Looking closely at the high brick walls, you might be able to spot a tiny Gothic window. This provides one of the most delightful, and least familiar, views in Bruges, as we will soon discover.

Once across the bridge we pass a bust of a sixteenth-century humanist, Juan Luis Vives from Valencia, who spent much of his life in Bruges. We now head down a lane squeezed between the mossy buttresses of the church and the lofty walls of the Gruuthuse mansion. Once under a bridge (about which more later), we come upon a building of gleaming white stone attached to Onze-Lieve-Vrouwekerk. This is the **Paradijsportaal** (Gate to Paradise), although it is now not a portal but a baptistry. It was added to the church in 1465 in the ornate style characteristic of Brabant Late Gothic architecture. Like the Stadhuis on Burg, it seems rather out of place in this windswept northern port, where most of the buildings are old and crumbling brick edifices.

We turn right now to enter the courtyard of the **Gruuthusemuseum**. The Gruuthuse family owed their extraordinary wealth to a right granted in the thirteenth century to levy tolls on *gruut* (grout), a mixture of herbs used by mediaeval brewers to flavour ales. Most beers are now seasoned with hops, but *gruut* is still used in the production of at least one Bruges beer, *Stropken Grand Cru*, an amber-coloured brew with a pleasant taste hovering between a *Duvel* and a *Bière Blanche*. This beer was launched some years ago by the Hopduivel café in Ghent. Its name *Stropken* (a noose) sounds rather ominous, as do other Belgian beers, such as *Duvel* (Devil), *Lucifer* and *Verboden Vrucht* (Forbidden Fruit). However, *Stropken* merely recalls an episode in the fifteenth century when the leading citizens of Ghent were forced to humble themselves before Philip the Good wearing hangman's nooses around their necks.

Despite appearing somewhat diffident in the portrait in the Groeningemuseum, Lodewijk van Gruuthuse was one of the most powerful nobles in the Burgundian Netherlands. He was a knight of the Order of the Golden Fleece, Governor of Bruges and Oudenaarde, Governor of Holland, Zeeland and West Friesland, and Commander of the Burgundian armies and fleets. His friends included King Edward IV of England, who stayed here with his brother Richard from October 1470 to April 1471 during their exile from England. Van Gruuthuse lent money to Edward IV to help him to regain the throne of England, and in return was granted the title of Earl of Winchester to add to his long list of honours.

Lodewijk van Gruuthuse was also a great patron of the arts, and built up a library of illuminated manuscripts that was considered the finest private collection in the Burgundian Netherlands. After his death in 1492, however, his son defected to the side of the French and moved to Abbeville. The famous library was sold, and now forms part of the Bibliothèque Nationale in Paris.

The Gruuthuse mansion then lay empty until 1628, when a charitable lending bank known as the *Mons Pietas* or *Berg van Barmhartigheid* was established here. This was modelled on the *Monte di Pietà*, an institution that existed in many Italian cities. The Dutch name, which means literally 'Mountain of Charity', derives from an erroneous translation of the Italian term *monte*, which in this context means a sum of money, or a loan, but not a mountain. These new banks lent money at a very low rate of interest, and sometimes charged nothing at all, thus breaking the monopoly of the bankers of Lombardy, who allegedly caused much suffering in Flanders by the extortionate rate of interest they charged on loans. The first charitable bank in Flanders was established at Ypres in 1534, followed by one at Bruges in 1573. The bank in the Gruuthuse mansion was one of several founded in the 1620s by the Archduchess Isabella. There are similar lending banks in Ghent, Antwerp and Mechelen.

The former lending bank now contains a captivating collection of Flemish sculpture, furniture, altarpieces, musical instruments, paintings, tapestries and lace. This collection was begun in 1865 by a society of local antiquarians, whose members included William Brangwyn, the Victorian architect, and James Weale, an expert on the Flemish Primitives. A third British expatriate in Bruges, John Steinmetz, presented the museum with his extensive collection of Flemish drawings, engravings, etchings and woodcuts. Steinmetz had arrived in Bruges in 1819 bound for Venice, but this northern Gothic city so captivated him that he abandoned his plans and settled here.

The antiquarian society originally displayed its collection in a room on the first floor of the belfry, but in 1900 the museum was moved to the Gruuthuse mansion, which had just emerged from an eight-year-long restoration by Louis Delacenserie. Having piously removed everything that did not belong to the fifteenth-century fabric, Delacenserie then went on to add certain Neo-Gothic features of his own, with the result that the building is now a somewhat baffling mixture of fifteenth-century and nineteenth-century elements. The equestrian statue of Lodewijk van Gruuthuse above the entrance, for example, is a pure nineteenth-century invention, and so is the magnificent ceiling in the entrance hall. The extraordinary mantelpiece in room 1, another nineteenth-century caprice, is adorned with a delightful scene depicting a walled city and trumpeters blasting from the battlements. This is not entirely fanciful, however, for the heraldic devices and symbolic motifs here are culled from authentic fifteenth-century windows, ceilings and mantelpieces in the house. It is therefore a catalogue, of sorts, of the mottos and motifs of Lodewijk van Gruuthuse, including his ubiquitous device *'Plus est en vous'*, and the symbol of a blasting mortar, both alluding to the superiority of his artillery. A more romantic device shows the initials of Lodewijk and his wife Margaretha united by a cord.

The most striking object in room 1 is a terracotta and wood bust of Charles V probably carved by the German Renaissance artist Konrad Meit in about 1520. Charles, aged about 20, is wearing the collar of the Golden Fleece, and a curious removable wooden hat.

Room 4 is an enticing Gothic interior reminiscent of paintings by the Master of Flémalle. The mantelpiece dates from the early fifteenth century, and once stood in a house in the nearby Mariastraat. The two stained-glass windows decorated with St George and St Michael were made in about 1500 for the chapel of the guild of painters.

In room 6 we should note particularly the attractive sculpture of *The Madonna Reading* by Adriaen van Wezel of Utrecht. This lovely figure formed part of an extraordinary retable carved in 1477 for the Brotherhood of Our Lady at 's-Hertogenbosch. Hieronymus Bosch, who was a member of this Brotherhood, was asked in 1508 to advise on the polychroming of the work. The retable is now split into many parts; museums in 's-Hertogenbosch, Amsterdam, Cologne and Berlin all possess fragments.

Room 13, often overlooked, is where we discover that tiny Gothic window we spied from the Bonifaciusbrug. Looking through it, we obtain a curious and captivating view reminiscent of the landscapes of Memling. Continuing to room 16, a mystery is finally solved, for here we come upon a bridge leading to a Late Gothic oratory with a bay window. This is the curious window that we saw from the choir of Onze-Lieve-Vrouwekerk. In 1472, after protracted negotiations with the church authorities, Lodewijk van Gruuthuse finally obtained permission to construct this small private chapel overlooking the choir, so that he and his family could attend Mass without the inconvenience of having to leave the mansion. The oratory contains some delightful features, such as the gilded paper flowers that bespangle the vaulted wooden roof, and the ingenious skylight windows to admit daylight to the chapel.

Another interesting feature of the mansion is the loggia reached from room 18, which offers a magnificent view of the choir and spire of Onze-Lieve-Vrouwekerk. Standing here, we can see another tiny Gothic window on a nearby wall. Room 22 contains some unusual mementoes of the young Charles II of Great Britain, who lived in exile in Bruges from 1656-9. It seems that Charles and his two brothers whiled away the days in the shooting butts of the three guilds of civic guards. Each of the guilds was delighted to have such distinguished members, and they all commissioned splendid Baroque paintings or sculptures of Charles II and his brothers to decorate their banqueting halls. A magnificent memorial to Charles II still hangs above the fireplace in the guild house of the archers on Carmerstraat. The other two guild houses were demolished in the nineteenth century and their Caroline memorabilia found its way into the Gruuthuse collection. A portrait of Henry, Duke of Gloucester, was brought here from the guild house of the crossbowmen, while another painting depicting a shooting competition came from the guild house of the arquebusiers.

On leaving the museum, we should glance at the small lapidary museum in the arcade opposite. This contains a baffling miscellany of Gothic gravestones, architectural fragments and fifteenth-century cannon. Hanging from the gatehouse is an ornate wrought-iron sign bearing a crescent moon, the trade mark of the Henri Maes brewery. Notice, too, the fascinating stone frieze embedded in the outside wall of the mansion, depicting a fifteenth-century military campaign. If we now turn right on Gruuthusestraat we can walk back to Markt along Dyver, a lovely stretch of water shaded by elm trees.

Bruges Explored Further

For anyone with time to spare there is still much to be seen in Bruges. On summer days, you can head out to the ramparts, and walk along landscaped paths laid out in the nineteenth century, as the locals with their rollicking dogs tend to do on Sundays after church. Although the city walls, built in 1297-1300, are no more, four magnificent mediaeval gates are still standing: the **Kruispoort**, **Gentpoort**, **Smedenpoort** and **Ezelpoort**. The Ezelpoort is a particularly beautiful weathered edifice of dark red brick that has been guarding the northern approach to Bruges since 1367. The finest walks are around the Smedenpoort, a contemporary of the Ezelpoort, and the Kruispoort, a sturdy white sandstone gate built, together with the Gentpoort, in 1401 by Jan van Oudenaerde and Maarten van Leuven. Not far from the Kruispoort is a sad and almost forgotten spot, the **Muur der Doodgeschotenen** (Wall of the Executed Prisoners). Still pock-marked with bullet holes, the wall is a memorial to 12 Belgians and a British soldier executed here in World War I.

When the centre of Bruges becomes unbearably crowded, we might spend time exploring the quiet streets in the neighbourhood of the St Annakerk. Here we come upon the strangest church in Bruges, the **Jeruzalemkerk** at Peperstraat 3. It is a private church built in 1428 by Pieter and Jacob Adorno, descendants of a thirteenth-century Genoese merchant named Oppicino Adorno who joined the crusading army of Guy de Dampierre and later settled in Bruges. According to a local legend the two brothers modelled the church in Bruges on the Church of the Holy Sepulchre in Jerusalem, which they had seen on a pilgrimage to the Holy Land. It is certainly a curious design, consisting of three separate chapels. We enter by a lower chapel, in which are several family tombs. A steep flight of stairs ascends to an upper chapel. Below this, there is yet another chapel, with a tiny crypt off it containing an imitation of the Holy Sepulchre, complete with the figure of Christ.

The most striking tomb is the black marble mausoleum with the recumbent figures of Anselm Adorno, son of Pieter, and his wife Margaretha van der Back. Anselm Adorno served the Duke of Burgundy on several diplomatic missions, including one to the court of James III of Scotland. As a result of this contact with Scotland, Anselm Adorno was appointed by James III as keeper of the privileges of the Scottish mercantile community in Bruges. He was murdered on a visit to Scotland in 1483 and his body buried at Linlithgow Palace, although later his heart was returned to Bruges in a lead casket to be buried here.

Another curiosity in this quarter of Bruges is the Café Vlissinghe at Blekersstraat 2. Baedeker's 1905 guide book described it as 'a resort of artists, with quaint fittings', and it scarcely seems to have changed since then. Although it strikes one initially as somewhat private, like a nineteenth-century debating society that has convened in the dining room of its most eccentric member, Café Vlissinghe is a very friendly old place.

Onze-Lieve-Vrouw van de Potterie, at number 79, is a hospice for elderly women founded in 1276 on the site of an ancient pottery. Standing on the quayside, you will see three dusky old brick gables. They look as if they all date from roughly the same period, but in fact each belongs to a different century. The middle gable, the oldest, is the hospice chapel, which dates back to 1359. The gable to the left is the hospital ward, built in 1529, while to the right is another chapel added in 1623. Thoroughly Brugean in its sober piety, the only decorative element is the Late Gothic chimney of the hospital.

This old hospice, like the St Janshospitaal, owns a collection of paintings and sculpture donated by benefactors. The collection at the Potteriemuseum is rather disappointing, however, as the works here mainly date from the sixteenth and seventeenth centuries, when artistic creativity in Bruges was at a low ebb. Nevertheless, we do see some interesting paintings in the style of the Antwerp Mannerists, and an attractive fourteenth-century statue known as the Madonna of the Pevelenberg. The seventeenth-century

Plate 9 Vismarkt

Baroque chapel is marvellous, crammed with curiosities including a striking Neo-Gothic mausoleum erected in memory of St Idesbald, an abbot of the Cistercian abbey of Ter Duinen.

Some time might also be spent in Bruges looking at almshouses, of which there are 48 still standing, many of them simple and dignified mediaeval buildings with whitewashed walls and intimate courtyards. Known in Dutch as *godshuizen*, they were established by wealthy citizens to accommodate the poor and elderly. My favourite is the **Godshuis de Moor** at Boeveriestraat 52-76, founded in 1480 by Donaas de Moor, a city official, and his wife Adriana de Vos. The 13 simple dwelling houses of de Moor were allocated to the guilds of carpenters, masons and coopers, each of which was given three houses, while the remaining four went to a hospice dedicated to St Julian the Hospitaller. The first nine houses in the row bear the coats of arms of the different guilds to which they belonged, while the others have the hospice's coat of arms. Depicting a boat, it recalls the legend of St Julian, who atoned for the accidental murder of his parents by setting up a hospice by a ford. Eight years after the foundation of this beautiful *godshuis*, Donaas de Moor was forced to flee Bruges because of his association with the imprisoned Emperor Maximilian, and he died in exile in Middelburg.

Another attractive row of whitewashed almshouses, the Schoenmakersrente at Rolweg 40, once accommodated retired shoemakers. It now houses the **Museum van Volkskunde**, a small folk museum containing, for example, a reconstructed school classroom, a shop interior and an old tavern.

Before leaving Bruges, I recommend taking a final short stroll from the fish market (pl. 9) along Steenhouwersdijk, past the **Godshuis de Pelikaan** at Groenerei 8-12. This almshouse, founded in 1634 for seven elderly women, is called 'The Pelican'. A relief above the door shows a pelican feeding its young with its own blood, a conventional Christian symbol of Charity. Following the Reie as it bends around to the right, then crossing the bridge and turning left, you come to a quiet quay with one of the finest views in Bruges.

CHAPTER 2: GHENT

Ghent, the capital of East Flanders, is a bustling and industrious old city, with a port and a university. Our first impression of Ghent may be one of utter exasperation, as it was for the Victorian writer Martin F. Tupper who, on a visit here in 1856, lamented: 'A trifle of time in such a town as this is bewildering; it is like having to describe a curiosity shop.' However, if we stay here longer than a trifle, we will discover Ghent to be a fascinating and stimulating city, with many delightful spots, such as the waterfront along Graslei, and the Van der Doncktdoorgang, a restored nineteenth-century glass-roofed arcade off Brabantdam.

Visiting Ghent in 1641, John Evelyn wrote: 'The Leys and the Scheldt melting in this vast city divide it into 26 islands, which are united by many bridges, somewhat resembling Venice.' The 1534 prospect (pl. 10) clearly shows the many islands which make Ghent somewhat like Venice. One of the delights of Ghent is to chance upon an unexpected stretch of water as, for example, at the end of St Widostraat (where you obtain a striking view of Ghent's castle), or down the lane called Zwaardsteeg off Brabantdam.

From its earliest days, Ghent has been a tumultuous city, always ready to fight for its independence. Its fiery spirit makes Ghent quite

different from the sleepy Burgundian backwater of Bruges, a mere 26 miles away. In the nineteenth century, while Bruges crumbled and languished, producing little else but lace, Ghent was industrialising at full tilt, and it is now one of the most prosperous cities of Flanders. However, we may not always applaud the consequences of Ghent's restless energy, for it sometimes leads to a neglect of historical buildings, such as the unfortunate Baroque fish market on St Veerleplein, which is now occupied by a garage. Yet the city still has many beautiful buildings, and some travellers even prefer Ghent to Bruges as it is never overcrowded with tourists.

Ghent grew up around two abbeys founded here in the seventh century. The St Pietersabdij, built on a hill of alluvial sand above the Scheldt, stands in the southern quarters of Ghent. Its church, designed in 1629 by Baroque architect Pieter Huyssens, was inspired to some extent by its namesake in Rome. The St Baafsabdij, built on another branch of the River Scheldt about a mile to the north, is now a romantic ruin.

Plate 10 Prospect of Ghent in 1534

A castle, 's-Gravensteen, was erected in about 867 to the west of the St Baafsabdij on an artificial hill above the River Leie. Like the Burg in Bruges, 's-Gravensteen was built by Baldwin of the Iron Arm, the first Count of Flanders, to protect his lands from the Vikings.

A sprawling city gradually grew up around the abbeys and castle. In the thirteenth century a considerable area of flooded land was reclaimed, and in 1251-69 the Lieve canal was cut between 's-Gravensteen and the Minnewater harbour in Bruges. The Lieve was one of the main routes through Flanders up until the construction of the railways; John Evelyn travelled along it in 1641, as did the Duke of Wellington's troops bound for Waterloo in 1815.

The cloth industry developed in Ghent, as in other Flemish cities, in the thirteenth century. By the mid-fourteenth century some 4,000 weavers and 1,200 fullers worked here, out of a total population of about 50,000. The harsh working conditions led to many revolts and disturbances,

Ghent

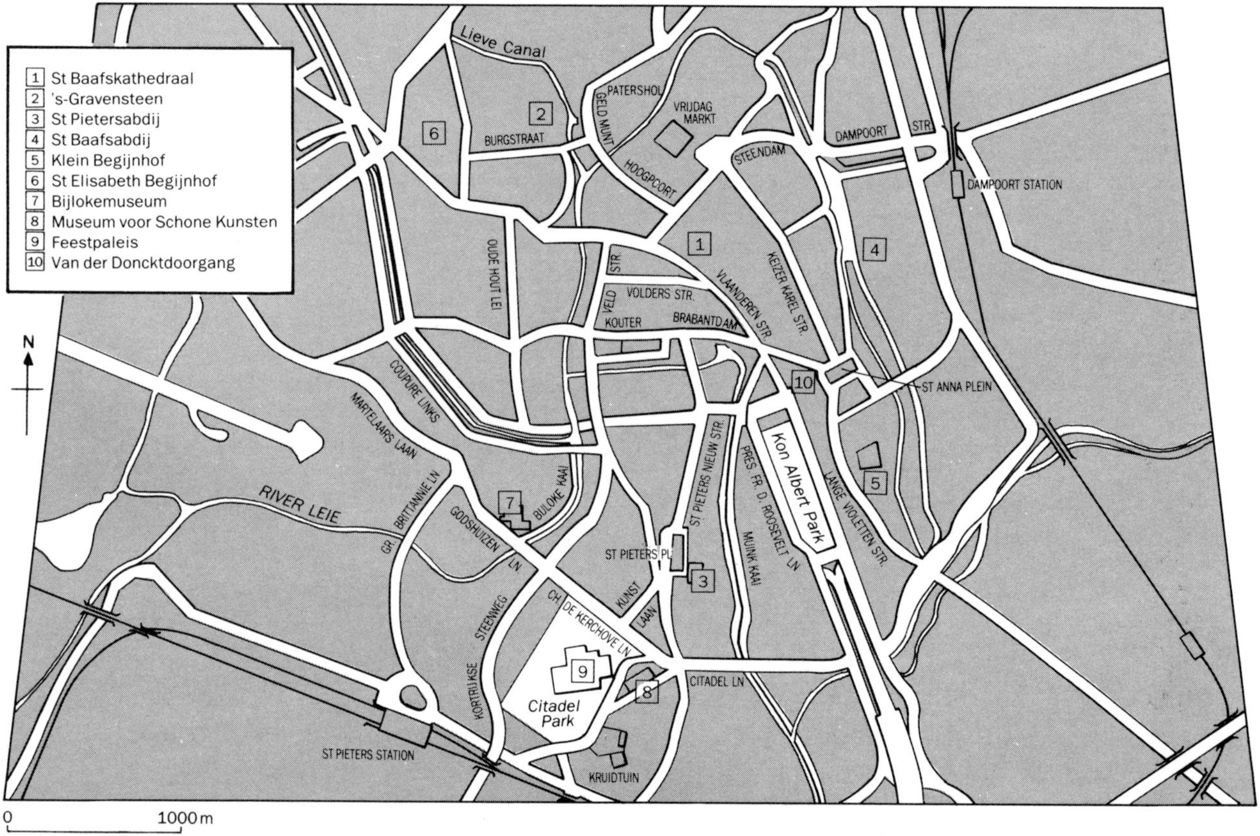
1 St Baafskathedraal
2 's-Gravensteen
3 St Pietersabdij
4 St Baafsabdij
5 Klein Begijnhof
6 St Elisabeth Begijnhof
7 Bijlokemuseum
8 Museum voor Schone Kunsten
9 Feestpaleis
10 Van der Donckdoorgang
N
Lieve Canal
PATERSHOL
GELD MUNT
VRIJDAG MARKT
BURGSTRAAT
HOOGPOORT
STEENDAM
DAMPOORT STR.
DAMPOORT STATION
OUDE HOUT LEI
STR.
VOLDERS STR.
VELD
KOUTER
BRABANTDAM
VLAANDEREN STR.
KEIZER KAREL STR.
ST ANNA PLEIN
COUPURE LINKS
MARTELAARS LAAN
Kon Albert Park
PRES. FR. D. ROOSEVELT LN
ST PIETERS NIEUW STR.
MUINK KAAI
LANGE VIOLETTEN STR.
RIVER LEIE
GR. BRITTANNIE LN
GODSHUIZEN LN
BIJLOKE KAAI
ST PIETERS PL
KUNST LAAN
CH. DE KERCHOVE LN
KORTRIJKSE STEENWEG
Citadel Park
CITADEL LN
ST PIETERS STATION
KRUIDTUIN
0
1000 m

including one remarkable incident in 1274 when all the weavers and fullers left the city in a mass protest.

Class conflict is a constant motif in the history of Ghent. In the Early Middle Ages, its patrician families were loyal to the Counts of Flanders, who in turn were bound feudally to the kings of France. The cloth-workers, however, relied on steady supplies of high-quality English wool, and so tended to support the English. In the tense atmosphere that developed, the patrician families prudently shut themselves away in rugged stone town houses with crenellated battlements. A few of these austere *stenen* (fortified houses) are still standing, such as the Grote Sikkel on Hoogpoort, the Borluutsteen on Korenmarkt and the Geraard de Duivelsteen on Limburgstraat.

At the Battle of the Golden Spurs in 1302, the Ghent workers' militia, led by Jan Borluut, played a decisive role in defeating the knights sent by Philip the Fair of France. The armed workers of Ghent also fought the French in the Hundred Years War, persuaded by Jacob van Artevelde of the advantages of supporting Edward III of England. Van Artevelde, although born into an aristocratic family, became a champion of the Ghent guilds and in 1337 was appointed Captain of Ghent. However, he later outraged the townspeople by suggesting that a son of Edward III be appointed Count of Flanders, and in 1345 he was murdered when a mob stormed his home. His son, Philip van Artevelde, later led the Ghent militia against Louis de Male, Count of Flanders. He defeated the Count's army in 1381, but the following year Charles VI of France marched into Flanders and crushed his rebellious vassals at the Battle of Westrozebeke.

Always spoiling for a fight, the folk of Ghent defied the Dukes of Burgundy, as they had defied the Counts of Flanders. In 1448 they refused to pay a hefty tax imposed by Philip the Good on salt and grain. Somewhat remarkably, Ghent was resilient enough to repel the Duke's forces for five years, but in 1453 its army was finally defeated at Gavre, where some 16,000 townspeople perished. After imposing a crippling fine on the city and cancelling its ancient privileges, Philip the Good indulged a theatrical whim by compelling the leading burghers of Ghent to walk out of a city gate wearing hangman's nooses around their necks, then to kiss the dust at his feet.

Yet the pugnacious spirit of Ghent was far from being quashed, as Charles V was to discover. Charles had been born in Ghent in 1500 in the Prinsenhof (pl. 11), a magnificent palace of which all that remains is a fifteenth-century gate on Bachtenwalle called the Donkere Poort (Black Gate). The birth of Charles V to Joanna the Mad is romantically portrayed in Browning's famous poem *How They Brought the Good News from Ghent to Aix*. However, when Ghent defied him in the 1530s by refusing to pay a tax, Charles V had no qualms about punishing his native city. In 1540 he ordered the St Baafsabdij to be demolished to make way for a massive Renaissance citadel. A contingent of loyal Spanish troops was garrisoned there, ready to crush any further signs of rebellion.

As might have been expected, Ghent sided with the Dutch rebels in the revolt against Philip II of Spain. In 1576 the Spanish troops were expelled from the city, and the massive citadel which had been standing a mere 36 years was razed to the ground. In the same year, representatives from the provinces of the Netherlands met at Ghent to sign the Pacification of Ghent. Had this document achieved its aims, the Spanish would have withdrawn from the Netherlands. But Philip II was determined to crush the Protestant revolt in his northern lands and sent Alexander Farnese, Prince, later Duke, of Parma, to recapture the cities from the rebels. Ghent fell to the Spanish in 1584, and with this defeat its spirit of independence finally seems to have been crushed.

French armies marched into Ghent in 1678, 1708, 1745 and again in 1794. The French occupations led to a revival of the ancient class division in Ghent between the French-speaking aristocracy and the Dutch-speaking townspeople. The rich settled in the southern quarters of the city, building the beautiful Baroque and Rococo palaces on Veldstraat and Kouter (an elegant square where a flower market is held on Sundays), while the workers inhabited the decaying northern areas such as the Patershol.

In 1800 Ghent was rescued from two centuries of ruin by Lieven Bauwens, a daring local who

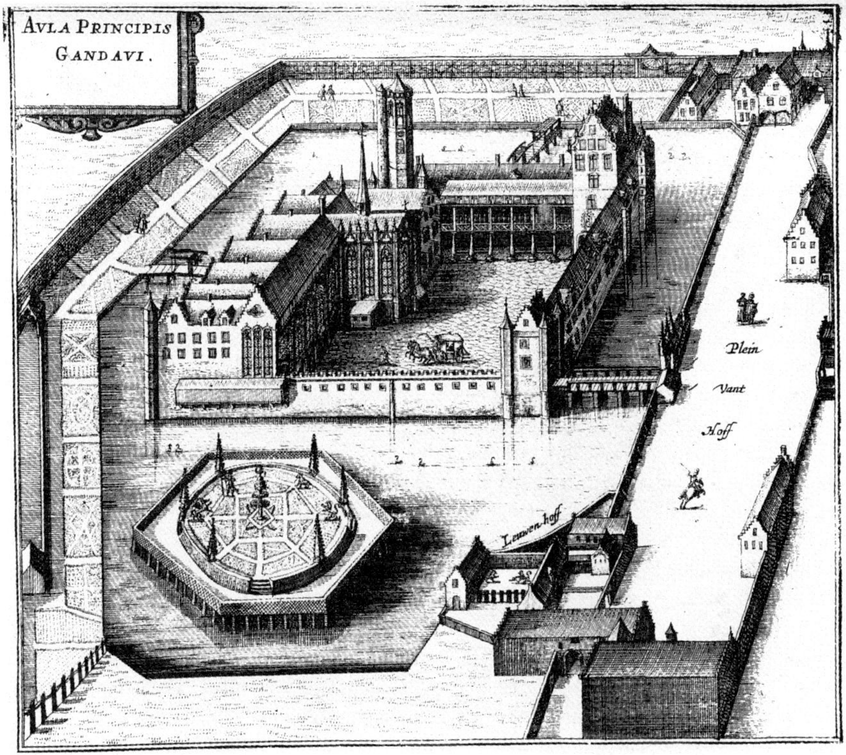

Plate 11 Prinsenhof

smuggled a spinning jenny out of Britain and set up a cotton-spinning mill in the former charterhouse of Ghent. This swashbuckling deed formed the basis of a flourishing textile industry. Factories were established in 's-Gravensteen, the Prinsenhof and in the many abandoned monasteries, and proved so successful that the population of Ghent trebled in the nineteenth century, reaching 160,000 in 1900. To facilitate transportation, a new canal was cut between Ghent and Terneuzen, and a large port built to the north of the city. But the conditions of the nineteenth-century textile workers were almost as harsh as those endured by the weavers and fullers in the fourteenth century, prompting the establishment of strong trade unions, which served much the same purpose as the 52 mediaeval guilds. As if to prove the point, several socialist buildings were erected on Vrijdagmarkt, where the guilds had traditionally gathered.

The World Fair of 1913 was held in Ghent's Citadelpark, prompting the city to embark on an ambitious programme of improvements. Much of the old city was restored, including the marvellous row of gable houses along Graslei. Two great buildings erected for the World Fair are still standing: the Feestpaleis, where a flower show is held every five years, and St Pieter's Station, which still has a splendid restaurant of banqueting hall proportions, decorated with gleaming ceramic tiles, polychrome capitals and eccentric lamps. This mood of optimism in Ghent was crushed by World War I, when the townspeople again fought hard to protect their freedom, as the many war memorials reveal.

Even today, there is a sharp contrast in Ghent between the old Flemish quarters to the north and the elegant French districts to the south. The dividing line is clearly marked by the row of towers of St Niklaasskerk, the belfry and St Baafskathedraal. The streets of French Ghent such as Veldstraat and Brabantdam have fashionable boutiques, elegant tea rooms and gleaming shopping arcades, whereas Flemish Ghent is an area of narrow cobbled lanes with old brick houses, dark taverns and dusty curiosity shops. It is this contrast, I think, that makes Ghent so fascinating and diverse a city, with an atmosphere very different from Bruges.

Walk 1: The Waterfront

Our first walk takes us along the old quays of the River Leie, where we obtain beautiful views of old gables and mediaeval church towers. After darkness has fallen, a stillness descends upon the old quarters of Ghent like the aftermath of a battle. The quays along the River Leie are particularly delightful at this hour, with floodlit spires and castle walls reflected in the water. 'Now it is merely a city of twenty-six slumbering islands filled with fantasies,' as the Italian poet Giuseppe Ungaretti wrote in a travel article in 1933.

We perhaps do not think of Ghent as a port, but from early times canals have laboriously been dug to provide the city with an outlet to the North Sea. The oldest harbour at Ghent was established on the Leie waterfront in the Early Middle Ages. Grain was shipped here from Artois in northern France and stored in massive Romanesque granaries. The fish market and meat market were also erected on this quayside. Nowadays only tour boats use the river, but the magnificent old meat hall is still standing on the waterfront, and there are fishmongers and vegetable stalls on the bustling Groentenmarkt nearby.

Let us begin this walk (*see page 82 for map*) on **Korenmarkt**, a bustling square where several tramlines converge. Most of the buildings overlooking this former grain market date from the seventeenth century, but there is one austere stone relic from the Early Middle Ages at Korenmarkt 6-7. Known as the **Borluutsteen**, this thirteenth-century stone house was built for the Borluut family in a rugged Romanesque style. At the Battle of the Golden Spurs in 1302, Jan Borluut, who then lived here, led some 700 Ghent militiamen to victory against the French knights. Isabella Borluut, one of the donors of the *Adoration of the Mystic Lamb* in the cathedral, also came from this family.

We now walk down **Veldstraat**, where we might

Ghent

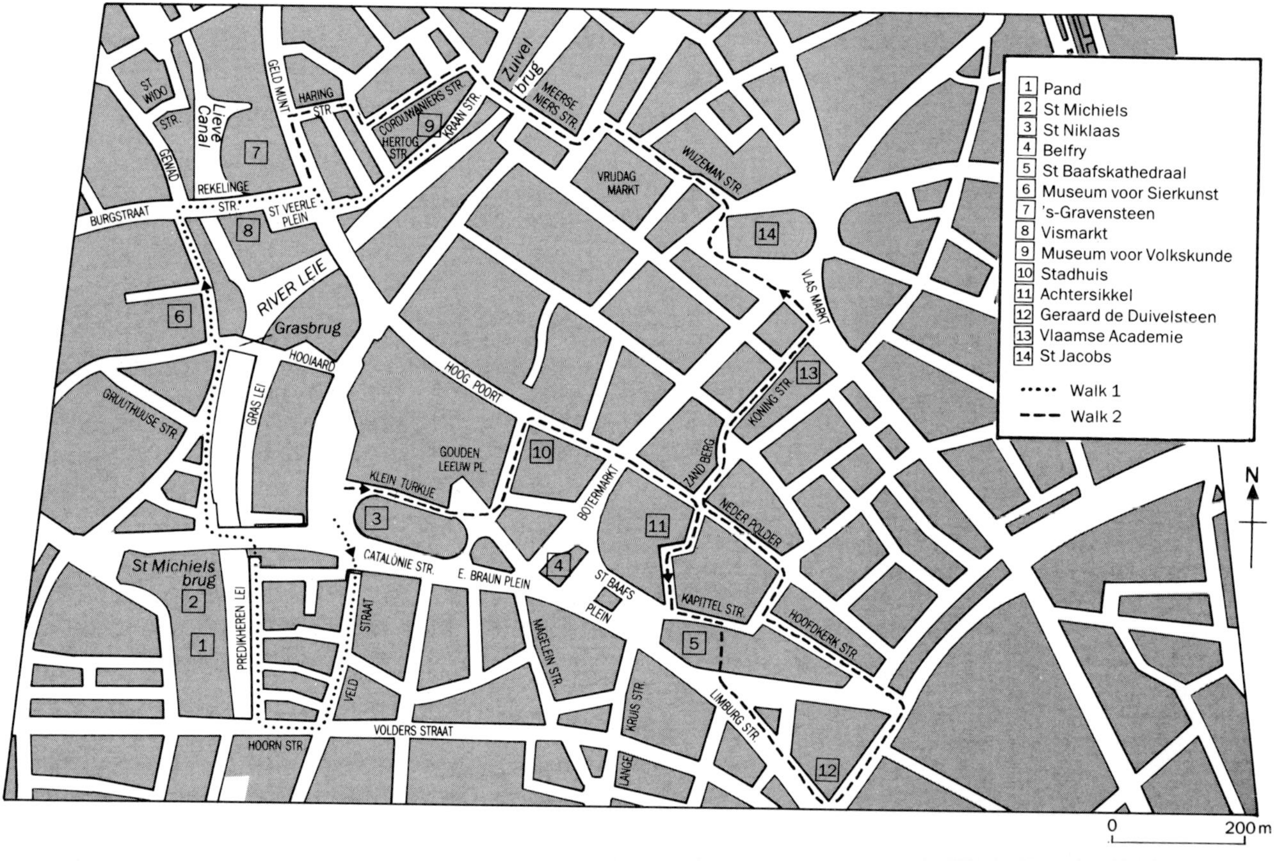

1 Pand
2 St Michiels
3 St Niklaas
4 Belfry
5 St Baafskathedraal
6 Museum voor Sierkunst
7 's-Gravensteen
8 Vismarkt
9 Museum voor Volkskunde
10 Stadhuis
11 Achtersikkel
12 Geraard de Duivelsteen
13 Vlaamse Academie
14 St Jacobs
Walk 1
Walk 2
N
0
200 m
ST WIDO STR.
Lieve Canal
GEWAD
GELD MUNT
HARING STR.
CORDUWANIERS STR.
HERTOG STR.
KRAAN STR.
Zuivel brug
MEERSENIERS STR.
VRIJDAG MARKT
WIJZEMAN STR.
REKELINGE STR.
BURGSTRAAT
ST VEERLE PLEIN
RIVER LEIE
Grasbrug
HOOIAARD
VLAS MARKT
HOOG POORT
GRUUTHUUSE STR.
GRAS LEI
GOUDEN LEEUW PL.
KLEIN TURKIJE
KONING STR.
ZAND BERG
BOTERMARKT
NEDER POLDER
St Michiels brug
CATALONIE STR.
E. BRAUN PLEIN
ST BAAFS PLEIN
KAPITTEL STR.
HOOFDKERK STR.
PREDIKHEREN LEI
STRAAT
MAGELEIN STR.
VELD
KRUIS STR.
LIMBURG STR.
VOLDERS STRAAT
HOORN STR.
LANGE

fortify ourselves with coffee and pâtisserie at Bloch, a traditional Alsatian bakery on the corner of Veldstraat and Hoornstraat. Veldstraat is the main shopping street of Ghent, but there are still a few elegant eighteenth-century town houses that have somehow managed to survive amidst the modern department stores. In the case of one eighteenth-century house just off Korenmarkt, all that remains is the façade. It was behind this splendid frontage that the Treaty of Ghent was signed in 1814, bringing to an end the 1812-14 war between Britain and the United States. The house occupied by the American delegate John Quincy Adams stood on the corner opposite Bloch's, where there is now a tobacconist's shop. Other important people have also stayed in Veldstraat; in the Hôtel d'Hane-Steenhuyse at number 82, for example, Louis XVIII of France was offered sanctuary by Count d'Hane during the Hundred Days of Napoleon's return to power. The Duke of Wellington once stayed in the Hôtel Vander Haeghen opposite, a decaying palace now used for exhibitions of urban planning in Ghent.

From Bloch we turn down Hoornstraat to reach the River Leie, then follow Predikherenlei to the right. The waters of the Leie lap against the crumbling brick walls opposite of a former Dominican friary, the **Pand**, founded about 1420. Adjoining it is the **St Michielskerk**, one of the many Late Gothic churches in Flanders that for one reason or another were never completed. Work began on this church in about 1440 but was halted in 1566 because of Protestant disturbances. The choir was finally completed in 1623-50 in an anachronistic Late Gothic style. A Baroque sacristy, added in 1650 in the corner between the north transept and the radiating chapels of the choir, was partly demolished when the high bridge to the right was constructed, and then rebuilt in Neo-Baroque style. The west tower is a very sad-looking stump; a seventeenth-century plan to add a soaring Gothic spire was abandoned due to financial difficulties.

We ascend a flight of steps on to the **St Michielsbrug**, a bridge built across the Leie in 1905. From here we obtain a magnificent view eastwards to the mediaeval, or mainly mediaeval, towers of Ghent. We see, from left to right, the sober grey sandstone tower of the St Niklaaskerk, the belfry encrusted with gilded details, and the honey-coloured sandstone tower of St Baafskathedraal. The Neo-Gothic post office clock tower on the far left, built in 1904, is very much in keeping with the Gothic spirit of Old Ghent with its encrustations of gargoyles, statues and coats of arms.

Once across the bridge, we descend the steps in front of the Graaf van Egmont (a restaurant described on page 88 to reach the quiet quay of Korenlei. From here we can look across the river to the splendid row of buildings on **Graslei**, which were fastidiously restored for the World Fair of 1913. The **Gildehuis van de Vrije Schippers** (guild house of the free boatmen) at number 14 reminds us that this quiet stretch of water was once a bustling harbour. This powerful guild monopolised inland shipping in much of Flanders. The guild house, a confident Late Gothic building of 1531 designed by Christoffel van den Berghe, is faced with a golden-toned sandstone that is particularly beautiful in the light of the setting sun. The tympanum above the entrance incorporates a relief depicting a sixteenth-century three-masted caravel, while two bas reliefs at the top of the gable show boatmen weighing anchor.

A narrow alley that once served as a firebreak separates this guild house from the **Korenmetershuis** at number 11, a Renaissance guild house built in 1698 for the grain measurers. To the left, we see a tiny step-gabled house at number 10 that has been squeezed into another narrow firebreak. This Flemish Renaissance building was erected in 1682 as a toll house, where shipments of grain were taxed. A delightful café called **'t Tolhuisje** now occupies the building, an interesting feature of which is the glass-roofed room at the back, built in the former alley. The exposed stone side wall of a massive Romanesque granary contrasts strikingly with the tasteful pale yellow walls and fragile modern lighting. 't Tolhuisje is open daily from 11.30am, serving coffee, cakes and Belgian beers.

The importance of the grain trade to Ghent is evident when we look at the rugged Romanesque granary next to the toll house. Erected in the twelfth century, this was used to store grain up until 1734. To its left stands the old guild house of the grain measurers, a sixteenth-century Flemish Renaissance building.

Four years before he designed the guild house of the free boatmen, Christoffel van den Berghe built the **Gildehuis van de Metselaars** (guild house of the masons) at number 8. But he did not build it here; the edifice was originally erected in 1527 opposite the St Niklaaskerk, and only moved here in 1912 to improve the appearance of the quay for the World Fair. The building is an attractive example of Brabant Gothic style, with pinnacles and blind tracery, which gives it an appearance that is both soaring and ethereal.

At the end of Korenlei we come upon a building known as **Het Anker** (The Anchor) at number 7. This striking Baroque building painted a shrill tone of orange was erected in 1739 for the Onvrije Schippers, another guild of boatmen. After being subject to the jurisdiction of the free boatmen for many centuries, this guild was finally granted various concessions in the eighteenth century. The boatmen celebrated by building this jaunty guild house festooned with anchors, dolphins, lions, and a weathervane in the form of a ship.

Standing upon the **Grasbrug** at the end of the quay and looking north, we see the River Leie joined from the left by the Lieve canal. The magnificent old standstone building on the right bank of the Leie is the former **Groot Vleeshuis** (Great Meat Hall). Built in the early fifteenth century in a sober Gothic style, its roofline is punctuated with dormer windows, rather like a Bruges almshouse.

The nineteenth-century fish market stands at the confluence of Leie and Lieve. Perhaps you can see the three prongs of a trident glinting in the sun. This is wielded by a splendid figure of Neptune who stands above the entrance to the old fish market on St Veerleplein.

We make our way there along Jan Breydelstraat, a street running behind the houses on our left. This takes us past the **Museum voor Sierkunst**, a museum of decorative arts occupying a large and decaying Baroque mansion at number 7, built in 1754. At present the museum consists merely of a series of rooms furnished in period style, the most notable of which is a Rococo dining room with a painted ceiling and lofty mirrors (room 7). Hanging over the table is an extraordinary wooden chandelier borne aloft by an eagle. The other rooms are, in comparison, rather drab and lifeless, although the temporary exhibitions held here are often quite interesting. At the time of writing, the rear wing of the mansion was being rebuilt to house a large collection of Art Nouveau objects.

On reaching Burgstraat, we will see a striking Renaissance house opposite, the **Graven van Vlaanderen** (Counts of Flanders), decorated with 14 medallions bearing portraits of the Counts of Flanders and Dukes of Burgundy. This façade was put up in preparation for a visit to Ghent by Philip II of Spain, its proud owner aware that the stately procession would pass this way to reach the Prinsenhof.

Turning right across a bridge, the **Hoofdbrug**, we see the massive buttressed walls of 's-Gravensteen rising from the waters of the Lieve canal like a grey cliff. Continuing down Rekelingestraat takes us past the Neo-Gothic fish market, built in 1872 and decorated with 12 stone reliefs illustrating different types of fish. Then we reach **St Veerleplein**, where Neptune stands sentinel over a bombastic Baroque portal that once led into the old fish market. Built in 1689 and restored after a fire in 1872, this portal now leads to a garage. Nevertheless it is still a splendid sight to behold, decorated by half columns with seaweed-like encrustations. The maritime theme is echoed in the pediment, where Neptune is surrounded by seahorses and dolphins. The window below is flanked by two female figures representing the rivers that meet in Ghent. The Leie is symbolised by a reclining man holding a billowing sail, while the Scheldt is a voluptuous Rubensian woman with a catch of fish at her side.

After crossing St Veerleplein, we continue along Kraanlei, our destination now being the **Museum voor Volkskunde** at number 65. This captivating museum of local history occupies a beautiful quayside almshouse called the Kinderen Alynshospitaal. The story behind the foundation of this almshouse starkly illustrates the atmosphere of violence and vengeance in fourteenth-century Ghent. The building stands on the site of a town house owned by Hendrik Alyn, the leader of the guild of fullers. Hendrik Alyn wanted to marry a girl called Godelieve, the daughter of a weaver, but for a fuller to marry a weaver's daughter in Ghent was as unacceptable as for Romeo to marry Juliet. The two guilds were constantly feuding, and in one clash that took place on the Vrijdagmarkt in 1345 some 500 people were slain. To make matters worse, Godelieve was already pledged to a weaver named Simon Rym. However, she broke with him and married Hendrik Alyn in 1354. This so enraged Simon Rym that he murdered both Hendrik and his brother Zeger. To expiate this crime, the Rym family was ordered to build an almshouse and chapel on the site of the Alyns' home.

The almshouse was rebuilt in 1519 in a sober Renaissance style, and adorned merely with a statue of St Catherine above the entrance. In 1940 a folk museum was established here, aiming to evoke everyday life in Ghent at the turn of the century. What is appealing about the museum is the diversity of material contained in its 77 tiny rooms, which we are led through by an intriguing route of narrow corridors and winding stairs. The exhibits include numerous photographs, postcards, paintings, toys and utensils. Many of the rooms contain reconstructed old interiors, such as a grocer's shop, a cobbler's, a weaver's workshop, a tavern with a wall-rack of clay pipes, a candlemaker's shop, a barber's, and a clog-maker's workshop decorated with the mementoes of a dedicated pigeon fancier. There is also a small puppet theatre which puts on shows in Dutch on Saturday afternoons.

Entering the chapel, which was rebuilt in the 1540s, we are surprised by two giant figures standing beside the polychrome wooden altar. These rather unflattering effigies purport to represent the Archduke Albert and Archduchess Isabella, and were once paraded through the streets during *Reuzen Ommegang* (Giants' Parade). Mock identity papers issued in 1947 for the giant couple are displayed in a glass case, the Archduke's height being given as three metres.

There are also several bourgeois rooms, including a bathroom with an uninviting zinc bathtub and a salon with a brass statuette of Napoleon I on the mantelpiece, revealing that the upper classes in Ghent still harboured French sympathies in the nineteenth century. In one of the last rooms, we come upon some souvenirs of World War I, including a fragment from a Zeppelin shot down by a British pilot near Ghent, and some makeshift chessmen fashioned from spent bullets by Belgian soldiers in the trenches.

On leaving the museum, we may end the walk in a nearby café. Tempting on summer afternoons, the Waterhuis aan de Bierkant, which stocks some 100 types of beer, has a terrace on the right bank of the Leie at the Groentenmarkt. On chilly days, the fashionable **Caffé Wolff** at Kraanlei 27 is a pleasant place to pause for a coffee, beer or aperitif. Occupying a Renaissance step-gabled house built of a delightful pinkish brick, this tastefully furnished café recalls the interiors painted by the Flemish Primitives. It is decorated with red floor tiles, bare stone walls and a lofty ceiling of wooden beams resting on stone corbels; on wintry days a few logs smouldering in the stone fireplace add to the atmosphere.

When it comes to dinner, there are several attractive restaurants occupying old houses on the quays of the Leie and Scheldt. The Graaf van Egmont at St Michielsbrug 21 is a convivial restaurant situated in a Baroque gable house with a striking view of the towers of Ghent. It offers traditional Flemish specialities such as stews of one sort or another, and *paling in 't groen* (eel in a green sauce made with chervil).

Another possibility is Tap & Tepel at Gewad 7, an enchanting and somewhat surreal wine and cheese house open from 7pm. Its wines are listed in a weighty and scholarly tome, while the cheeses are displayed on a sideboard called the 'cheese altar'. The atmosphere is decidedly mediaeval, with candles dripping hot wax, old Flemish paintings of saints and cherubs, and wooden shelves lined with a miscellany of bizarre objects. I cannot imagine a more fitting end to a day in Ghent than to sit at one of the heavy wooden tables here sipping a glass of mulled wine, beneath a hovering angel or a massive iron lamp decorated with dangling bunches of illuminated grapes.

Walk 2: The Old City and the Van Eyck Altarpiece

On this walk we explore the island known as the **Kuip**, on which the oldest part of the city stands. Originally a neck of land at the confluence of the Leie and Scheldt, the Kuip became an island when the Ketelkanaal was dug. Although the Scheldt now runs underground, leaving only a short stretch of water in which the towers of the Geraard de Duivelsteen are mirrored, we can still clearly see the outline of the island on the map of Ghent. This walk takes us along the quiet, crooked streets of Old Ghent and into the cathedral and the castle. The highlight of the walk is the altarpiece of the *Adoration of the Mystic Lamb* by Jan and Hubert van Eyck—the most beautiful mediaeval Flemish painting in Belgium, if not in the world.

Let us begin this walk (*see page 82 for map*) in front of the post office on Korenmarkt, where we can admire the west front of the **St Niklaaskerk**, the parish church of Ghent's merchants and guilds. St Niklaas is a marvellous example of Tournai Gothic, a sober form of Early Netherlands Gothic, modelled on the great cathedrals of northern France. The nave, aisles, transepts, choir and the tower above the crossing were built in the thirteenth century in this austere Gothic style. In the fourteenth century, new chapels were added to the aisle by various guilds, and in the fifteenth century the choir, surrounded by radiating chapels, was completed in Late Gothic style. St Niklaas became rather dilapidated over the years, but at the time of writing it was being expertly restored to its old splendour.

On leaving St Niklaas, we walk down **Klein Turkije**, a dark street of ancient, blackened buildings facing the north side of the church. This takes us past a row of small buildings clinging to the north wall of the church, including a curious kiosk with a miniature mansard roof. Klein Turkije's ancient stone houses are now occupied rather incongruously by cafés, restaurants and even a throbbing discotheque. In 1521 Albrecht Dürer lodged at an inn within the sombre thirteenth-century building known as Den Rooden Hoed (The Red Hat) at number 2, which is now occupied by a café ominously named Catastroph.

Upon reaching **Gouden Leeuwplein**, stand in front of the Hotel De Fonteyne (named after a sixteenth-century chamber of rhetoric which met here) to obtain a striking view of the **Belfry**. The sturdy base of Tournai limestone was laid in about 1314, and by 1323 the first four floors had been built. Fifteen years later, the two graceful upper tiers were added using a lighter freestone, and the top was decorated with four corner turrets bearing statues representing the armed officials who guarded the belfry. Only one of the original figures has survived, and is now displayed within the belfry.

The ornate spire with gleaming gilt details was added in 1911-13 as part of the World Fair celebrations. Its design is based on the original fourteenth-century elevation drawing, now in the Bijlokemuseum. The spire is surmounted by a copper dragon, modelled closely on the belfry's fourteenth-century weathervane. The privileges granted to Ghent by the Counts of Flanders were once kept in a strongbox, fitted with three locks, which sat in a ground-floor room of the belfry. This room was in turn protected by two doors each secured by three more locks.

The belfry also contained a set of bells which were rung on important occasions, including one cast in 1325 bearing the inscription, 'My name is Roeland, if I toll, then there is a fire at hand, if I peal, then there is victory in Flanders land.' Roeland ceased to herald good news or bad in 1540 when Charles V ordered its removal. The great bell was eventually melted down in 1659 and recast by the Dutch bell-maker Pieter Hemony into a 37-bell carillon, which now hangs on the fifth floor. Hemony also cast three large bells known as the Triomphanten, one of which later cracked after an ill-advised attempt to strike it using a charge of electricity. The damaged bell was lowered from the tower and now sits in the square below.

The long Gothic building adjoining the belfry was once the **Lakenhalle** (Cloth Hall). Begun in

1425, it was left unfinished in 1445 and only finally completed in 1903. Its vaulted crypt, used as a prison from 1742 until 1902, now contains a cavernous restaurant rather like the *Ratskellern* restaurants situated in the cellars of many German town halls. The delightful Baroque building attached to the north side of the cloth hall was, rather surprisingly, also a prison. Built by David 't Kind in the eighteenth century, it was nicknamed *Mammelokker* (The Suckling) after the Baroque relief in the pediment illustrating the story of Cimon and Pero. In this Roman legend, Cimon, an old man, was languishing in prison awaiting execution when his daughter Pero visited him and quenched his thirst from her breast.

Let us now look at Ghent's magnificent **Stadhuis** (Town Hall), which we reach by turning up Stadhuissteeg, a narrow lane beside the Novotel, then right along Hoogpoort. We need to cross the street to appreciate the town hall's Late Gothic façade, which was designed by Rombout Keldermans and Domien de Waghemakere in 1516 (pl. 12). We will come upon other Late Gothic buildings on our wanderings in Antwerp, Brussels and Mechelen, but none quite so delicate and delightful as the frontage of the town hall of Ghent, which resembles a frail curtain of lace. The main features are the ornate balcony where proclamations were read, the projecting choir of the magistrates' chapel, and the striking polygonal tower on the corner of Hoogpoort and Botermarkt. On studying the tracery at close quarters we will discover delightful details amidst the abstract designs, such as oak leaves and acorns, and vines laden with tiny bunches of grapes.

The problem with buildings in this florid Flemish style was that they were extremely laborious and costly to build. Many of them were therefore abandoned long before they reached completion. Such was the case with Ghent's town hall, of which only one quarter had been built by 1535, when work was halted due to the worsening relations between the city and Charles V. In Ghent's Bijlokemuseum are two detailed elevation drawings made by Keldermans and De Waghemakere in 1517, showing how the town hall should have looked. One drawing depicts the façade on Hoogpoort, which was originally

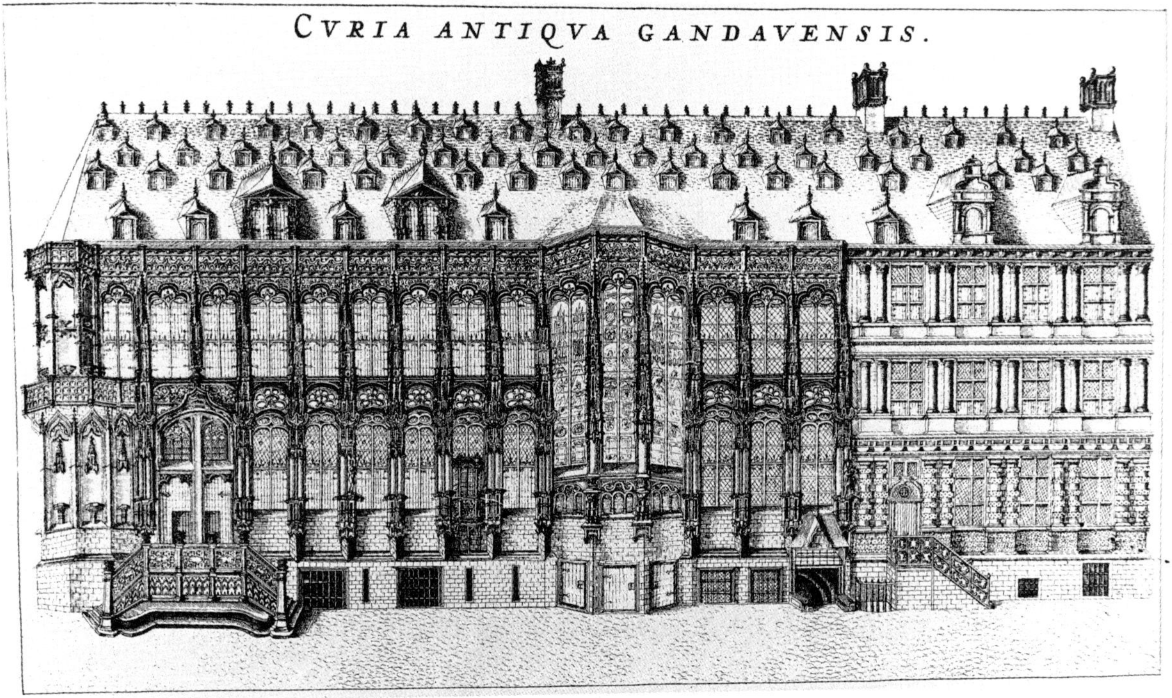

Plate 12 Stadhuis

planned to be 21 bays wide, though only 15 bays were ever built. The other shows the façade on Botermarkt, where only four out of 17 planned bays were built. The elaborate niches on the façade were earmarked for statues of the Counts of Flanders and Dukes of Burgundy, rather like those on the town hall in Bruges, but these were never produced. Some niches are now occupied by nineteenth-century Neo-Gothic inventions, including the figure of Rombout Keldermans stroking his chin contemplatively as he examines a drawing of the town hall, and a rather glum Domien de Waghemakere holding a model of an elaborate double niche. Nineteenth-century Ghent Gothic enthusiasts once went so far as to propose tearing down several buildings so that the town hall envisaged by Keldermans and De Waghemakere could finally be built. This would have entailed the demolition of the Renaissance extensions built in 1572 on Hoogpoort, and in 1620 on Botermarkt, but the plan was quashed by the Belgian Commission for the Protection of Historic Monuments.

Many historic events have taken place in Ghent's town hall. In 1576 representatives of the provinces of the Netherlands assembled in the hall which runs most of the length of Hoogpoort to sign the Pacification of Ghent, a document which unfortunately proved of little consequence in securing peace and religious freedom in the Low Countries. A curious feature of this hall, now known as the Pacificatiezaal, is the intricate maze picked out in the floor in tiles of two different colours. Apparently, offenders in the Middle Ages who had been sentenced by the court to embark on a pilgrimage might instead follow this labyrinth.

Standing on the corner of Hoogpoort and Botermarkt, we will see the **St Jorishof** opposite at Botermarkt 2. This hotel claims to be the oldest in Europe, dating back to 1228. The ancient step-gabled building of blackened stone that we see on Botermarkt was erected in 1469-77 as the cross-bowmen's guild house. St George, the patron saint of this guild, can be spotted slaying a dragon on the gable top. It was in the St Jorishof in 1477 that Mary of Burgundy, succeeding her father Charles the Bold, was forced to sign the Great Privilege, in which she promised to uphold the privileges of the

Flemish cities. Later that year she gave a sumptuous banquet here in honour of the ambassadors sent by the Emperor Frederick III to woo her on behalf of his son, the Archduke Maximilian. The proposal was accepted and Mary married Maximilian that year. Charles V, whose statue stands on the corner of the town hall opposite, also stayed several times in the St Jorishof, and in 1805 Napoleon I spent two nights here.

The coats of arms on the front of the hotel recall episodes in its rich history. They are the arms of Ghent, Flanders, Austria, Burgundy, Spain and the guild of St George. At the top of the gable is a window with attractive tracery, where the crossbowmen had their chapel. Notice, too, the Madonna on the corner of the hotel, a rarer sight in Ghent than in Bruges.

We now cross Botermarkt, of which Dorothy Wordsworth wrote, 'I can hardly endure to call a place so dignified by such a name.' The butter market which gives this square its humble name was once held in the cellars of the town hall, where Ghent's tourist office is now situated.

Continuing along Hoogpoort, we come upon a row of ancient stone houses. Just beyond the St Jorishof are two fifteenth-century houses known as the **Grote Moor** (Great Moor) and the **Zwarte Moor** (Black Moor). Then come two magnificent houses flanking Biezekapelstraat, built by the Van der Sickelen family. To the left of the lane, at Nederpolder 2, is the **Kleine Sikkel**, a rugged Romanesque town house built in the thirteenth century of unhewn stone, with a crenellated curtain wall at the top. The family's coat of arms, much weathered, can still be seen above the door. In 1418 the family quit this fortified town house and moved into the **Grote Sikkel**, a less sombre step-gabled house on the opposite side of the lane.

Venturing down the alluring Biezekapelstraat, we discover a third house once owned by the Van der Sickelen family—the **Achtersikkel**—situated, as its name suggests, behind the Grote Sikkel. This secret dwelling house overlooking a small courtyard is the most attractive of the three Sikkels, particularly at night when it is floodlit. Various Gothic and Renaissance buildings and arcades are picturesquely grouped around a lofty round tower of white stone dating from the fifteenth century. The little turret behind is a fourteenth-century relic.

The Grote Sikkel, Kleine Sikkel and Zwarte Moor now house the Ghent Conservatory of Music, which generates the curious cacophony of noises that we hear as we wander down Biezekapelstraat. A stone tablet attached to a rear wall of the Achtersikkel depicts, appropriately, Orpheus soothing the wild animals with his lyre. My guess is that this stone was placed here when the building was converted to a conservatory in 1900.

Biezekapelstraat takes us by a delightfully crooked route to the cathedral, past a strange and somewhat eerie Neo-Renaissance house dated 1901 and covered with floral decorations in stone and rusting wrought iron. We then turn left along Kapittelstraat to enter the **St Baafskathedraal** (Cathedral of St Bavo) by the north portal. Let us now sit down in the nave to read the history of this great church.

The St Janskerk, as the cathedral at Ghent was originally named, was constructed in three phases. Following mediaeval custom, the choir was built first. Grey Tournai sandstone was used in the construction, which proceeded at a snail's pace from the late-thirteenth to the mid-fifteenth century. The choir rests on an immense and impressive crypt, where there are some traces of a twelfth-century Romanesque church. Another interesting feature of the crypt is its 15 radiating chapels, some still containing family tombs and religious paintings.

In the second phase of construction, lasting from 1462-1534, the tower was built in Brabant Gothic style, a more ornate Gothic than that of Tournai, and more appealing because it used a warm, crumbly sandstone from the quarries of Lede. In the third period of construction, from 1533-59, the nave and transepts were erected, these too in Brabant Gothic style.

This church was the setting for two chapters of the Order of the Golden Fleece. The seventh chapter of the Order was convened here by Philip the Good in 1445, and in 1559 the twenty-third chapter was called by Philip II of Spain, just before he left the Netherlands for the last time. The 51 coats of arms of the knights who attended in 1559 now hang in the south transept, including one above the portal bearing the Medici coat of arms, decorated with the Florentine family's device of five balls. Two years after this chapter, Philip II elevated Ghent to a bishopric and this church, which already in 1540 had been renamed the St Baafskerk after the old abbey in Ghent of that name, then became St Baafskathedraal.

The Rococo pulpit in the cathedral is a masterpiece of Counter-Reformation sculpture. Carved by Laurent Delvaux in 1745, it is a lavish work of marble, oak, gilt and stucco. It represents Time, an old man, being awakened from his slumbers by Truth, a young maiden holding a book with an admonition of St Paul's to the spiritually asleep. A magnificent double staircase leads up to the pulpit, to which two carved figures are pointing, as if to direct the attention of the congregation towards the priest's words. Yet it would be rather difficult to concentrate on the priest, given the rollicking drama that is unfolding above, as two angels wrestle with a large cross, while a third places an apple in the mouth of a golden snake entwined around a gnarled tree trunk.

Behind the pulpit is a portrait of Bishop Triest, who donated this work to the cathedral. The bishop paid for many other sumptuous Baroque embellishments to replace the art treasures destroyed in the religious troubles of the sixteenth century. He made a gift of the marble choir screen, and the set of four copper candlesticks placed on the high altar. The candlesticks are decorated with the coat of arms of Henry VIII of England, and were designed by Benedetto da Rovezzano to support a canopy above the royal tomb at Windsor. Bishop Triest's mausoleum, which stands in the ambulatory, was carved in 1654 by Hieronymus Duquesnoy the Younger, and shows the sad and aged bishop reclining wearily on his tomb.

The ambulatory and radiating chapels of this church had scarcely been finished, and the tower and nave not yet begun, when Jan and Hubert van Eyck painted the famous altarpiece of the *Adoration of the Mystic Lamb* to hang in a chapel of the church. This work, which took some twelve years to complete, is one of the most remarkable achievements of mediaeval European art. Returning to his inn after seeing it in 1521, Albrecht

Dürer wrote in his diary, 'I saw the St John panel, a stupendous painting of great intelligence.'

In about 1420 Burgomaster Joos Vydt and his wife Isabella Borluut commissioned Hubert van Eyck to paint a polyptych to hang within their family chapel in the St Janskerk, as the church was then called. However, Hubert van Eyck apparently died in about 1426, when the altarpiece was still very far from completion. His brother Jan was called to Ghent from Bruges to take over the work, and it was finally completed in 1432. The interesting question of who painted what is far from being resolved, and some scholars have even cast doubt on the existence of Hubert.

As long ago as 1510, the Flemish Renaissance poet Jean Lemaire de Belges described Jan van Eyck as 'the king of painters, whose perfect and minute works will never fall into vain oblivion'. He was absolutely right, as we discover on entering the chapel in which the painting hangs, joining, probably, a crowd of art-enthusiasts talking excitedly in a dozen or so different languages. The painting, which has drawn travellers to Ghent for more than 500 years, is a large winged altarpiece comprising 26 separate scenes painted on 12 oak panels. It is a truly encyclopaedic work illustrating 14 separate episodes from the Old and New Testaments. The seventeenth-century art critic Karel van Mander counted 330 complete faces in the painting.

The altarpiece is teeming with delightful details, such as the glint of light on precious jewels, and the almost legible words of an illuminated manuscript. There are numerous tiny Gothic inscriptions in the work, sometimes incorporated into a length of fabric, or hidden in a floor tile. Van Eyck has also skilfully depicted the natural world; a botanist once studied the altarpiece and identified some 40 different types of flower.

The figure of God (or Christ, say some critics) fills the middle panel of the upper register. He is portrayed in a cloak of vivid scarlet cloth, the most costly material woven by the Flemish weavers. The Virgins in Jan van Eyck's *Madonna with Canon Van der Paele* in Bruges and *Madonna with Chancellor Rolin* in Paris also wear cloaks made from this sumptuous cloth.

Mary, who is seated to the left of God, has a face

of astonishing beauty. Her lips, Karel van Mander observed, 'seem to utter the words that she is reading in a book'. To the right of God is the figure of John the Baptist, who is wearing a hair shirt beneath his sumptuous green cloak, a quaint reminder of the preaching in the wilderness. The inner panels of the wings are decorated with angels singing and making music. The faces of the singers, though not particularly beautiful, are meticulously realistic, capturing the angels in an unguarded moment as they strain to pitch their voices precisely. Notice, too, the bellows operator who is just visible behind the portable organ in the right panel.

We then come to the extraordinary naked figures of Adam and Eve on the outer panels of the wings. Never before in the history of painting were naked figures depicted with such realism. Look at Eve's foot, which seems to be balanced on the very edge of the picture frame. Then compare Adam's right foot, which seems to be stepping out of the frame! This uncanny realism was perhaps intended to remind the mediaeval viewer that Adam and Eve are part of our world, the world of flesh, whereas God, Mary and the choirs of angels are not.

The panels in the lower register are linked together into a unified composition. The middle panel shows the Adoration of the Mystic Lamb, a theme taken from the Gospel of St John. 'Behold the Lamb of God, which taketh away the sins of the world,' is inscribed in Latin on the rim of the altar upon which the lamb stands, but the letters are too minuscule to read from afar. To the fore stands the Fountain of Life, a symbol of redemption. The prophets are kneeling to the left of the altar, and the apostles to the right. Four other groups of figures converge on the altar. At the bottom left are the patriarchs, who were, according to mediaeval scholars, the founders of the human race. The figure wearing a white gown and carrying a twig of laurel is sometimes identified as Virgil. Emerging from a copse of exotic bushes behind are bishops and confessors dressed in blue vestments and bearing palm branches. This group is balanced by the virgin saints emerging from the copse to the right, including Agnes, with a lamb, and Barbara, carrying a miniature tower. The final group, occupying the bottom right corner, are saints and martyrs. St Stephen is identified by the stones, symbolising his martyrdom, which he carries in his vestment.

The landscape is painted with supreme clarity, recalling those sunny spring days in the Low Countries when the light inundates the flat landscape. The rolling hills in the distance are rather more southern European, and the horizon is bristling with exotic Mediterranean trees, probably added by Jan van Eyck after his journey to Portugal, where he had been sent by Philip the Good to paint a portrait of his intended bride. Some of the mediaeval spires may also be based on buildings that Van Eyck saw on his travels. In the middle stands the spire of Utrecht Cathedral, which also appears in Van Eyck's Rolin altarpiece in Paris. We may also recognise Cologne Cathedral and the Romanesque church of Gross St Martin on the summit to the right; Memling's *St Ursula Shrine* in Bruges also includes views of these buildings. There is one discrepancy in Van Eyck's version, however, for Cologne Cathedral is shown with twin spires; although these were begun in the Middle Ages, they were not in fact completed until the nineteenth century.

Now let us look at the side panels, in which groups of figures advance towards the altar over symbolically rough and stony ground. On the far left are the just judges, whose expressive faces and contemporary costumes suggest that they may be portraits of eminent Burgundians. According to an old legend, the horseman in the foreground is Hubert van Eyck, while the figure fourth from the left is said to be his brother Jan. In the adjoining panel are the warriors of Christ, including St George bearing a shield with a red cross, on which there is an inscription, but again illegible from our vantage point. The two panels to the right show the holy pilgrims led by an overlarge St Christopher, and the holy hermits led by St Antony Abbot, the founder of monasticism.

Lastly, we should look at the 12 panels on the back of the wings. The donors appear on the outer panels of the lower register. Above we see the Annunciation, set in a lovely Flemish interior with views through windows to the streets of Ghent. These panels, which are in the style of the

Master of Flémalle, were probably painted by Jan van Eyck after a visit to the Master's shop in Tournai in 1427. The four panels are linked together by common features such as the roof beams and floor tiles. A gilt inscription in ornate calligraphy fills the gap between the two figures of the Annunciation. '*Ave Maria!*' the angel declares. The Virgin replies, '*Ecce ancilla Domini*' (Behold the handmaid of the Lord). Notice that the Virgin's reply is upside-down, apparently an odd mediaeval convention to allow God to read the message.

The tumultuous story of the Ghent altarpiece began in the 1550s when Philip II attempted to ship the work to Madrid. The church authorities refused to permit this, and Philip II had to make do with a copy painted by the Mechelen artist Michiel Coxie, who laboured for two years on this task. At about this time, the predella of the altarpiece, apparently showing a scene of Hell, was mysteriously lost.

The Ghent altarpiece would almost certainly have been destroyed during the Protestant disturbances in 1566 had the church authorities not hidden it in the church tower. During the period of Protestant rule, the altarpiece was moved to the town hall, and the aldermen on one occasion came close to presenting the work to Queen Elizabeth I of England to repay a loan. After Ghent was recaptured by the Spanish in 1584 it was moved back into the church, where it remained undisturbed for the next two centuries, until in 1781 Emperor Joseph II of Austria expressed his distress at the naked figures of Adam and Eve. The church authorities dutifully removed the offending panels and replaced them with copies in which Adam and Eve are clothed in shaggy cloaks. These ridiculous panels now hang at the west end of the nave.

After Napoleon I invaded the Low Countries, the four middle panels were carried off to Paris to be displayed along with other war booty, but the side panels were concealed from the pillaging army. Following Napoleon's defeat, the panels were returned to Ghent, but a few months later the church authorities sold the six remaining side panels to an antique dealer for 3,000 florins. This dealer promptly resold the panels to a collector in Britain for the princely sum of 100,000 florins, and in 1821 the shrewd British dealer earned an even more handsome profit by selling the panels to the Kaiser Friedrich Museum in Berlin for 400,000 florins. To add to Ghent's sorrow, the four panels left hanging in the cathedral were badly damaged by a fire. During the three years spent restoring these panels, there was nothing at all to see of the Van Eyck altarpiece in Ghent.

A series of fortuitous events then brought the scattered pieces of the altarpiece together again. In 1861 the Adam and Eve panels resurfaced, having been lost since 1781, and were purchased by the Musée des Beaux-Arts in Brussels. At the end of World War I, under the reparation terms of the Treaty of Versailles, Germany was required to give Belgium a number of works of art, including the panels sold to the Berlin gallery in 1821. The original Adam and Eve panels were then returned to Ghent in 1920, and the altarpiece was again complete, for the first time in 141 years. But this happy reunion was of short duration, for in 1934 a thief broke into the church and removed the panel at the bottom left-hand corner, with the just judges on one side and the grisaille St John the Baptist on the other. This was one of the panels that had been sold to the Berlin gallery, and the wooden frame had been carefully sawn down the middle so that the two paintings could be hung separately. The thief prised apart the two pieces, keeping the painting of the just judges and depositing St John the Baptist in a left-luggage locker. He then demanded an enormous sum of money for the return of the second painting. The authorities refused to pay the ransom, however, and the painting has never been recovered. In its place is a copy painted during the German occupation in World War II. There is a further twist to this bizarre story, for the artist who made the copy apparently expressed his patriotism by secretly altering the face of one of the just judges to resemble King Léopold III, who was then being held prisoner in the palace at Laeken.

Later in the war the altarpiece was removed from Belgium for safety, first to Pau, then to 'Mad' King Ludwig's castle of Neuschwanstein, and finally to Munich. It was returned to Ghent after the war, and has only moved once since then, when it was transferred from the Vydt chapel to its present secure location in a windowless chapel in the nave.

Once we have explored the cathedral, we head down Limburgstraat, past a bronze sculptural group of Jan and Hubert van Eyck surrounded by admirers. This work was unveiled, as so much in Ghent was, for the World Fair in 1913. Further on we come to a bridge where the River Scheldt makes a brief appearance before vanishing below the streets. Under the terms of the Treaty of Verdun in 843, the Scheldt formed a frontier between the lands of the French kings to the west and those of the German emperors to the east. Rising like a cliff from the water is the **Geraard de Duivelsteen**, a massive fortified town house of blackened Tournai sandstone. This *steen*, once much larger than it is today, was erected in the thirteenth century for Geraard de Duivel (Gerald the Devil), whose sinister epithet was apparently due to his extremely dark skin.

We now turn left along Reep, left again up Hoofdkerkstraat and right into Kapittelstraat. On reaching Nederpolder we turn left, then right into **Zandberg**, an attractive little square with a curious pump surmounted by an obelisk, put here in 1810 by the Napoleonic administrators. In Koningstraat, straight ahead, we come upon the **Vlaamse Academie** (Flemish Academy) at number 18, which occupies a beautiful Rococo town house designed by David 't Kindt in 1746. A pleasing effect is achieved by the mock drapery, which seems to flutter from the window ledges and balustrades. In the setting sun the golden-hued sandstone of the building is particularly striking. This street leads to the **St Jacobskerk**, a sober church with twin Romanesque towers, and a thirteenth-century Gothic choir and nave.

Wijzemanstraat leads thence into **Vrijdagmarkt**, a cheerful square surrounded by cafés and restaurants. Vrijdagmarkt is particularly lively on Fridays, market day, when the heavy smell of waffles and *frites* wafts around stalls selling clothes, smoked sausage and boiled sweets. Many important events in Ghent's history have taken place on this square. The imposing Neo-Gothic statue of Jacob van Artevelde in the middle commemorates the rousing speech he made here urging the citizens of Ghent to support Edward III of

England against the King of France. The three bas reliefs on the base are decorated with allegorical female figures representing the treaties concluded by Van Artevelde. The polychrome coats of arms of the guilds of Ghent also appear on the base, recalling that Van Artevelde was at one time captain of each of the 48 guilds. It was also here, on a day in 1345 that became known as Evil Monday, that the weavers and fullers clashed following a dispute about wages, leaving some 500 people dead.

Of the many guild houses that once stood on Vrijdagmarkt, only one remains. Built in about 1450 for the guild of tanners, **Het Toreken**, as it is called, stands on the corner of Kammerstraat, its elegant round watchtower attractively restored and emblazoned with the guild colours. On the opposite side of the square is a warehouse designed in 1899 by Ferdinand Dierkens for the Ghent socialist society *Vooruit*, bearing the Dutch equivalent of 'Workers of the World Unite'.

Meerseniersstraat leads down to the River Leie, a short distance downstream of a fifteenth-century cannon known as Dulle Griet. Facing us on the other side of the bridge are two interesting Baroque houses. **De Fluitspeler** (The Flautist) at Kraanlei 79 is decorated with six terracotta reliefs representing the five senses, and a flying deer. The house takes its name from a delightful figure of a flautist in a medallion at the top. Allegorical figures on the cornice representing Faith, Hope and Charity finish off this crowded composition. **De Zeven Werken van Barmhartigheid** (The Seven Works of Charity) at Kraanlei 77 is decorated with six panels. The top three represent the charitable works of burial of the dead, comforting prisoners and visiting the sick; the lower ones depict feeding the hungry, refreshing the thirsty and clothing the naked. The seventh work of charity—lodging travellers—was represented by the building itself, which was once an inn.

Rodekoningstraat leads straight ahead into the **Patershol**, a picturesque mediaeval quarter first settled in the tenth century by leather workers. After years of neglect, the lanes and houses in this corner of Ghent are being carefully restored, and attractive cafés, restaurants and art galleries are transforming an area that was once a notorious slum. The street to the left named Corduwaniersstraat (Cordwainers Street) is a reminder of Ghent's old leather trade. The word cordwainer derives from Cordoba in Spain, which produced luxurious leather products. Spanish leather workers were particularly renowned for *guadamacil*, a gilded leather introduced to Spain by the Moors, and used in Flanders for wall hangings. There is a beautiful room in the Plantin-Moretus Museum in Antwerp that is hung with this sumptuous Spanish leather.

If we turn right from Corduwaniersstraat along Hertogstraat, we come upon a lane to the left named Haringstraat. Here we glimpse the grey stone walls of 's-Gravensteen, a lowering castle which we reach by walking down the lane and turning left along Geldmunt.

Dark and dank, bristling with turrets and battlements, **'s-Gravensteen** (The Count's Castle) (pl. 13) is a stark symbol of mediaeval power. On a chilly winter's day, the castle is rather gloomy, but when the sun shines, it is delightful to climb up to its breezy battlements and look down upon the old city.

's-Gravensteen is a motte-and-bailey castle, consisting of a raised mound (the motte) surmounted by a tower, and surrounded by a courtyard (the bailey) enclosed by an elliptical outer wall with 24 turrets. It stands on the site of a castle erected in the ninth century by Count Baldwin of the Iron Arm, which was rebuilt in 1180 by Count Philip of Alsace, Duke of Flanders, to curb the rebellious spirit of the townspeople of Ghent.

Entering 's-Gravensteen, you will see a rather sinister cruciform window with eerie dripping stalactites, flanked by twin octagonal towers of blackened stone. This curious window may have been intended by Philip of Alsace to remind his vassals of his crusading zeal. Eleven years after erecting this castle, Philip of Alsace died in the Holy Land at the siege of 'Akko.

In the thirteenth century a building known as the Count's Residence was added alongside the keep. It was a rather less severe style of architecture, with stepped gables and Romanesque windows. Despite this improvement, the castle was not a comfortable place to live. By the fourteenth century, the Counts of Flanders had moved to a

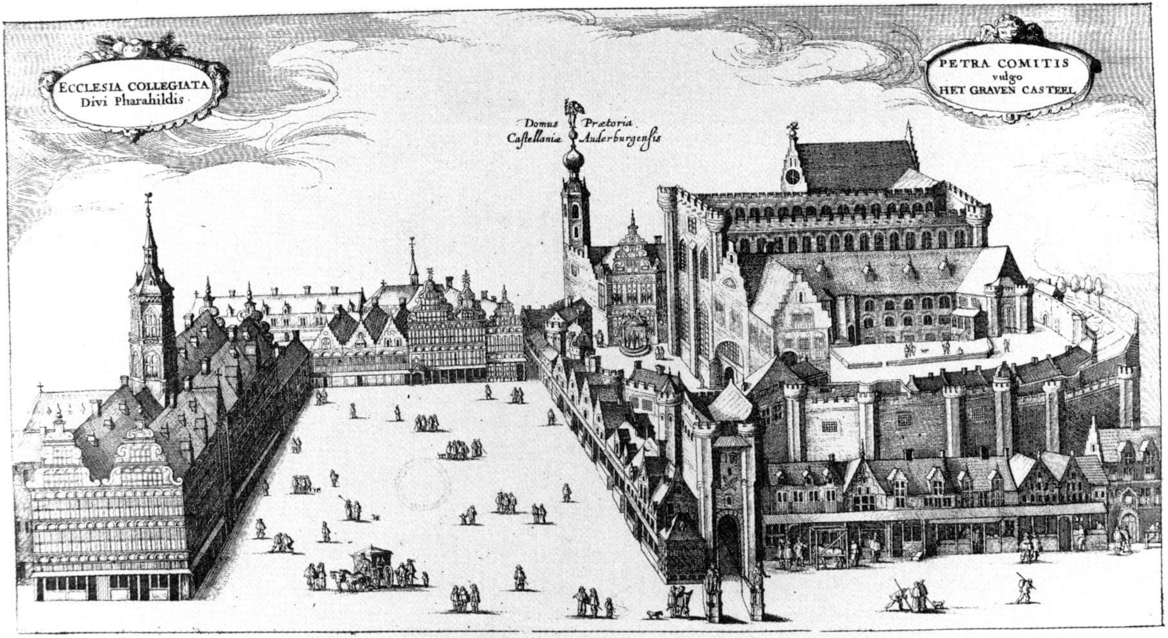

Plate 13 's-Gravensteen

new residence built on the island to the west. This eventually became the magnificent Prinsenhof, where Charles V was born in 1500.

In 1779 the abandoned 's-Gravensteen was sold to a local architect who conceived an ambitious plan to convert the buildings into dwelling houses and artists' ateliers, but this was never realised. During the industrial revolution, 's-Gravensteen was one of many old buildings in Ghent used as a textile mill, and looms clattered in the vacated rooms of the Count's Residence. In 1888 a zealous restoration of it was begun; families living within the castle were evicted and the houses that had been built against its walls were torn down. The old castle buildings were then purged of looms and litter, and rebuilt in a style that owed as much to Victorian values as to the architecture of the Early Middle Ages. A century on, weeds have sprung up on the battlements and pigeons have returned to their old haunts in the stone walls, thereby restoring a patina of desirable decay to this ancient hulk.

Many of the rooms of 's-Gravensteen seem to have been used at one time or another as prisons, including the room in the gatehouse with the cruciform window. The most dreadful sight in the castle is the oubliette sunk deep below the floor in one of the rooms in the Count's Residence. Another unlovely feature of 's-Gravensteen is a small room containing an exhibition of torture instruments. The gloomy impressions that these rooms inevitably leave are quickly dispelled, however, when we ascend the dark spiral stairs to emerge on the windy battlements, where we obtain a magnificent panoramic view of Ghent's old stone and brick houses, the magnificent row of towers, and the cluster of cranes around the port.

Ghent Explored Further

If time permits you should venture further afield in Ghent, for there are numerous interesting sights outside the centre. Many can be reached by tram from Korenmarkt, although it is also pleasant to wander along the quays of the Leie, Scheldt and Lieve to reach the outlying quarters.

I. Southern Ghent

Southern Ghent has an elegant nineteenth-century character, with broad, leafy avenues and imposing mansions. The main attractions of this quarter are the antiquities collection of the Bijlokemuseum and the paintings in the Museum voor Schone Kunsten. We might also stroll into the **Citadelpark**, an attractive park laid out in the 1870s. It stands on the site of a citadel erected in 1819-31 by the Duke of Wellington at the time of the short-lived Kingdom of the Netherlands. A solitary gate is all that survives of the citadel, which was once one of the strongest fortresses in Europe. A sonorous Latin inscription above the gate proclaims, *Anno XI Post Proelium ad Waterloo Exstructa* (Erected nine years after the Battle of Waterloo). Another device in French declares, *L'union fait la force* (Strength through unity). This slogan did not convince the Belgians, who in 1830 severed their links with the Dutch.

Behind the park is the attractive, if small, **Kruidtuin**, a botanical garden tended by the university. Here some 7,000 species of plants from all over the world thrive in alpine gardens or shady glades. A lake bordered with magnolias and pines adds a certain romance to this scientific garden.

Opened in 1904 beside the Citadelpark, the **Museum voor Schone Kunsten** (Museum of Fine Arts) houses a diverse collection of paintings by Flemish, Dutch, British and French artists. Ghent has always been more interested in industry than art, one feels, and its collection of old paintings does not compare with the galleries at Brussels, Antwerp and Bruges, although its contemporary art collection contains many pleasing works. Before visiting the gallery, we might pause for a coffee in the airy Neoclassical apse at the centre of the building.

Room 1 contains a curious long and narrow painting which once formed part of a retable. It depicts the conquest of Jerusalem by Titus in a most detailed manner. Also in this room is a sixteenth-century set of three double portraits representing Philip the Good and his third wife Isabella of Portugal, John the Fearless and Maria of Bavaria, and Charles the Bold and his second wife Isabella of Bourbon.

The most remarkable paintings in the collection are two works by Hieronymus Bosch in room 2. The *Bearing of the Cross* is a nightmarish painting filled with 17 of the ugliest physiognomies in the history of art. Besides Christ's, the only remotely attractive face is that of a woman who is turning her head away from the scene. Even she is not an entirely appealing character, however, and looks mildly amused by the mockery that Christ is suffering. The other work by Bosch is a *St Jerome*, set in a bizarre landscape with curious plants and animals.

The rooms of nineteenth-century art contain many attractive works, including some beautiful views of the River Leie by Emile Claus. The river was known to the English in the Middle Ages as 'The Golden River' because it flowed through extensive fields of flax. The peaceful landscape of the Leie attracted Flemish Impressionists in the nineteenth century, rather as the Seine attracted French Impressionists.

Not far from the Citadelpark, the **Bijloke-museum** at Godshuizenlaan 2 occupies an attractive Cistercian abbey founded in 1228 by Ferrand of Portugal. The oldest buildings still standing are the fourteenth-century infirmary and refectory. The rest of the abbey was destroyed when the Dutch rebels built new ramparts here. After the Spanish recaptured the city, a relatively stable period followed when the Cistercian nuns slowly rebuilt their abbey, sometimes (as we will discover) in an unexpectedly ostentatious style. The abbey was used as a hospital up until the 1920s, then converted to house a museum of antiquities established in 1884.

The museum has amassed a diverse collection of local curiosities, including furniture, guild relics, armour, decorated tiles, ship models, paintings, maps, plans, sculpture, old doors, coins and ironwork. The collection is not so carefully tended as the Gruuthusemuseum in Bruges, I suspect because Ghent looks towards the future rather than the past. Nevertheless it is an interesting museum to explore, fascinating in much the same way as the overcrowded attic of an old stately home might be.

We first explore the four walks of the lower cloister, where we come upon a surprising room decorated with lavish stucco. Dated 1715, it looks as if it might have once been a ballroom in one of the palaces on Veldstraat. Not so; this room was built by the Cistercian nuns *inside* the ancient abbey refectory. During a recent restoration of the abbey, this Baroque oddity was removed, thankfully, and rebuilt here. An interesting painting in this room shows the *Inauguration of Charles II of Spain as Count of Flanders*, a splendid ceremony that took place on the Vrijdagmarkt in 1666. A magnificent Baroque stage was erected on the east side of the square for the occasion, behind which the watchtower of the guild house of the tanners is just visible.

The lower cloister contains several rooms furnished in period style, including an Empire drawing room furnished with a few mementoes of the Napoleonic era. The most attractive of these rooms is the former Treasury of the Stadhuis at Ghent, a rich and dark Baroque interior, rendered rather mysterious by the greenish light that filters in from the overgrown courtyard. The walls are hung with sumptuous gilt leather of Mechelen, and a magnificent polychrome mantelpiece dated 1682 is decorated with a painting of the *Four Seasons* by Joos van Cleef.

Mid-way up the staircase, we come upon the abbey's fourteenth-century refectory, a majestic Gothic structure with a painted oak roof resting on columns of grey Tournai sandstone. On the west wall is a fourteenth-century fresco with John the Baptist and St Christopher. Pilgrims often lodged at the abbey, which explains the figure of St

Christopher, patron saint of travellers. The fresco at the east end is a Last Supper, a subject often found in abbey refectories. The long side walls are decorated with Neo-Gothic frescoes. Placed in the middle of this vast room is the tomb of Hugo II, chatelain of Ghent, who died in 1232. The recumbent figure is dressed in chain mail, and rests on a stone slab supported by four fantastic animals. A castle at his head recalls his function as chatelain (keeper of the castle), and a dog at his feet symbolises his duty of fidelity.

At the top of the stairs we enter the former dormitory where an interesting collection of guild relics is displayed. Notice the 18 wooden guild emblems once carried in processions, including those of the carpenters, boatmen, millers (a windmill), weavers (a loom) and porters (a figure in eighteenth-century dress carrying an enormous sack on his head). The upper cloister contains further curiosities, including a strange little room decorated entirely with Delft tiles.

On leaving the cloister, we enter a little garden with a clipped hedge, there obtaining a good view of the west gable of the refectory. It is a magnificent brick Gothic design dating from the 1320s, with a large trefoil cornice surrounded by niches, rose windows and blind arches.

The former house of the abbess, which we enter from the garden, contains various furnished rooms including an attractive Flemish kitchen. On leaving this house, we still have one room to visit, which we might easily overlook. Situated at the end of the corridor opposite the porter's lodge, it is the Room of the Governors of the Poor Board, a splendid Baroque interior designed in 1689, with panelling by Norbert Sauvage. A chimneypiece painting by Joos van Cleef depicts the foundation of the Poor Board at Ghent by Charles V in 1531, the spires of Ghent looming in the background. The other paintings in the room depict the Seven Works of Charity.

II. Begijnhofs in Ghent

Ghent has three large Begijnhofs, all of them interesting to explore if you have time to spare. The oldest in the city, and probably in Flanders, is the **St Elisabeth Begijnhof**, to the north of

Begijnengracht. In 1234 Countess Joanna of Constantinople granted the Beguines this site, which was then an area of marshy ground beyond the city boundary. Although the walls of the St Elisabeth Begijnhof are no longer standing, it has not entirely lost its enclosed and protective atmosphere. Proveniersterssstraat is particularly attractive, with houses dating from the sixteenth and seventeenth centuries, their doorways delightfully adorned with iron grilles, elaborate bell-pulls and saints in niches.

The **Klein Begijnhof** on Lange Violettenstraat is the most appealing of Ghent's Begijnhofs. Founded in 1234 by Countess Joanna of Constantinople, it has the advantage of retaining its walls and portal, so that the outside world is kept at bay. Leaving behind the furore of traffic, we enter its secluded precincts to hear the birds singing in the lime trees. The houses, dating mainly from the seventeenth and eighteenth centuries, surround a spacious grassy square rather like an English village green. Each house has its own small portal with a statue of a saint to identify it. The doors, as always, have elaborate if rusty bell-pulls and tiny iron grilles through which to scrutinise each visitor.

There is another Begijnhof, the **Groot Begijnhof**, in the eastern suburbs of the city, beyond Dampoort station. Built in 1874 to rehouse the women of the St Elisabeth Begijnhof, this large Neo-Gothic complex is rather less appealing than the older Flemish Begijnhofs, though it has a certain dusty and dilapidated charm.

III. St Baafsabdij

With its crumbling slate walls and overgrown Romanesque windows, the ruined **St Baafsabdij** is perhaps the most romantic spot in Ghent. After the roar of traffic along the quays of the Scheldt, it is particularly pleasing to enter this unexpected ruin and hear only the cheerful twitter of the caretaker's budgerigars.

A Benedictine abbey was founded here in about 630 by St Amandus, a missionary from Aquitaine. It is named after Bavo, a Brabant landowner who lived a debauched life until his wife died, whereupon he mended his ways, giving away his possessions and living as a hermit in a hollow tree near Ghent. The abbey was later granted to Eginhard, Charlemagne's biographer. When Charlemagne visited Ghent in 811 to inspect the fleet he had assembled to fight the Vikings, he probably stayed here as a guest. Despite Charlemagne's efforts, the Vikings reached Ghent in 851, and this abbey was one of the buildings sacked.

The monks returned in the tenth century, and in 940-50 rebuilt the abbey in splendid Romanesque style. It was here that Edward III of England and Queen Philippa stayed when they visited Ghent in 1341. Their third son, John of Gaunt, was born in the abbey, his epithet being an anglicisation of Gand, the French name for Ghent. Twenty-eight years later the marriage of Philip the Bold and Margaret of Flanders took place in the abbey church.

Little now remains of the abbey church or of the guest quarters where John of Gaunt was born. In 1540, enraged by Ghent's refusal to pay a new tax, Charles V ordered much of the abbey to be destroyed. In its place a huge Renaissance citadel was erected, designed by the Italian military architect Donato Buoni de Pellezuoli. Modelled on a citadel at Verona, the Spanish citadel, as it was called, was a square fortress with pointed bastions at the corners, surrounded by a moat. It was the first Renaissance fortress built in the Low Countries, soon to be followed by similar oppressive strongholds at Antwerp and Utrecht. The abbey church, which appears in the foreground of the prospect of Ghent (pl. 10), was demolished. Only the choir was spared, to serve as a chapel for the Spanish troops. The parish church on this island and numerous houses in the neighbourhood were also razed to the ground in this military operation.

After a long siege in 1576, the Spanish troops garrisoned here surrendered to the Dutch rebels, and much of the citadel was then demolished. The last vestiges were finally removed in 1831, leaving only street names such as Spanjaardstraat, and two tombstones inscribed in Spanish, to recall the existence of the citadel.

The abbey buildings have been left as romantic ruins, unlike 's-Gravensteen, which was restored to almost mint condition for the 1913 World Fair.

The wistful decay of these ancient buildings provides a fitting setting for the fascinating **Museum van Stenen Voorwerpen** (Lapidary Museum) established here in 1887. In the mysterious and melancholy cloisters, we discover an enchanting miscellany of tombstones, columns, boundary stones, capitals, urns, balustrades, doorways and tympana.

The chapter house, dormitory and refectory are still standing, the Spanish garrison having used these as barracks and store rooms. The oldest part to survive is an unusual octagonal building off the east walk of the cloister, erected in 1171 in a sober Romanesque style. The ground floor originally served as a lavatory, and a sanctuary above held the relics of St Macharius, an eleventh-century saint who allegedly saved Ghent from an outbreak of plague. The cult of St Macharius revived during an outbreak of plague in the seventeenth century, and the lavatory was then converted into a small chapel.

An Early Gothic chapter house was added to the east of the cloisters in the thirteenth century. In this now sadly dilapidated building, we see fragments of the stone benches on which the monks sat, and a few broken columns from which the vaulting sprung. There are also a number of unusual stone tombs set into the floor.

The north cloister contains two tombstones (number 25 and 26) bearing Spanish inscriptions. Rescued from the chapel of the Spanish citadel, these tombstones, both dated 1625, mark the graves of the garrison commander, Luis Espinola, and its chaplain, Franco Henriquez. Above, we see three curious tympana reliefs (number 31) salvaged from a house dating from 1660. The original owner was a local surgeon who commissioned the reliefs to advertise his trade. They depict an unfortunate woman undergoing bloodletting, the Good Samaritan helping the injured traveller, and the dissection of a corpse.

Three rooms off this cloister contain an interesting collection of sculptural fragments which have been imaginatively exhibited on scaffolding, as if in a mason's yard. The most striking work is a Romanesque baptismal font (number 119) with reliefs on its four sides depicting Adam and Eve in Paradise, the Expulsion, the Magi before Herod, and (now rather damaged) the Adoration of the Magi. This twelfth-century font is presumed to have come from the parish church, which was demolished during the construction of the Spanish citadel.

We also see an interesting tombstone of a Ghent boatman named Jan van den Poele (number 154), decorated with a three-masted caravel of the type used to ship goods to Ghent during the sixteenth century. Notice, too, the rather enigmatic fragments of a head and hands (number 171) which were salvaged from the Baroque fish market after the fire in 1872.

The third room we enter was designed in a graceful Late Gothic style in 1495. Known as the **Mercatelzaal**, it was built for Abbot Raphael de Mercatel, a bastard son of Philip the Good born in Bruges and given the name of the Venetian merchant his mother married. From the paintings and engravings reproduced in this room, we can form an impression of the vanished abbey buildings, and also of the citadel erected by Charles V. A seventeenth-century engraving by Sanderus (number 194) shows us the plan of the citadel, with the abbey cloister clearly visible in the top left corner.

Directly above the Mercatelzaal is the extraordinary Romanesque refectory, to which we ascend by a flight of steps off the cloister. Extending along the entire north walk of the cloister, this vast and gloomy hall dates from the end of the twelfth century. The solemn rhythm of the arched windows along the south wall is broken only once by a niche, where a monk would read from the Benedictine orders during meals. After being used by the Spanish garrison as an arsenal, the refectory served as a parish church in the nineteenth century. It now houses a collection of mediaeval tombstones, which came here in a rather curious way. Up until the eighteenth century, churches and monasteries in Ghent were accustomed to raise funds by selling off ancient tombstones to the city authorities. These were then used in the foundations of bridges, sluices and other public works. In the nineteenth century, when many of these buildings were renovated or demolished, several old tombstones were uncovered. These were presented to the newly established lapidary museum, and are now displayed here. The most interesting find was the probable tombstone of the artist Hubert van Eyck (number 79) discovered in 1892.

Further curiosities salvaged from Ghent's past are displayed in the overgrown garden to the west of the cloisters, where the guest house and kitchens once stood. The gigantic head of a river god (number 199) is all that remains of a nineteenth-century bridge blown up in World War II. Equally impressive is a large eighteenth-century figure of Diana the huntress, which adorns a tympanum (number 203). Notice, too, the chimney stack planted in the grass, and the Miraculous Well of St Macharius, moved here in the nineteenth century when the Neo-Gothic church that looms above us was built on the site of the well.

Before leaving the abbey, we should briefly explore the delightfully overgrown corner to the south of the cloisters, where the nave of the church once stood. The forest of columns nonchalantly planted in the grass came from the cellars of various mediaeval Ghent houses. The museum guide book has nothing to say about other odd fragments, such as an upturned leg and a pile of three capitals. This enigmatic corner is a rather appropriate place to end a tour of Ghent, the most curious and baffling of Flemish cities.

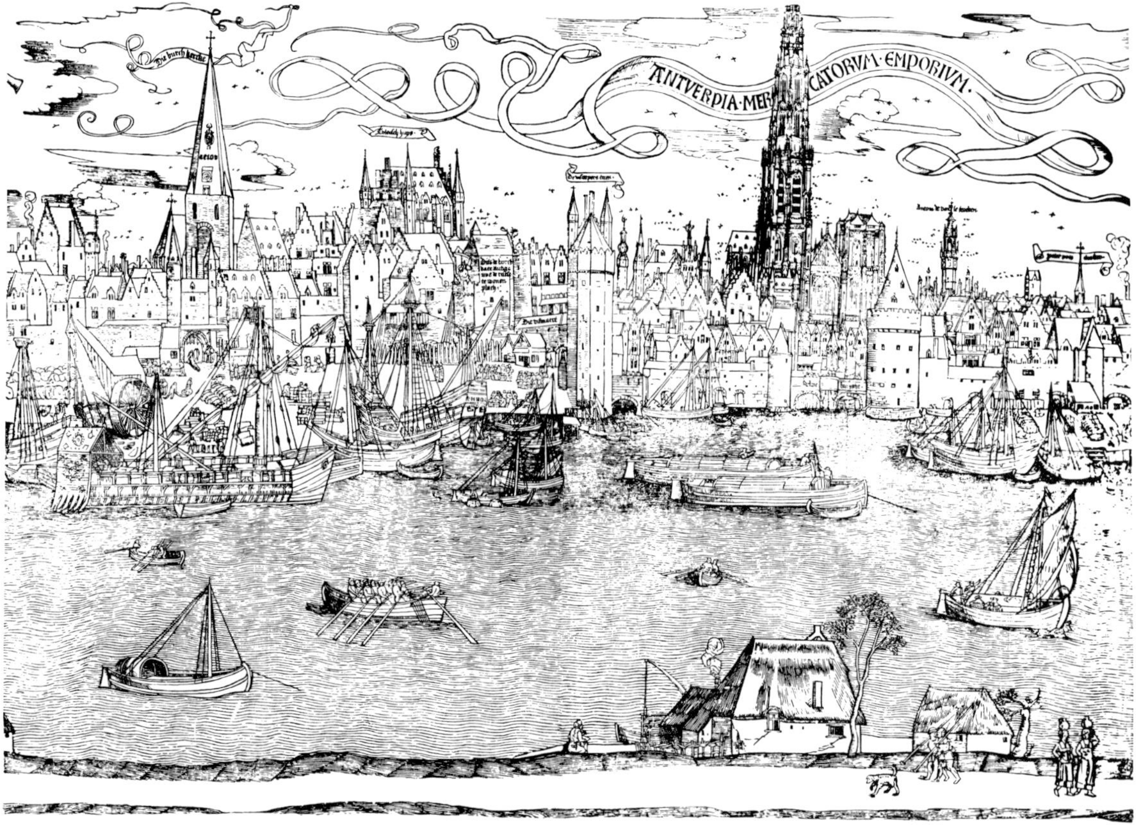
ANTVERPIA·MER CATORVM·EMPORIVM·

CHAPTER 3: ANTWERP

The maritime city of Antwerp stands upstream of Ghent on the broad River Scheldt. On a visit there in 1641 John Evelyn wrote in his diary, 'Nor did I ever observe a more quiet, cleane, elegantly built, and civil place, than this magnificent and famous Citty of Antwerp.' Anna Roemers Visscher, a seventeenth-century Dutch poet, was equally impressed, proclaiming it to be: 'The fairest town the Netherlands has ever seen.' Antwerp is still one of the most beautiful and artistic of Europe's northern cities, with many hidden delights, including exquisite Gothic chapels, secret Baroque gardens, and beautiful Renaissance interiors hung with gilt leather. At the end of our explorations, we may agree with Victor Hugo, who said of Antwerp in 1837, 'The city is delightful: paintings in the churches, sculpture adorning the houses, Rubens in the chapels, Verbruggen on the gables; the city is literally overflowing with art.'

There is a marvellous woodcut showing the harbour at Antwerp in 1515 (pl. 14). Bruges was in decline by that time, and Antwerp was fast becoming the main seaport of northern Europe. Up until then, the city's main role had been as a fortress at the western frontier of the loose confederation of German states known as the Holy Roman Empire, a frontier which, under the terms of the Treaty of

Plate 14 Harbour at Antwerp in 1515

Verdun, had followed the River Scheldt. However, Antwerp's fortunes improved dramatically after 1505, when the Fuggers of Augsburg moved their trading house here from Bruges. The powerful German bankers erected a splendid Late Gothic building, which is no longer standing, in the southern quarter of the city. Other trading nations followed the Fuggers to Antwerp, and the old Bruges trading houses on Oosterlingenplein and Vlamingstraat were left to decay. Late Gothic buildings spread through Antwerp like wildfire, each with an ostentatious watchtower to espy ships as they sailed up the Scheldt.

Antwerp enjoyed a period of extraordinary prosperity during the reign of the Emperor Charles V. Born in Ghent and raised by his aunt, Margaret of Austria, in Mechelen, Charles V chose Antwerp as the principal port of his domains. The 19 states he governed formed one of the greatest empires ever to exist. It encompassed the Burgundian Netherlands, which he inherited in 1515, the Spanish Empire, including lands in South America, acquired through his mother in 1516, and the Holy Roman Empire, which fell into his hands in 1519.

Antwerp eventually became the most important commercial centre of the sixteenth-century world, eclipsing Bruges, Genoa and even Venice. The commodities which passed through its warehouses must have seemed unbelievably rich compared to the wool and cloth which until then had formed the basis of Flemish trade. Sugar and exotic spices, including pepper and cinnamon, were trans-shipped from Portugal; velvet, silk and cloths of silver and gold filigree were brought from Italy; wines came from the Rhineland and fruits were imported from Spain. The paintings of the Antwerp Mannerists provide us with a vivid impression of the jewel-encrusted objects of the age of Charles V, just as the paintings of Jan van Eyck depict the fabrics and furnishings of the Burgundian world. A favourite Biblical theme of this sixteenth-century school was the Adoration of the Magi, for this afforded an ideal opportunity to depict the opulent clothes and ornate objects which were flooding into Antwerp from all parts of the world.

The old warehouses in the northern quarter of Antwerp now lie empty, although a few have been put to new uses as jazz clubs or bars. However, the confidence of the sixteenth century is still reflected in the Renaissance architecture of the town hall, and the splendid merchants' palaces that we sometimes glimpse behind sturdy portals. Even in the somewhat shabby streets of the northern quarter, there are still some imposing edifices, such as the **Hessenhuis** at Falconrui 53, a vast Renaissance building erected in the 1560s to provide stabling and lodgings for the wagoners who shipped goods between Antwerp and the German cities.

The abdication of Charles V in 1555 brought an end to Antwerp's golden age. His son, Philip II, inherited the Spanish Empire and the Netherlands from his father, while the Holy Roman Empire passed to the Hapsburgs. Philip II's passionate Catholicism quickly brought him into conflict with the traditionally free-thinking and tolerant people of the Low Countries. Antwerp's troubles began in 1566 when a group of zealous Protestants broke into Catholic churches and monasteries, destroying religious paintings and sculpture. Philip responded in 1567 by sending an army under the Duke of Alva to erect a huge Renaissance citadel to the south of the city, similar to the one built by his father at Ghent in 1540. In 1576 the Spanish troops quartered in Antwerp plundered the city during a horrifying episode known as the Spanish Fury, which left some 7,000 townspeople dead. The Spanish troops were briefly expelled in 1577 by the Protestant leader William the Silent, but they were soon back led by Alexander Farnese, then Prince of Parma, and after a gruelling siege lasting 14 months the city was recaptured in 1585.

We can obtain an impression of the disastrous turn of events if we look at the population figures. In 1526, some 55,000 people lived in Antwerp, and by 1567 the population had almost doubled, to 100,000, according to the *Description of All the Low Countries* published in Antwerp by Ludovico Guicciardini, son of the famous Florentine historian and at one time Tuscan ambassador to the Netherlands. At the outbreak of the Dutch Revolt in 1568, the population had climbed yet further to 125,000, but then it dropped rapidly, as citizens were brutally slain or forced to flee to

Holland or England. By 1589 the population had fallen to 55,000, while in the eighteenth century a mere 40,000 people lived here. James Howell, who saw Antwerp in 1619, described the city as: 'a disconsolate Widow, or rather some super-annuated Virgin, that hath lost her Lover, being almost quite bereft of that flourishing commerce wherewith before the falling off of the rest of the Provinces from Spain she abounded to the envy of all other Cities and Marts of Europe.'

We may find it surprising that this observation was made at the time when the painter Pieter Paul Rubens was active in Antwerp, for his paintings suggest a boundless energy and creativity. Rubens, however, was painfully aware of Antwerp's decline, and he once described the city as 'languishing like a consumptive body, declining little by little'. His Baroque painting and architecture was a heroic attempt to rescue the dying northern city by importing the vivacious style he had encountered on his travels in Italy. Numerous works by Rubens have remained in Antwerp: ten in the Museum voor Schone Kunsten, 18 portraits in the Museum Plantin-Moretus, two works in the Rubenshuis, four altarpieces in the cathedral, a religious painting in the St Pauluskerk, and two works in the Rockoxhuis. Rubens' palatial home is also still standing, as is a magnificent Jesuit church built partly to his designs. The indefatigable Rubens also undertook various diplomatic missions on behalf of the Archduchess Isabella, in the hope that peace in Europe might rescue Antwerp from economic ruin. In 1630 he successfully negotiated a treaty between England and Spain, which led to a temporary hiatus in hostilities.

The Treaty of Münster of 1648, signed eight years after Rubens' death, secured a more lasting peace in the Low Countries. But its terms were disastrous for Antwerp: the Scheldt was closed to shipping, and Antwerp's hopes of economic recovery were dashed. Amsterdam and Rotterdam became the main ports of northern Europe, and Antwerp followed Bruges into decline and decay.

And so it remained until well into the nineteenth century. There was some recovery under Napoleon I, when a new naval dock, the Bonapartedok, was built to the north of the city.

But Napoleon, like Philip II, was interested only in Antwerp's strategic position, which he pugnaciously described as 'a pistol pointed at the heart of Britain'.

After three centuries of stagnation, Antwerp finally revived as a commercial city in the 1860s with the abolition of the Dutch right to levy tolls on ships navigating the Scheldt. Its economy suddenly boomed, and a second golden age dawned. The elegant boulevards, railway station, museum of fine arts and Stadspark are mementoes of this confident period in Antwerp's history.

But perhaps the most remarkable nineteenth-century creation is the boulevard in the southern suburbs known as **Cogels Osylei**. Two nineteenth-century entrepreneurs, Baron Edouard Osy and his sister Joséphine Cogels Osy, shrewdly realised that this corner of Antwerp was an ideal residential area for commuters, due to two suburban railway stations nearby. They bought an old castle called Zurenborg that stood on the site and

Plate 15 Cogels Osylei

promptly demolished it. In the 1880s architects began to erect opulent Victorian mansions on Cogels Osylei and neighbouring streets in every imaginable architectural style. There is a Greek Classical building at Transvaalstraat 23, a reconstructed Renaissance house at number 59, a magnificent Venetian palace at Cogels Osylei 65, and several beautiful Art Nouveau houses at the southern ends of Cogels Osylei and Waterloostraat (pl. 15).

Antwerp again became an important military stronghold in the nineteenth century. Although the sixteenth-century walls had been demolished in 1859, new forts were built around the city in the nineteenth century, making it again one of the most heavily fortified cities in Europe. But the elaborate defences, parts of which survive in the modern suburbs, failed to halt the German advance in 1914. British troops led by Winston Churchill rushed to the defence of the city, but succeeded only in stalling the German army for a few days. The British were pushed back to the Channel ports, and the Belgian army dug in beyond the River Ijzer. The tiny corner of Belgium west of the Ijzer was heroically defended throughout the war, and the small town of Veurne, with a population of only 11,000, became the country's capital.

Antwerp was also badly bombed in World War II, and the damaged quarters have still not been completely rebuilt. Although a huge modern port was constructed after the war to the north of the old Napoleonic dock, the city still sometimes has the look of a 'disconsolate Widow', particularly in the neighbourhood of the Stadswaag and the Waalse Kaai. Yet Antwerp is, I think, one of the most captivating of northern European cities, its architecture and art a curious blend of Amsterdam, Rome, Paris, London and New York.

Antwerp

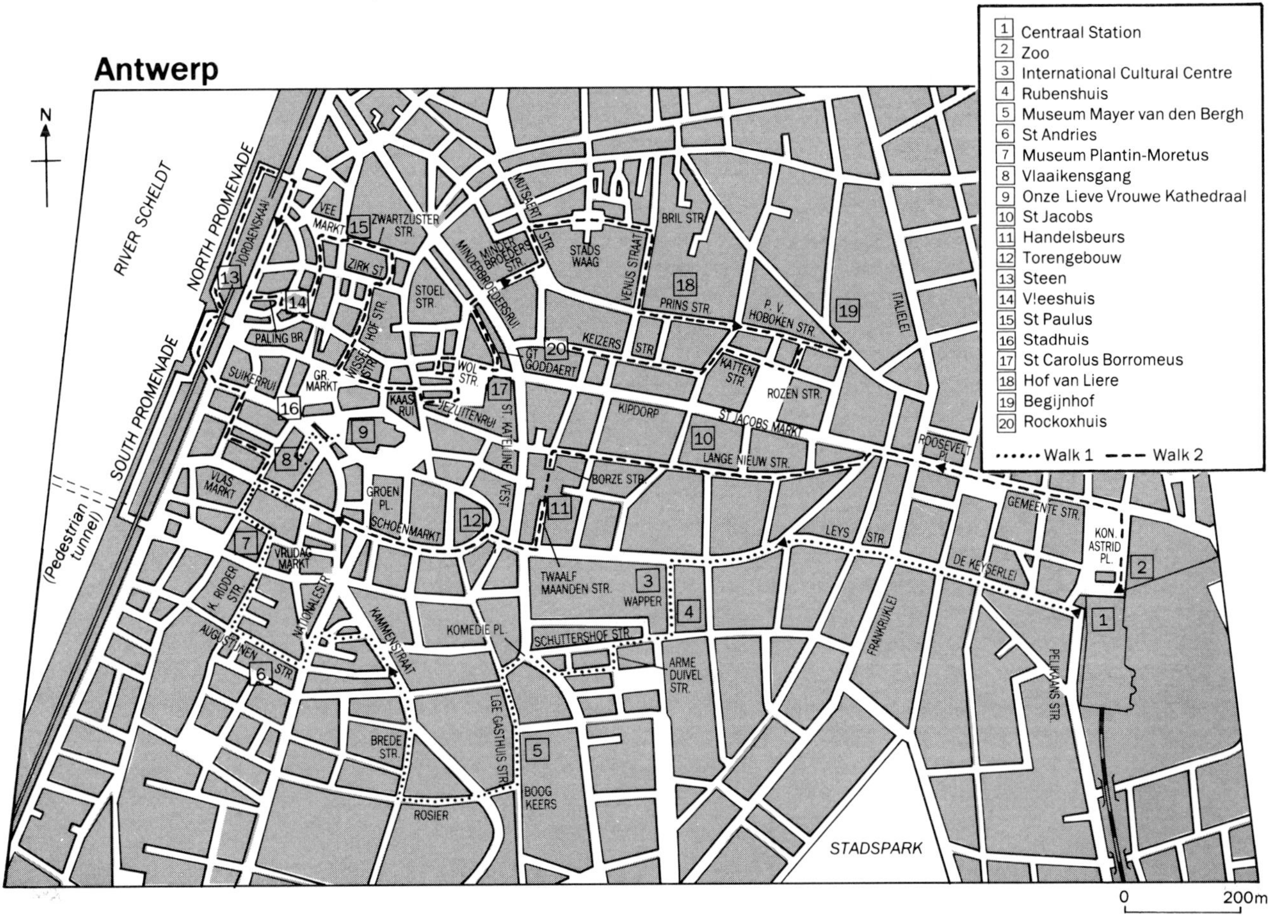

N
1 Centraal Station
2 Zoo
3 International Cultural Centre
4 Rubenshuis
5 Museum Mayer van den Bergh
6 St Andries
7 Museum Plantin-Moretus
8 Vlaaikensgang
9 Onze Lieve Vrouwe Kathedraal
10 St Jacobs
11 Handelsbeurs
12 Torengebouw
13 Steen
14 Vleeshuis
15 St Paulus
16 Stadhuis
17 St Carolus Borromeus
18 Hof van Liere
19 Begijnhof
20 Rockoxhuis
Walk 1
Walk 2
RIVER SCHELDT
NORTH PROMENADE
SOUTH PROMENADE
(Pedestrian tunnel)
JORDAENSKAAI
VEE MARKT
ZWARTZUSTER STR.
ZIRK ST
MINDER BROEDERS STR.
MINDERBROEDERSRUI
MUTSAERT STR.
STADS WAAG
VENUS STRAAT
BRIL STR.
STOEL STR.
HOF STR.
PALING BR.
WISSEL STR.
SUIKERRUI
GR. MARKT
KAAS RUI
WOL STR.
JEZUITENRUI
GT GODDAERT
KEIZERS STR.
PRINS STR.
P. V. HOBOKEN STR.
ITALIELEI
KATTEN STR.
ROZEN STR.
KIPDORP
ST JACOBS MARKT
ROOSEVELT PL.
LANGE NIEUW STR.
BORZE STR.
ST KATELIJNE VEST
VLAS MARKT
GROEN PL.
SCHOENMARKT
GEMEENTE STR.
KON. ASTRID PL.
LEYS STR.
DE KEYSERLEI
VRIJDAG MARKT
TWAALF MAANDEN STR.
WAPPER
K. RIDDER STR.
NATIONALESTR.
KAMMENSTRAAT
KOMEDIE PL.
SCHUTTERSHOF STR.
ARME DUIVEL STR.
FRANKRIJKLEI
PELIKAANS STR.
AUGUSTIJNEN STR.
LGE GASTHUIS STR.
BREDE STR.
BOOG KEERS
ROSIER
STADSPARK
0
200m

Walk 1: Rubens, Bruegel and Plantin

On our first walk in Antwerp we will explore the Baroque home of Rubens and the fascinating former printing works of Christopher Plantin and Balthasar Moretus. 'Our City of Antwerp is proud to possess two such great citizens as Rubens and Moretus,' wrote Jan Woverius, a councillor to the Archduke Albert and Archduchess Isabella in the seventeenth century. 'Foreigners will stare at the houses of both, and travellers will admire them,' he said.

This walk also takes in the Museum Mayer Van den Bergh, a remarkable and virtually unknown art collection, which includes the only two paintings by Pieter Bruegel the Elder to remain in Antwerp, where he lived from 1555-63. As this walk is mainly concerned with museums, each deserving at least an hour of our time, it is an ideal way to pass a rainy day in Antwerp.

We begin at **Centraal Station**, the main railway station, which was designed in 1895-1905 in the extravagant Neo-Baroque style favoured by Léopold II. We may notice that Léopold's monogram, a florid *L*, appears on numerous cartouches, as if he sought to model his little kingdom on the absolute monarchies of Baroque Europe. The architect of this palatial railway station, we may be surprised to discover, was Louis Delacenserie, who hitherto had made his mark as the fastidious restorer of Burgundian Gothic buildings in Bruges, such as the Gruuthuse mansion. Present-day Belgian railways do not have the funds necessary to maintain this enormous edifice, but at least no cheap attempt at modernisation has been attempted, and we can still enjoy the splendid, albeit run-down, station café situated next to platform 1, with its ballroom mirrors and its ornate and enormous clock.

Antwerp's **Zoo**, situated next to the station, is one of the oldest in Europe, dating back to 1843. It was once, according to Baedeker's 1905 guide book, 'a favourite resort of the fashionable world', and it still boasts some splendid architecture, although many of the buildings were destroyed in World War II. There is a delightful Greek temple set on an artificial hill, a Moorish villa which is home to the rhinoceroses and an Indian temple where Central African okapis ruminate. But the most astonishing building is a large Egyptian temple, which serves as an elephant house. This spectacular souvenir of the Victorian cult of Egyptology was designed by Charles Servais, who modelled it upon the Egyptian Court at the Crystal Palace in London. It is decorated with intriguing hieroglyphics composed by an Antwerp Egyptologist, including one sonorous inscription which declares, 'In the Year of Our Lord 1856, in the reign of His Majesty the King, Sun and Life of Belgium, Léopold the First, this building was erected as a book for the glorification of Antwerp and the edification of its inhabitants.'

Perhaps we should leave the delights of the zoo for another day, however, and proceed at once down De Keyserlei, then cross Frankrijklei, one of the *leien*, or boulevards, laid out in 1859 on the site of the Renaissance city walls. Continuing down Leysstraat, we should pause to admire the nineteenth-century house at **Leysstraat 15**. The balcony is in the shape of a ship's prow and there are also reliefs decorated with whales, suggesting that the original owner had the sea in his blood.

We come to the beautiful street **Meir**, whereupon we soon turn left down Kolveniersstraat, there discovering an unexpected delight at number 16. Through an open door we see the Renaissance courtyard of the **Kolveniershof**, built in the 1630s as the guild house of the arquebusiers.

The drill yard of the arquebusiers happened to back on to Pieter Paul Rubens' garden. Inspired by the formal Baroque gardens he had seen during his eight-year stay in Italy, Rubens resolved to create his own Italianate garden in Antwerp, and he approached Burgomaster Rockox, captain of the arquebusiers, to buy the land he needed. Rockox was already an enthusiastic patron of Rubens, and in 1608 commissioned an *Adoration of the Magi*—now in the Prado—to hang in the town hall. The Burgomaster therefore proposed to Rubens that he pay for the plot of land with a painting. The subject

Plate 16 Courtyard and portico of the Rubenshuis

was to be a portrait of St Christopher, the guild's patron saint, for the banqueting hall. Rubens responded with characteristic gusto and, instead of a portrait of St Christopher, the arquebusiers received the magnificent *Triptych of the Descent from the Cross*, now in Antwerp Cathedral. The members of the guild were apparently none too pleased at this breach of contract and ordered Rubens to add a portrait of St Christopher (who had not appeared on the original) to one of the wings.

We return to Meir, to see facing us at number 85 the elegant **Osterriethhuis**, now a bank, built in Flemish Rococo style by Jan Pieter van Baurscheit in 1748. Turning left along Meir, we soon come upon another fine Rococo palace at number 50, completed by the same architect three years earlier. Occupied briefly by Napoleon in 1811, this palace now houses the **International Cultural Centre**. Interesting exhibitions are held in the first-floor rooms of this decayed palace, and if time permits, we should glance inside. The ballroom is now empty and tragic, but the stables at the far end of the courtyard have been maintained in immaculate condition and the polished wood and brass fittings are gleaming.

Now let us visit the **Rubenshuis** at Wapper 9. We can begin our tour of the house at once, if we wish, though should the sun be shining we may be tempted to pause on a bench in the garden to read about the building.

Plate 16 shows the handsome portico that links the two wings of the house, framing a charming little temple in the garden. The portico and temple, both designed by Rubens in Italian Baroque style, appear in many of his paintings. They also feature in several works by his pupils, such as the portrait of Isabella Brant by Sir Anthony van Dyck in Washington's National Gallery, and *Diana in the Bath* by Jacob Jordaens in the Prado.

The Baroque garden designed by Rubens provided a setting for many of his most felicitous paintings, such as *Amidst Honeysuckle* in Munich's Alte Pinakothek, and *The Garden of Love* in Madrid's Prado. These paintings greatly influenced later artists such as Watteau, Fragonard and Gainsborough. The Munich painting (pl. 17) is a tender portrait of the artist with his

Plate 17 Rubens and his Second Wife in the Garden

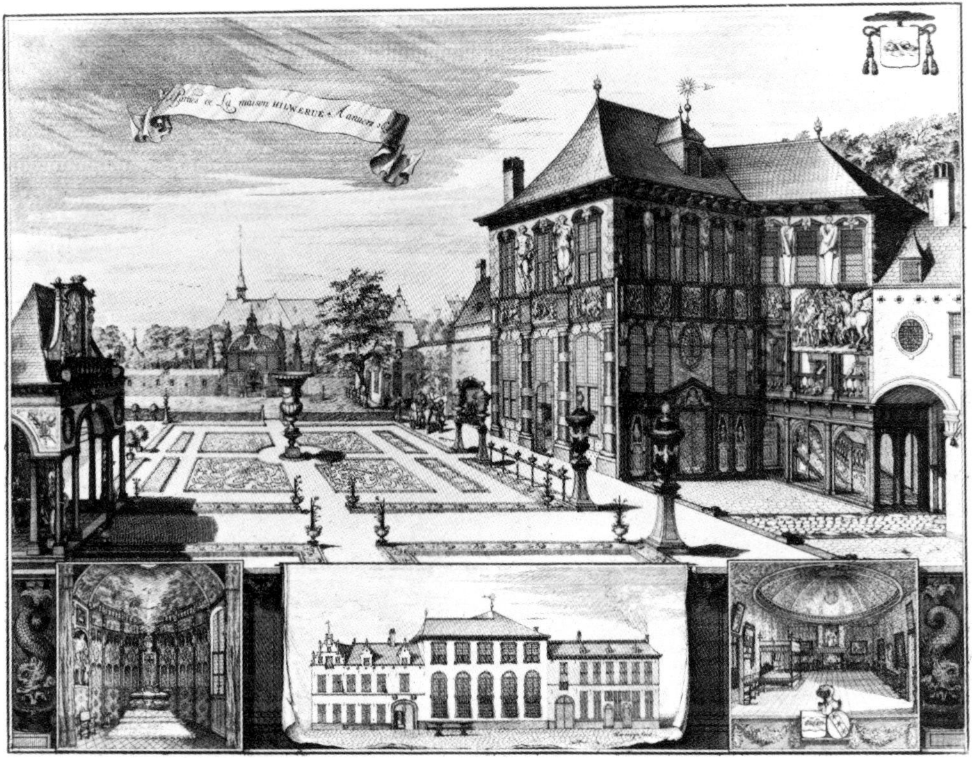

Plate 18 Garden of the Rubenshuis in 1692

second wife, Hélène Fourment, whom he married in 1626, four years after Isabella Brant, his first wife, died. 'I am determined to remarry,' Rubens wrote somewhat defensively, 'considering myself not yet old enough to surrender to the abstinence of celibacy and, as it is sweet after one has been thrown into desolation to enjoy permissible pleasures, I have taken myself a young girl.' Many of the charming scenes painted in this garden feature Rubens' voluptuous second wife, who was only 16 when she married. Hélène was also cunning, however, for when Rubens died in 1640 she immediately sold off his huge collection of paintings and antiques to prevent the children of his first marriage from inheriting anything.

When Baedeker's 1905 guide book was written, only the portico and pavilion (on the left in plates 17 and 18) were still standing. The house was painstakingly reconstructed in 1938-45 using as guidelines paintings by Rubens and his pupils, or old prints (pl. 18). The building to the north of the portico is a reconstruction of the original sixteenth-century house bought by Rubens, a typical Flemish Late Gothic building with alternating courses of brick and sandstone. The reconstructed kitchen, dining room, picture gallery and bedrooms are in this wing. Annexed to the picture gallery is a curious apsidal Pantheon where Rubens displayed his collection of Classical busts.

Rubens also designed the magnificent Baroque wing to the south of the portico (on the right in plate 18). This wing is almost entirely taken up by Rubens' lofty atelier, where he and his many pupils laboured tirelessly to produce scores of Baroque paintings that now hang in art galleries throughout the world. An interesting feature of the atelier is the viewing gallery at the far end, where Rubens took his clients to show them the large canvases in progress. It is interesting to reflect on how little we would see of a Flemish Primitive painting if it were to be viewed from this upstairs gallery.

A youthful study by Rubens of *Adam and Eve*, with a rabbit in the foreground to symbolise fecundity, hangs in the atelier. But the most interesting painting in the house is not by Rubens at all; it is *The Picture Gallery of Cornelis van der Geest* by Willem van Haecht, who was keeper of the picture gallery depicted in the painting. The work (pl. 19) now hangs in Rubens' picture gallery. Painted in 1628, it is a fascinating example of a curious type of work called a *kunstkamer* painting. The object of these paintings, which were very popular in seventeenth-century Antwerp, was to depict the interior of a private picture gallery, often with the patron's family and friends.

Most of the guests in the painting by Van Haecht can be identified, including the Archduke Albert and Archduchess Isabella, who are sitting on the left. Van der Geest is showing them a *Virgin and Child* by the Antwerp artist Quinten Metsys. Rubens, who is also among the guests, looks to the Archduke, while Anthony van Dyck stands behind Van der Geest. Burgomaster Rockox is also in the painting, standing directly behind the Archduchess Isabella, and the figure entering the room from the street may be the artist himself. The house of Cornelis van der Geest overlooked the Scheldt, and some ships can be seen through the windows of the picture gallery.

The painting shows three walls of the picture gallery, which is crammed from floor to ceiling with works of art. A number of paintings are propped against the furniture, presumably having been taken down from the fourth wall to allow the entire collection to be depicted. Of the 43 works copied here in miniature, 24 have been identified. One of the best known is Rubens' *Battle of the Amazons*, now in the Alte Pinakothek in Munich, which is given pride of place by the window. Above it hangs a small portrait by Metsys of the Swiss physician Paracelsus. The Musée d'Art Ancien in Brussels owns a copy of this painting made by Rubens.

The most intriguing work displayed in the collection of Van der Geest hangs in the right-hand corner above a statue of Venus and Cupid. It depicts a naked woman taking a bath in the company of another woman. The woman on the right is holding a phial (symbolising cleanliness) and an orange (symbolising fertility), suggesting that the scene represents a prenuptial bath. Some scholars have argued that this is a lost work by Jan van Eyck painted as an accompaniment to the *Arnolfini Wedding Portrait*, now in the National Gallery in London. The rooms in both paintings are

Plate 19 The Picture Gallery of Cornelis van der Geest

strikingly similar; each has a window on the left with three wooden shutters, and a convex mirror reflecting the people in the room. A dog (symbolising marital fidelity) also appears in both works, and similar wooden shoes lie discarded on the floor. Giovanni Arnolfini, the husband in the wedding portrait in London, was a merchant from Lucca who had settled in Bruges in 1420. Jan van Eyck was a witness to the wedding that took place in 1434 in Arnolfini's home in Bruges, when Arnolfini married Giovanna Cenami, also from Lucca. If the painting in Cornelis van der Geest's *kunstkamer* is indeed a lost prenuptial portrait, then it would seem to cast some doubt on the popular belief that Giovanna Cenami, who is wearing a voluminous dress in the London painting, was pregnant when she married.

The painting of Van der Geest's *kunstkamer* also includes a small drawing lying on the table in the foreground. It is a work by Johan Wierix, dated 1600, of *Alexander in the Studio of Apelles*. The drawing depicts the Greek legend in which Alexander the Great commissioned the renowned Greek artist Apelles to paint a nude portrait of his favourite mistress, Campaspe. While working on the painting, Apelles fell in love with Campaspe. To demonstrate his admiration for Apelles, Alexander made him a gift of his mistress. By a curious coincidence, the drawing by Wierix is now in the collection of the next museum we will visit.

On leaving the Rubenshuis we turn left down Wapper, right along Schuttershofstraat, and left into Arme Duivelstraat, where we might be tempted to stop for lunch in De Varkenspot, an attractive Flemish bistro. Turning right along Kelderstraat, right again on Komedieplaats, and then left on Huidevettersstraat, we reach Lange Gasthuisstraat.

Our destination is the marvellous **Museum Mayer van den Bergh** at Lange Gasthuisstraat 19. This museum boasts a large collection of paintings, sculpture, stained glass, tapestries and rare manuscripts. The works were amassed in the nineteenth century by Fritz Mayer van den Bergh, a passionate art connoisseur, whose portrait hangs on the main staircase. When he died, aged only 43, his mother resolved to create a museum next to the family home. A local architect was commissioned in 1904 to design the building in the rich Renaissance style of sixteenth-century Antwerp, incorporating heavy Mannerist furniture, gilt leather walls, and old leaded glass windows. The Mayer van den Bergh is now one of the best-preserved museums of the Victorian era, still furnished with its original Neo-Gothic display cabinets. The most intriguing of these is hidden behind a Renaissance door to the left of the fireplace in room 10. On opening the door, we find a cabinet containing some seventeenth-century drawings. According to the museum's guide book, the drawing by Johan Wierix of *Alexander in the Studio of Apelles* should be here, although it was not when I last looked.

Room 3, a curious vaulted room, contains two beautiful twelfth-century carved figures. These are rare relics from the monastery of Notre-Dame-en-Vaux, which once stood in Châlons-sur-Marne. The monastery was demolished in the eighteenth century, and its stones used locally as building material. However, recent excavations have unearthed some extraordinary fragments of sculpture, suggesting that this vanished monastery must have been one of the finest Early Gothic buildings in France.

Room 4 contains a *Crucifixion Triptych* by Quinten Metsys, an Antwerp painter who lived for the last nine years of his life in a house on Schuttershofstraat, a street we have just walked down. The wings bear portraits of the donors, whose identities are unknown, although we can deduce their Christian names from the patron saints alongside. Mary of Egypt—the woman's patron saint—was a penitent whore who lived naked in the desert, sustained by three small loaves.

Perhaps the most delightful mediaeval work in the museum is the double panel from the *Antwerp-Baltimore Polyptych*, displayed in a glass case in room 6. Painted in about 1400 by an artist living in the vicinity of Aachen, it formed part of a travelling altar, the rest of which is now in a museum in Baltimore. One panel is decorated with a scene showing St Christopher, the patron saint of travellers, crossing a stream. Looking closely in the water, we see numerous fish and even a mermaid admiring herself in a looking-glass. Another panel of the polyptych depicts a charming, if fanciful, Biblical episode in which Joseph cuts his stockings to provide swaddling clothes for the infant Christ. Some photographs displayed in the case show what there is to see of this work in far-off Baltimore.

The undoubted highlights of this collection are the two paintings in room 9 by Pieter Bruegel the Elder. There are only seven works by this great artist still in Flanders: five are in Brussels, and the other two are here. The most famous of the two paintings in Mayer van den Bergh's collection is *Dulle Griet*, painted in about 1562-4. If we tend to think of Bruegel as the painter of hunters in the snow and merry peasant weddings, we may be rather shocked by this work; it is in the style of Hieronymus Bosch and shows an irate, perhaps insane, woman rampaging through the chaos of war. The meaning of the work is not clear; some scholars have interpreted it as a warning by Bruegel about the dangers of allowing women to rule, while others say that it is an allegory of folly. The other work by Bruegel is an engagingly whimsical study of *The Twelve Proverbs*, with 12 miniature scenes illustrating popular Flemish sayings, such as falling between two stools and belling the cat.

On leaving the museum, turn left and walk down Lange Gasthuisstraat. At number 33 is the beautiful **Maagdenhuis**, an orphanage for girls founded in 1564 by Jan van der Meeren and Gilbert van Schoonbeke. Van Schoonbeke, a typical figure of the Flemish Renaissance, was constantly occupied with schemes to improve the city of Antwerp, several of which we come across in our wanderings. Not all, however, were popular with the folk of Antwerp, and eventually he had to flee to Brussels, where he died at the age of only 36.

Above the entrance to the orphanage is a delightful Mannerist relief dating from 1564. It depicts orphaned girls being admitted to the Maagdenhuis, and a classroom scene so finely detailed that it even includes shelves lined with school books. If the gate is open, we can glance into an arcaded courtyard dating from 1636, with a seventeenth-century wooden figure of an orphan girl.

A short distance further, we turn right along Boogkeers, continue along Rosier, then right up Bredestraat. This brings us out on a little square where a statue of the Virgin illuminated by a quaint old iron lamp smiles down on us. As in Bruges, there are numerous statues of the Virgin in Antwerp. The difference is that the Virgins of Bruges look frail and pious, whereas those of Antwerp are voluptuous Rubensian women wearing glittering crowns and surrounded by gaudy ornaments.

Continue along Kammenstraat, past a Baroque church designed in 1615 by Wenceslas Coeberger, then turn left into Ijzeren Waag. This brings us to a square where, if tempted, we can buy *frites* at a small wooden chalet. After crossing Nationalestraat, we continue down Augustijnenstraat, watched over by another magnificent Virgin and Child illuminated by a dusty iron lamp. Standing opposite the north transept of the **St Andrieskerk**, we obtain a marvellous view of the Baroque church tower rising above a picturesque cluster of roofs. St Andries was built in 1514-23, and the tower added in 1756-63. Inside the church, which is unfortunately rarely open, there is an unusual memorial to two ladies-in-waiting to Mary Queen of Scots, who both died in exile in Antwerp.

This corner of Antwerp was badly damaged in World War II and it has only recently been redeveloped. There remains one intriguing sixteenth-century lane, the Maesganck, at Korte Ridderstraat 23. Continuing down Korte Ridderstraat, we then cross Steenhouwersvest and into Vrijdagmarktstraatje. This little lane emerges on the **Vrijdagmarkt**, the scene every Wednesday and Friday morning of a market in second-hand goods. The market was established here in 1549 by Gilbert van Schoonbeke, co-founder of the girls' orphanage.

But we have not come to the Vrijdagmarkt to buy bric-à-brac. On the south side of the square stands the **Museum Plantin-Moretus**, a fascinating and beautiful museum of books and printing presses, suffused with the genial warmth of the Flemish Renaissance. In a Renaissance arcade overlooking the courtyard, we can sit on a worn bench beside an old seventeenth-century pump to read about the history of the great publishing house that occupied this building for several centuries.

Christopher Plantin, who founded the business,

was a French printer from the vicinity of Tours who moved to Antwerp in 1549. In 1576 he established the Plantin Press on the Vrijdagmarkt, adopting as his trade mark a pair of compasses with the motto *Labore et Constantia* (by work and reliability). This trade mark decorates several wooden consoles in the arcade. In the *Description of All the Low Countries* by Ludovico Guicciardini, published in 1567, the Plantin Press is singled out for praise. 'Such an establishment has never been seen in the whole of Europe,' declared the well-travelled Italian author, 'with more presses, with more types of various kinds, with more prints and other instruments, appertaining to so excellent an art; with more capable and competent printer's assistants, earning higher wages by working, correcting and revising in all languages, both rare and familiar, none excepted, which are employed throughout the whole of Christendom.' It was Christopher Plantin, incidentally, who published Guicciardini's guide book to the Low Countries, which may explain this rather lengthy eulogy.

Plantin's first publication was an etiquette manual for young ladies, presumably an invaluable book to have around the house as all five of his children were girls. The main activity of the Plantin Press, however, was to print religious works. Plantin's first major success in this field was the publication in 1572 of a five-language *Biblia Polyglotta* (Multilingual Bible), a copy of which is displayed in room 16. This four-year undertaking so impressed Philip II that he granted Plantin the monopoly of the right to print liturgical works throughout the Empire. This brought commissions which, as a humanist, he would have found distasteful, such as the printing of lists of heretical works. Perhaps it was to atone for this work that Plantin clandestinely published several anti-Spanish tracts.

Following Plantin's death in 1589, the business was taken over by Jan Moretus, his son-in-law. He introduced a new trade mark, a star, which appears on several consoles in the arcade. The publishing house remained in the hands of the Moretus family up until 1879, when it finally closed down. The fully-furnished complex, consisting of the family home and the publishing house, was then bought by the city of Antwerp and lovingly restored to its original state.

The first three of the museum's 33 rooms originally formed part of the family's dwelling house. Hanging in these rooms are several portraits by Rubens of prominent persons associated with the publishing house, among them a gaunt Christopher Plantin, his wife Jeanne Rivière, Jan Moretus and his wife Martina, the geographer Ortelius and the classicist Lipsius.

The bookshop (room 4) is entered from the arcade. Several well-known people have visited this shop to make purchases, including John Evelyn, who noted in his diary, 'Returning by the shop of Plantine, I bought some bookes for the namesake onely of that famous printer.' The dusty old books on the shelves are not for sale, but we can buy an excellent little guide to the museum written by Leon Voet and printed in a handsome Plantin typeface.

Sales of books were once recorded in a large ledger by the book-keeper, who perched in the little office next door. The old account books are still preserved, including a seventeenth-century ledger displayed in room 19 in which Rubens' account is entered. He is debited for the purchase of various books on architecture, and credited for furnishing the designs of frontispieces for a number of books published by Balthasar Moretus.

The adjacent wing contains an evocative series of rooms in which the printers, editors and proof readers worked. In room 9 is the aged wooden desk at which the proof readers worked, marking the texts with symbols still used today (as we see from the old proof copy displayed in a glass case). Room 10 is hung with gilt leather from Mechelen, which bathes the interior in a captivating golden light, like a shaded glade on a summer day. Even more exquisite is the sixteenth-century gilded leather of Cordoba known as *guadamacil*, which hangs in room 12. This is believed to be the room in which Justus Lipsius worked when he visited the Plantin Press. We then walk through a room with cases of old type to enter the remarkable printing workshop built by Plantin in 1579, with sturdy wooden beams anchoring the old printing presses to the roof. The smell of printers' ink still pervades this room, and occasionally one of the old presses is put back into service to turn out copies of Plantin's ode, *Le bonheur de ce monde*. The printer's assistants here are still apparently able to work in 'all languages . . . employed throughout the whole of Christendom', for Plantin's ode to contentment is available in seven European languages. There is even a Russian version, presumably for the benefit of the Soviet sailors who are often to be seen roaming the streets of Antwerp in search of souvenirs.

We then leave the printing works and ascend the creaking stairs to the first floor. Room 19 contains a collection of books and prints recalling Rubens' long association with this publishing house, which began in 1608 when he and his brother Philip published a book on the social customs of Rome.

One of the most amusing books to be published by this house is the *Dictionary in Seven Languages* written by the humanist Ficardus in 1616 and displayed in room 20. This provided seventeenth-century travellers with essential phrases such as 'You seeke noothing but to begyle me', the Flemish equivalent of which, should we

Plate 20 Antwerp in 1565

ever find ourselves being unwantedly *begyled*, is *Ghy en soeckt niet dan my te bedrieghen*.

Room 23 is filled with fascinating maps, including the only surviving copy of the 1565 map of Antwerp (pl. 20) by the Renaissance cartographers Virgilius Boloniensis and Cornelis Grapheus. We then ascend to the second floor, there to visit the stone-floored attic room. The type founders were banished here to minimise the danger of them setting fire to the building with molten metal. The typeface known today as Plantin was based on the designs of Claude Garamond, a French designer, after whom another typeface is named. Standing by the ancient stove which once took the chill off this room, we may glimpse through the small window a nearby watchtower embellished with a curious onion-shaped dome. This marks our next destination.

Upon leaving the museum, we turn down the lane to our left, Heilige-Geeststraat, and enter the courtyard of the **Huis Draeck** at number 9. A city official built a house here in the fifteenth century, of which all that survives is the small chapel on the left. In 1540 the building was bought by Wolf Puschinger, a merchant from Leipzig, who rebuilt it in Late Gothic style and added the octagonal watchtower that we spied from the attic foundry of the Plantin Press.

We see this watchtower again from another angle upon entering the nearby courtyard of the **Jordaenshuis** at Reyndersstraat 4. To reach it, turn right at the end of Heilige-Geeststraat into Hoogstraat, then again right. The attractive, if somewhat decayed, Baroque house was built by Jacob Jordaens, a pupil of Rubens and painter of numerous rather fleshy and grotesque Baroque works, such as *The King Drinks* in the Musée d'Art Ancien in Brussels.

On leaving the courtyard of Jordaens' house, turn right and soon you come upon yet another secret courtyard, at Reyndersstraat 18. There is a pleasant café here, De Grote Witte Arend, and on summer days long wooden benches are set outside. Some 34 types of beer appear on the menu, including the unusual bottle-fermented Corsendonk ales.

Pelgrimstraat, directly opposite the café, was once, as its name suggests, the route taken by pilgrims bound for the cathedral. The view of the soaring cathedral spire from the end of the street is breathtakingly beautiful. From here, I suggest that we take a somewhat indirect route to the cathedral, retracing our steps and turning down the passage at Pelgrimstraat 8. This takes us into the **Vlaaikensgang**, an undisturbed sixteenth-century corner of Antwerp, where narrow crooked lanes run between whitewashed houses with bluestone pumps, all overgrown with rambling creepers.

We emerge from this almost rural warren of lanes on the bustling Oude Koornmarkt, from which no directions are needed to reach the cathedral. Begun in 1352, **Onze-Lieve-Vrouwekathedraal** (Our Lady's Cathedral) is one of the finest Gothic churches in the Low Countries. It was built on the site of a twelfth-century Romanesque church that was slowly demolished as the new church was built. The overall design was the work of the French architect Jean Appelmans, who is commemorated by a delightful statue at the foot of the unfinished south spire. The choir was built first, then the west front, and finally the nave, probably to the design of Herman de Waghemakere. The north spire of the cathedral, constructed in 1420-1518, is its greatest glory. For several centuries this graceful spire was the tallest structure in the Low Countries. The lowest tier (which see in Jan van Eyck's drawing of St Barbara in Antwerp's Museum voor Schone Kunsten) was designed by Master Everaert, while the two upper tiers were added later by Domien de Waghemakere in a thrilling Brabant Gothic style.

In 1519 Domien de Waghemakere and Rombout Keldermans the Younger were commissioned by Charles V to rebuild the choir in Brabant Gothic style. But following a fire in 1533 the project was abandoned, and ever since then the choir has been closed off from the nave by a screen.

The interior of the cathedral was badly damaged by the Protestants in 1566, and the main relic to survive from the Middle Ages is a bronze recumbent figure of Isabella of Bourbon, attributed to Jacob van Gerines. It was moved here when the St Michael's Abbey on Kloosterstraat was demolished. Isabella of Bourbon, the second wife of

Charles the Bold, died in the abbey in 1465.

The main glory of the cathedral is its collection of altarpieces by Rubens. The most impressive work is the *Descent from the Cross*, hanging on the wall that closes off the choir. We have already related the story of this painting, which was commissioned by the guild of arquebusiers. The other great work by Rubens in the cathedral is the *Elevation of the Cross*, an ambitious early work painted in 1610. Rubens had then just recently returned from an eight-year sojourn in Italy and his style was still heavily influenced by Michelangelo. This large painting is currently being restored, a laborious and painstaking undertaking not due to be completed until the end of 1991. The Treasury contains another work by Rubens, the *Resurrection Triptych*, painted in 1612 for the tomb of his friend Jan Moretus, the Antwerp printer.

The *Marriage at Cana* by Martin de Vos is an interesting example of Antwerp Mannerism. True to the artistic conventions of the day, the scene is set in a sixteenth-century Flemish interior complete with a minstrels' gallery. Notice, too, the little chapel on the north side of the cathedral, which contains several paintings in Pre-Raphaelite style, including an altarpiece called *Our Lady of Peace*, a strange and sad World War I memorial. The soldiers are depicted in the guise of mediaeval knights, and dark scenes at the base depict the bombardment of Antwerp.

As so often happens in the crowded cities of the Low Countries, the cathedral is enclosed by a jumble of dwelling houses. Baedeker stiffly condemned these 'mean houses', but I think that they add a certain picturesque charm to the scene. Many of these buildings now contain cafés and tea rooms, and there are many others on the nearby Groenplaats. The café terraces hereabouts are particularly delightful when concerts are given on the cathedral carillon.

A café with a hint of Surrealism in its decor faces the north transept of the cathedral at Torfbrug 10. Wickedly named De Elfde Gebod (The Eleventh Commandment), it has a most curious interior crammed with nineteenth-century plaster-cast saints and Neo-Gothic altars salvaged from old churches. One of the oddest features is the door to the kitchen on which, as a 'Homage to Diderot', all the parts have been labelled with a flourish of calligraphy.

There are also many attractive restaurants in the neighbourhood of the cathedral, including the celebrated Sir Anthony van Dyck at Oude Koornmarkt 16, where excellent Flemish cuisine is served in attractive rooms with flagstone floors, Renaissance cabinets and old Flemish paintings. More modest restaurants include Pita at Oude Koornmarkt 20, a good place for a pitta bread lunch, and Pasta at Oude Koornmarkt 32, a striking modern Italian restaurant with a magnificent view of the cathedral from the upper floor.

Walk 2: The Old City

There are many delightful buildings and engaging curiosities to be discovered in the winding lanes of the old city, yet we should be prepared too for a certain amount of decay and sad neglect. Already in 1789, Harriet Lynch Thrale, a friend of Samuel Johnson, complained that Antwerp was 'a dismal heavy looking town—so melancholy!' Despite the revival of Antwerp's trade in the nineteenth century, the old city still at times seems somewhat ravaged, but if we can ignore this we will find the old town fascinating to explore.

The walk (*see page 123 for map*), which will take a full day to complete, again begins at **Centraal Station**, but this time we leave by the north entrance to reach Koningin Astridplein. We cross this square, dodging the parties of children bound for the zoo, and turn left along Gemeentestraat, past the opera house and under an unsightly overpass, to enter the narrow streets of the old city. We then take a left fork down Lange Nieuwstraat (Long New Street), not quite so new as in 1315 when it was named. This gently curving street, with an enticing view of the cathedral spire to tempt us onwards, was one of the most desirable streets in Antwerp in the fifteenth and sixteenth centuries, though it is now rather the worse for wear.

We have come down this street to visit the **St Jacobskerk**, which is entered by a small door in the south transept, at number 73. The church was begun in 1491 by Herman de Waghemakere and continued, after his death, by Domien, his son, and Rombout Keldermans the Younger of Mechelen. In 1526 the work was halted because of lack of funds (a familiar story in sixteenth-century Flanders) and it was not until 1656 that the church was finally completed. But the tower, like so many Late Gothic towers in the Low Countries, remains unfinished, a symbol of failure, with its belfry terminated half-built. It was simply too costly to complete these ambitious Late Gothic towers, and in any case the style became totally outmoded in the sixteenth century.

Unfortunately the delicate Late Gothic interior of St Jacobs is now buried beneath masses of heavy Baroque sculpture added in the seventeenth century. The effect is overpowering and dizzying, as it was intended to be, for the aim was to win converts to the Catholic faith. A sign directs us to Rubens' mausoleum the ambulatory, one of the largest Baroque monuments in the church. It is far more impressive than the memorials to other northern Baroque artists such as Rembrandt and Vermeer. But we must remember that Rubens was a diplomat as well as a painter and architect; should we have forgotten the fact, there is a lengthy eighteenth-century inscription in Latin recalling his many achievements. The painting on the tomb of *The Virgin Surrounded by Saints*, executed by Rubens towards the end of his life, is virtually a family group portrait, for it has Rubens posing as a gallant St George, his two wives as saints, and his father, probably, as St Jerome. The Virgin is portrayed with deep tenderness and, interestingly, looks more like a Raphael Madonna than one of the typically plump models that Rubens usually preferred. Perhaps the elderly Rubens imagined Paradise to be like the Italy he had once known so well.

The tomb of Nicolaas Rockox, Rubens' faithful

patron and close friend, is in the north aisle of the church. Above it hangs a *Triptych of the Last Judgement* by Bernard van Orley of Brussels. The left wing includes a portrait of Rockox and his three sons, while the right wing shows his wife and ten daughters.

Looking at too many tombs can be a gloomy pursuit, so let us leave this church where so many eminent citizens of Antwerp are buried and continue along Lange Nieuwstraat. The Renaissance house at **Lange Nieuwstraat 43** was purchased in 1559 by the English diplomat and merchant banker Sir Thomas Gresham, who gave his name to Gresham's Law, the economic principle that bad money drives good money out of circulation. Gresham belonged to a community of 5,000 or so foreign merchants who carried on business in Antwerp's Handelsbeurs, the world's first purpose-built stock exchange. Gresham worked here intermittently from 1551-74 as financial agent of the crown, often securing large loans on behalf of Elizabeth I. So impressed was he with the Antwerp exchange that, on his return to London in 1566, he founded a similar institution, originally called the Bourse and later renamed the Royal Exchange.

Further along this street, the **Bourgondische Kapel** at number 31 is an elusive Gothic chapel which is open only six hours every week. The chapel, all that survives of the fifteenth-century palace of Jan van Immerseel, was built in 1496 by Herman de Waghemakere. It is decorated with murals commemorating the marriage in that year of Philip the Fair to Joanna the Mad of Castile. There is another concealed chapel in a picturesque courtyard at Lange Nieuwstraat 2.

The **Handelsbeurs** (Exchange) is situated at the point where four lanes meet. We reach it from Lange Nieuwstraat down one of the lanes called Borzestraat. The building is usually open to the public during office hours.

Named the Handelsbeurs after the Huize ter Buerze at Bruges where foreign merchants met in the fifteenth century, it was designed in 1531 by Domien de Waghemakere in Flamboyant Gothic style. Although the building we now see is not the exchange that Sir Thomas Gresham knew, which was destroyed by fire in 1868, it is a fairly faithful reproduction of the building. The main difference is that the courtyard of the original exchange was open to the sky, to ensure that all transactions were conducted in the eyes of God, whereas the new building is roofed over. The curious Moorish arcades of the original Handelsbeurs have been carefully reconstructed, but the murals are a nineteenth-century invention. Now gloomy and deserted, we might nevertheless still be able to imagine the Antwerp exchange in its heyday, when the courtyard rang to the voices of merchants from Italy, Spain, England, Scotland, Holland, France and Germany.

We leave the Handelsbeurs by the south entrance and walk down Twaalf Maandenstraat to reach **Meir**, Antwerp's elegant shopping street. This is a good area to stop for coffee; opposite the **Torengebouw**, built in 1929-32 as Europe's first twentieth-century skyscraper, Locus is an elegant tea room which sells tempting pâtisserie. A few doors down is Cuperus, a shop specialising in coffee, tea and chocolates, where elegant Antwerp ladies perch precariously on uncomfortable stools to enjoy the superb coffee served there.

From the Torengebouw, Schoenmarkt leads to **Groenplaats**, a bustling square surrounded by cafés. My favourite is the old-fashioned De Post, which serves excellent coffee and good lunches. Leaving Groenplaats on the south side, we proceed along Reyndersstraat, then turn right up Hoogstraat, a street lined with a strange mixture of fashionable boutiques and curiosity shops. The tea room Leonardo at number 28 is primly elegant, whereas the Frituur De Twee Vuistjes on the corner of Vlasmarkt is more down to earth, serving tempting *frites* in a building decorated with a splendid Baroque statue of the Virgin standing atop a globe with a snake entwined around it.

We in fact turn off Hoogstraat shortly before Leonardo, proceeding left down Korte Pieter Potstraat then right along Grote Pieter Potstraat. Suikerrui then leads left down to the waterfront, where we can ascend to a breezy promenade to admire the magnificent sweep of the Scheldt. Plate 14 shows the waterfront of Antwerp in 1515, when it was crammed with sailing ships of every description. The old quays that Baedeker described in 1905 as 'handsome and busy' are now empty and rather forlorn (pl. 24); nowadays almost all ships berth in the modern docks situated to the north of the old city.

The **Nationaal Scheepvaartmuseum** (National Maritime Museum) is situated in Antwerp's old castle, the **Steen**, which overlooks the river just north of here. The castle was built in the ninth century to protect the western frontier of the German Empire from the troublesome Counts of Flanders on the opposite bank of the Scheldt. It can be seen in the 1515 woodcut (pl. 14), below a Gothic inscription stating, 'This is the castle where the giant Antigoon lived.' We may be fairly certain that he did not, as Antigoon, if he ever lived, lived long before the ninth century.

Examining the woodcut, we will see that almost all the old buildings along the waterfront have now vanished. In the nineteenth century it was deemed necessary to modernise the port of Antwerp by straightening the harbour front and creating the broad quays that Baedeker admired. This could only be accomplished by demolishing some 600 houses, obliterating eight streets and destroying the old fish market. The only building to survive was the Steen, which now stands on the quayside like a beached whale.

As we ascend the inclined approach to the Steen, we can distinguish two distinct layers of masonry, as if the tide had receded leaving a high-water mark about mid-way up the walls. The dark lower courses of masonry date from the thirteenth century, while the lighter upper level was added in 1520, when the Steen was partly rebuilt by Domien de Waghemakere and Rombout Keldermans the Younger. We enter through a gate to emerge on a small terrace, which is all that remains of one of the eight streets destroyed in the nineteenth century.

After serving for a long time as a prison, the Steen was converted into a museum of antiquities in the late nineteenth century. It would appear to have been a rather gloomy place to visit, judging from Baedeker's 1905 guide book, which informed travellers that candles, walking sticks and umbrellas were available for hire. It is difficult to imagine why an umbrella was needed to visit a museum. The collection of antiquities is now in the Vleeshuis.

The Steen has been brightened up considerably and its jaunty collection of maritime curiosities is highly entertaining. It is all displayed rather haphazardly in a maze of little rooms with chronically creaking floorboards, but this casual confusion makes the collection all the more intriguing. A few of the rooms have the added attraction of containing enormous Renaissance fireplaces, which were left behind when the museum of antiquities moved to the Vleeshuis. The most striking of these is an ornate Mannerist fireplace decorated with Biblical scenes, designed by Pieter Coecke van Aalst for the Moelenaere house. Other relics that were rescued from this magnificent Renaissance house are now displayed in the Vleeshuis museum.

The maritime museum boasts a large collection of beautifully detailed ship models, figureheads, charts and instruments. Among the curiosities, there are ships in bottles and even one in an electric light bulb. The museum has also amassed a marvellous collection of old photographs of Antwerp harbour. Another interesting feature, in the basement, is a recently excavated cesspit containing detritus from the sixteenth and seventeenth centuries.

From the terrace in front of the Steen, we can see our next destination, the step-gabled **Vleeshuis** (Meat Hall), flanked by two Neo-Gothic buildings. We can reach it by an interesting, if somewhat indirect route; after walking along the north promenade, we descend to Jordaenskaai, turn right, then left up Palingbrug, where a flight of ancient steps ascends to the old meat market.

The Vleeshuis is another Late Gothic work of Herman de Waghemakere, who completed the building in 1503, shortly before his death. Its walls are built of alternating bands of brick and sandstone, a picturesque technique delightfully known as 'streaky-bacon style'. We see the meat hall quite clearly on the 1515 woodcut (pl. 14). It was then, and still is, one of the tallest buildings in Antwerp, a visible symbol of the power of the mediaeval guild of butchers. So powerful indeed was this guild that in 1585, when the Duke of Parma's army was besieging the city, it successfully vetoed a plan by the Dutch to flood the polders to the north of Antwerp. This desperate military strategy—successfully employed a few years before to rescue Leiden from the Spanish—would have enabled the Dutch fleet to sail up to the city walls unopposed. But the plan was unacceptable to the butchers of Antwerp because the land to be put under water was where they grazed their beef cattle. The guild of butchers was eventually abolished, as were all the other guilds, during the Napoleonic administration, yet the butchers continued to occupy their guild house for a further seven years before finally quitting.

The Vleeshuis is where we come to learn more about Antwerp's history, for its four floors are crammed with a fascinating miscellany of local antiquities. We begin on the ground floor, a vast vaulted space where meat was once sold. The heavy Baroque doors, fierce oak satyrs and voluptuous Virgins in this room reflect the robust and sensual spirit of Antwerp. Attached to the far wall are two oak brackets decorated with satyrs in a style known, not without cause, as Grotesque. They were carved by Pieter Coecke van Aalst in about 1549 to decorate the loggia of the Moelenaere house. The loggia was faithfully copied by a nineteenth-century architect in a Neo-Renaissance mansion at Transvaalstraat 59-61, not far from Cogels Osylei.

Ascending a staircase worn by the footsteps of many generations of butchers, we reach the first floor, which was formerly used by the guild for meetings and banquets. Several furnished rooms are preserved, including the very attractive Raadzaal, where the guild meetings were held. After looking at the exhibits on this floor, which include a rather gruesome model of a public mutilation, we ascend to the top floor. Here, to our surprise, we find an extensive collection of musical instruments, and a small room devoted to Egyptian relics collected by a nineteenth-century antiquarian at a time when Egyptology was in vogue. Yet the main reward for the stiff climb here is the view we obtain of the extraordinary mediaeval roof construction.

To leave the Vleeshuis, we must descend three flights of stairs to the basement and then ascend one flight to return to the ground floor. This lengthy route may seem tiresome, but it is amply rewarded by the lapidarium in the basement. This contains a fascinating variety of sculptural fragments, including façade stones, gravestones and obelisks that marked the boundaries of municipal jurisdiction. Many of the stones are decorated with a hand, the symbol of Antwerp. There are also two Renaissance busts of Jan van Eyck and Albrecht Dürer, carved in 1549 to decorate a house in Antwerp.

As we climbed the spiral stair of the Vleeshuis, we may have glimpsed the **St Pauluskerk** to the north. Let us now visit this church, which we reach by turning left along Vleeshouwersstraat, past some modern dwellings imitating the traditional Renaissance houses of Antwerp (such as those in Kaasstraat). **Veemarkt**, the old cattle market, upon which we emerge, is a somewhat nondescript square overlooked by the St Pauluskerk, a Late Gothic church built by Domien de Waghemakere in 1533-71. The church originally belonged to a Dominican friary, and in the eighteenth century was furnished by the friars with Baroque paintings and sculptures. The main painting of interest is a *Scourging of Christ* by Rubens.

The church has a curious little garden which many visitors miss, tucked into the corner of the nave and south transept; we reach it it through a door in the long corridor leading into the church from the street. Two devout Dominican friars laboured here for half a century, from 1697 to 1747, to create a mock Mount Calvary. The artificial hill built up against the church is crowded with Baroque statues of saints, angels and prophets in rather exaggerated poses of ecstasy or grief. At the foot of the hill is a dark cave with a grim vision of Hell. Baudelaire, the irascible French poet, dismissed the work as 'ridiculous', yet the fact that the friars devoted the best part of their lives to the construction of this calvary gives it a certain tragic grandeur.

From the church we turn left along Zwartzusterstraat. A right turn then takes us into Stoelstraat, one of the loveliest old lanes in Antwerp, even if its most picturesque house, at number 11, is merely a modern reconstruction of a mediaeval house rather than the genuine article. At the end of Stoelstraat we turn right along Zirkstraat, then left down Hofstraat. During office hours, we can glance into the courtyard of the **Oude Beurs**, at number 16. This handsome sixteenth-century palace has an attractive Late Gothic arcade, and one of the few surviving watchtowers of Antwerp. It is now occupied by the rather antiquated offices of the local education authority.

We turn right at the end of Hofstraat to reach, on the left, a little alley known as the Spanjepandsteeg. The sixteenth-century house at the end of this alley was built for the guild of archers. Named **Den Spieghel** (The Mirror), it was purchased in 1506 by Pieter Gilles (who preferred the sonorous Latin name Petrus Aegidius), Secretary of the City of Antwerp. Gilles was a leading Antwerp humanist whose friends included Erasmus and Thomas More. The inspiration for *Utopia* came to Thomas More in 1515 when he was visiting Gilles in Antwerp. More informs the reader at the beginning of *Utopia* that he had been sent to Bruges by Henry VIII to settle a dispute jeopardising the wool trade between Castile and England. While waiting for the Spanish envoy to return from an audience at Brussels, More seized the opportunity to travel to Antwerp to see Pieter Gilles, 'a very fine person and an excellent scholar'. In the opening scene of *Utopia*, More describes his encounter with Pieter Gilles and a certain Raphael Hythlodaye as he was walking back to his inn after attending Mass in the cathedral. Like many young men roaming the streets of sixteenth-century Antwerp, Raphael Hythlodaye had just returned from a long voyage around the world. As they sit in the garden at More's inn, he tells them of his adventures and of the remarkable island of Utopia.

Utopia was first published in Leuven in 1516 in a Latin edition proof-read by Erasmus. One year later Erasmus furnished More with a unique token of their friendship by commissioning the Renaissance artist Quinten Metsys of Antwerp to produce a double portrait of himself and Pieter Gilles (pls 21 and 22). The portrait of Gilles now hangs in Longford Castle, and there is a copy in Antwerp's Museum voor Schone Kunsten. The Erasmus portrait, a favourite book jacket illustration, has been lost, but there are several copies in existence, including a good one in the Palazzo Barberini in Rome.

If Erasmus appears rather yellowish in his

Plate 21 Portrait of Erasmus

Plate 22 Portrait of Pieter Gilles

portrait, it is because he was ill at the time. In a letter written to More in 1517, while Metsys was still working on his portrait, Erasmus complained, 'My doctor has taken it into his head to get me to swallow pills to purify my spleen and whatever he is foolish enough to prescribe I am foolish enough to do. The portrait has already been begun, but when I went back to the artist after taking the medicine he said that I didn't have the same physiognomy any more, and so the painting had to be postponed a few days until I looked a little more alive again.'

More was particularly impressed with the uncanny realism of the two portraits by Metsys. On looking closely at the portrait of Gilles, More was delighted to discover that his friend was holding a letter from him, in which the handwriting was clearly recognisable as More's. He subsequently wrote to Gilles asking for the letter to be returned so that he could hang it alongside the painting. 'If it has been lost,' he added, 'I will see whether I in my turn can copy the man who copies my hand so well.'

We now walk back along Oude Beurs and turn right down Wisselstraat, which provides a particularly dramatic approach into Antwerp's main square, the **Grote Markt**. To enjoy the architectural spectacle of this square, let us sit down on one of the café terraces, or at a window table indoors if the weather is bad. I recommend 't Ogenblik at number 12; both the view and the coffee are excellent.

Grote Markt is dominated by the Renaissance **Stadhuis** (Town Hall), designed by Cornelis Floris in 1561. Its construction marked the end of quaint Late Gothic architecture and the beginning of an era of disciplined and proportioned public buildings based on Italian principles. The Antwerp Stadhuis was also built in part using Italian materials, such as the rosy marble of the columns, which is a rare delight in these northern latitudes.

From our café table we can see also some of the guild houses on the market square. **Grote Markt 5** (the fifth building on the north side, beginning at the town hall) was built by the guild of coopers in 1579. **Grote Markt 7**, with a statue of St George on the pediment, was erected one year later for the guild of archers.

Now let us turn our attention to the extraordinary fountain which spouts water recklessly over much of the square. Designed in 1887, the **Brabo Fountain** depicts the legend of Salvius Brabo, a Roman soldier who freed the Scheldt from the tyranny of a giant called Druoon Antigoon. The giant had exacted a toll from every ship sailing down the Scheldt, and severed the hand of any captain foolish enough to resist. Eventually he met his match in Brabo, who is shown holding aloft the hand of Antigoon, just before hurling it into the Scheldt. According to one school of etymology, Brabo throwing the hand gives Antwerp its name; from the Dutch *hand werpen* (to throw the hand). A rather more prosaic explanation gives Antwerp's root as *aan 't werven* (on the waterfront). The omnipresent hand in Antwerp reveals that the people prefer to believe the romantic legend of Salvius Brabo.

Visiting Antwerp in 1520, the German artist Albrecht Dürer was solemnly taken to the town hall to be shown the skeleton of Antigoon. 'In Antwerp I saw a bone from the leg of the giant,' he noted in his diary. 'This bone measures five and a half feet in length and is extraordinarily heavy and very thick; the shoulder blade is likewise very broad, like the back of a strong man. This giant was 18 feet tall . . .' Dürer seems to have been the victim of a practical joke, however, for the bones he observed were apparently those of a whale.

We leave Grote Markt by the street facing the town hall, Kaasrui, then turn right along Korte Koepoortstraat and left down a narrow lane, Jezuitenrui, so called because it leads to a Jesuit church. And a most splendid Jesuit church it is, known as the **St Carolus Borromeuskerk**. Modelled on Vignola's Il Gesù church in Rome, St Carolus Borromeus was designed by Pieter Huyssens in 1614-21. He was assisted by Rubens, who probably designed the lovely Baroque tower and the clustered cherubs above the entrance. John Evelyn wrote, 'The church of the Jesuits is most sumptuous and magnificent, a glorious fabriq without, and within wholly incrusted with marble, inlay'd and polish'd into divers representations of histories, landskips, flowers, &c.' Much of the interior was destroyed by fire in 1718, and little of the original marble remains.

From the attractive square in front of the Jesuit church, we now follow a somewhat winding route to reach the house in which Albrecht Dürer lodged for some nine months in 1520. Heading first down Wijngaardstraat, we then turn right along Hoofdkerkstraat, and finally right into Wolstraat (Wool Street), so called because of the many English wool merchants who settled here in the sixteenth century. Notice the splendid Baroque portal at **Wolstraat 30** designed by François Duquesnoy. There is a very attractive portrait of this sculptor by Sir Anthony van Dyck in Brussels' Musée d'Art Ancien.

Dürer's house is at the end of Wolstraat, on the corner of Minderbroedersrui. In 1520 Dürer travelled from Nuremberg to Antwerp with his wife Agnes and his maidservant Susanna, paying his expenses as he went along by producing woodcuts and sketches of German merchants. He was an acutely observant traveller and filled his notebooks with detailed drawings and descriptions of the curiosities he encountered, from the mansions of Antwerp to the lions in the menagerie of Ghent's Prinsenhof. Through the diaries of Dürer we learn a great deal about the splendour of sixteenth-century Antwerp. Once he observed a magnificent procession as it rounded the corner into Wolstraat: 'Wagons were drawn along with masques upon ships and other inventions. Behind them came the Company of the Prophets in their proper order, and scenes from the New Testament, such as the Annunciation, the Three Holy Kings riding on great camels, and on other rare beasts, all very well arranged.'

A quiet lane behind Dürer's house, Grote Goddaert, leads us in a gentle curve along the course of the mediaeval city walls. We emerge on a small square named **Engelse Beurs**, the English Exchange, where a separate stock exchange was established for the English mercantile community. If we turn right here and proceed down Minderbroedersstraat we come upon the Neoclassical lodge of the **Academie voor Schone Kunsten** (Academy of Fine Arts), established in 1662 by the artist David Teniers the Younger. In 1810 it moved to its present location in a former Franciscan friary. Exploring the romantically overgrown garden, we come upon a weather-beaten statue of Teniers and some magnificent Baroque portals salvaged from demolished buildings.

Stadswaag, where the public weigh house once stood, is our destination now; we reach it by walking up Mutsaertstraat and then turning right. With the weigh house now demolished, a chilly silence has fallen upon this once animated square. Here, as nowhere else in Antwerp, we find that mood of melancholy which so struck William Beckford in 1783: 'No village amongst the Alps, or hermitage upon Mount Lebanon is less disturbed ... In its two hundred and twelve streets and twenty-two squares the grass grows in deep silence.' During the day the only sign of life on Stadswaag comes from a specialist beer café called 't Waagstuk, which is tucked away in a secluded courtyard at number 20. But at night the square becomes rather more animated, as jazz cafés and bars come to life in the old cellars and abandoned warehouses. Visitors who find themselves at a loose end in the evening might stroll back this way and visit, for example, the curious café De Trein der Traagheid at Lange Noordstraat 33, which is furnished with aged wooden Belgian railway carriage seats from the 1930s.

From Stadswaag we continue along Lange Brilstraat, and right down Venusstraat. The mouldering buildings numbered 11-15 were formerly warehouses used by the English Merchant Adventurers. Later they housed the Berg van Barmhartigheid, a municipal pawnbroking bank founded by Wenceslas Coeberger in the seventeenth century.

Continuing down Venusstraat, we then turn left along Prinsstraat. An old gateway at number 13 leads us into the **Hof van Liere**. This splendid Late Gothic palace was probably built by Domien de Waghemakere in 1515-20 for Burgomaster Arnold van Liere. Visiting Van Liere here soon after the completion of the palace, Albrecht Dürer praised the building in his diary and sketched its slender watchtower. In the 1550s the city fathers, who by then owned the palace, offered it to the English Merchant Adventurers as an incentive to remain in Antwerp. It was a successful ploy, if temporary, for the English merchants eventually quit Antwerp in 1611 to resettle in Hamburg. The Hof van Liere was then given to the Jesuits who used it as a religious college, adding two large quadrangles on the north side.

Our explorations in Bruges and Ghent have perhaps given us a taste for the Begijnhofs of Flanders. Antwerp, too, has a **Begijnhof**, although it is seldom visited by tourists. To reach it, we continue down Prinsstraat, then along Pieter van Hobokenstraat to reach Ossenmarkt, a likeable little square. The Begijnhof, concealed by a high brick wall, is entered through a portal at Rode Straat 39. We discover within its walls the familiar enticing prospect of a simple and secluded community of modest whitewashed houses grouped around cobbled courtyards and leafy squares. It is difficult to imagine a more pleasing place to live, combining as it does the intimacy of village life with the excitement of a metropolis.

We now retrace our steps along Pieter van Hobokenstraat and turn left into Rozenstraat. Our destination is the street named grandly Via Caesarea on the 1565 plan of Antwerp, which we reach by turning right along Kattenstraat, left into Prinsesstraat and then right into Keizersstraat.

Situated slightly off the beaten track, this street once contained the homes of many prominent Antwerp families. We have come here to visit one of the most splendid of these houses, the **Rockoxhuis** at number 12, a beautiful Flemish Renaissance house bought in 1603 by Burgomaster Nicolaas Rockox. As in the Rubenshuis and the Museum Plantin-Moretus, we discover here the alluring atmosphere of Baroque Antwerp.

We have already met Nicolaas Rockox in our wanderings, as captain of the guild of arquebusiers, and a friend and patron of Rubens. Rockox lived here with his wife and 13 children, all of whom we saw in a painting in the St Jacobskerk. When we enter the hall of the Rockoxhuis, we are following in the footsteps of Grotius, Ortelius and Lipsius, all friends of the Burgomaster.

The restoration of the house has been carried out with impeccable attention to detail: the rooms are furnished in solid Baroque style and the walls hung with an interesting collection of Flemish paintings. There is a landscape by Patinir, an astonishing sketch of two old men's heads by Sir

Anthony van Dyck, and a view of the fish market at Antwerp by Frans Snijders, who lived in the house next door to Rockox. But the principal delights of this tasteful little collection are the two works by Rubens. On our walks so far we have seen many, perhaps too many, of Rubens' large-scale religious paintings. In room 2 we obtain a glimpse of a different style of Rubens altogether. The *Madonna and Child*, executed by Rubens in 1613, is a tender study of his first wife Isabella and their son Nicolaas. There is also a sketch of the *Crucifixion*, drawn in about 1628. Delacroix greatly admired this work, which was owned once by his friend George Sand. The sketch was a preliminary study for a large religious painting, which Rubens was forced to abandon when in 1628 he was called away to mediate in the war between Spain and England. This diplomatic mission was successful and a peace treaty was signed between the two countries in 1630. Rubens received a knighthood from Charles II and an honorary degree from Cambridge University for his efforts.

Room 4, once the picture gallery of Burgomaster Rockox, is depicted in the painting of the *Feast in the House of Burgomaster Rockox* by Frans Francken the Younger (pl. 23). This *kunstkamer* painting includes allegorical figures representing the five senses; they are gathered around a table laden with food and drink. The painting depicted above the fireplace is Rubens' *Samson and Delilah*, now in London's National Gallery. Two other works represented in the picture gallery are now in Antwerp's Museum voor Schone Kunsten. Through the open doorway we see Rubens' painting of *The Incredulity of St Thomas*, commissioned by Burgomaster Rockox in 1613 to hang above the tomb of his dead wife. To the right of the fireplace is Quinten Metsys' diptych of *The Saviour of the World and Mary at Prayer*, one of the most beautiful and moving works by this Antwerp artist.

Plate 23 Feast in the House of Burgomaster Rockox

Antwerp Explored Further

I. The Museum voor Schone Kunsten and its Neighbourhood

The Museum voor Schone Kunsten (Museum of Fine Arts) occupies an imposing Neoclassical building in Antwerp's southern quarter. This district was developed in the boom years of the nineteenth century and it contains numerous splendid buildings from that era. As well as the delights of the relatively unknown Museum voor Schone Kunsten, there are two other interesting museums which have recently opened in this neighbourhood.

On entering the **Museum voor Schone Kunsten**, we are swept into the Great Vestibule, which is decorated with a panoramic frieze by Nicaise de Keyser depicting Flemish art and architecture through the ages. We then ascend a monumental staircase to enter Gallery I, a room devoted to religious paintings by Rubens.

The large panel of the *Baptism of Christ* is, astonishingly, merely a side panel from an early work painted in 1604. In 1600 Rubens set off for Italy, where he stayed for eight years. Soon after arriving in Venice he met Vincenzo Gonzaga the Elder, Duke of Mantua, who offered him employment in Mantua. In 1604 Gonzaga commissioned Rubens to paint a gigantic triptych for the Jesuit church in Mantua. The *Baptism of Christ* is part of this triptych, which is now divided between Mantua, Nancy and Antwerp.

Many of the other works by Rubens in this gallery were commissioned to hang in churches in Antwerp, including *The Adoration of the Magi* (which includes some wonderfully expressive figures), *Christ Crucified between Two Thieves*, *Christ on the Straw* (a tender study painted as an epitaph for his friend Jan Michielsen), and *Christ on the Cross* (a bleak painting commissioned in 1619 by Nicolaas Rockox). *The Incredulity of St*

Thomas was also commissioned by Rockox, Rubens' friend and steady patron; the wings have affectionate portraits of Burgomaster Rockox and his wife Adriana Perez. In the midst of so many monumental works, it is easy to overlook one small painting in a more intimate style. It is a portrait by Rubens of his friend Gaspard Gevartius, town clerk of Antwerp, seated at his desk with his pen poised. A bust of Marcus Aurelius is there to remind us that Gevartius had written a commentary on the Roman emperor. The study of Gevartius is one of the few portraits by Rubens in Antwerp; because they were easily sold and shipped abroad, the portraits now tend to be in far-off collections, whereas most of the large religious works have stayed in Antwerp.

After we have looked at the works by Rubens in Galleries I and G, it is logical to proceed to Galleries H and F where there are several paintings by his pupils. *The King Drinks* is a work of typically earthy humour by Jacob Jordaens, one of Rubens' many successful followers.

The Flemish Primitives occupy the rooms on either side of the Rubens galleries. Gallery Q is a quiet room containing an exquisite collection of miniature works by Flemish Primitives, including two by Jan van Eyck: a tiny sketch of *St Barbara*, dated 1437, and *The Madonna at the Fountain*, painted two years later. The study of St Barbara adopted a rather revolutionary approach to its subject. Mediaeval artists up until then had depicted Barbara holding a miniature tower in her hand to symbolise the building in which she was imprisoned by her jealous father. This is how St Barbara appears in the *Adoration of the Mystic Lamb* in Ghent by Jan and Hubert van Eyck. In the Antwerp sketch, however, Van Eyck realistically represents the tower as a full-scale Gothic edifice looming above the saint. The tower was modelled upon the north tower of Antwerp Cathedral, which at the time the sketch was done had reached about one-third of its final height. Van Eyck's minuscule study of the cathedral tower contains a plenitude of details concerning mediaeval construction methods, including a delightful sketch of the architect, who is shouting instructions to the masons at work at the top of the soaring edifice.

Also in this gallery is Roger van der Weyden's *Triptych of the Seven Sacraments* painted in 1445 for Jean Chevrot, Bishop of Tournai. Set in a large Gothic church, the Seven Sacraments depicted are, from left to right, Ordination, Marriage, Extreme Unction, Eucharist, Baptism, Confirmation and Penance. Notice the ingenious way that the picture frame has been designed to harmonise with the Gothic architecture.

There is also a marvellous portrait by Van der Weyden of Philippe de Croy. This originally formed one wing of a diptych; the other wing—a study of the Virgin and Child—is now in the Huntington Gallery in California. Van der Weyden captures the intelligence and sensitivity of the Burgundian noble, who is dressed entirely in black, with the result that his face and hands stand out vividly.

In room S we abandon for a moment the Flemish Primitives to look at Simone Martini's four miniatures depicting the Annunciation, the Archangel Gabriel, the Crucifixion and the Descent from the Cross. These four panels originally belonged to a polyptych of the Passion owned by the Charterhouse of Champmol. Founded by the Dukes of Burgundy to receive their mausoleums, this Charterhouse just outside the city walls of Dijon was endowed with a magnificent collection of Gothic painting and sculpture. After the French Revolution the Charterhouse was demolished and its remarkable collection sold off. An Antwerp collector bought these four Martini panels, but the other two were lost to Paris and Berlin. Van der Weyden's painting of the *Seven Sacraments* came from the same collection.

While we are in this room we may be struck by the strange study of *The Virgin and Child Surrounded by Angels*, painted about 1451 by the French artist Jean Fouquet. The extraordinarily pale Virgin has been tentatively identified as Agnes Sorel who, until her untimely death at the age of 28, was the mistress of King Charles VII of France. The bright red angels surrounding her are very puzzling. This room also contains a handsome *Portrait of a Young Italian* painted by Memling in about 1478.

Gallery R contains a miniature landscape by Joachim Patinir which we should not overlook.

Illustrating Patinir's most cherished Biblical episode, *Landscape with the Flight to Egypt* is dotted with delightful details such as some tiny rabbits and a goat perched on a mountain ridge. The strange rock formations in Patinir's paintings may look like fantastic creations, but in fact they are based on the extraordinary limestone gorge of the River Meuse between Namur and Dinant.

This gallery contains several beautiful works by the Antwerp painter Quinten Metsys, including his *Triptych of the Entombment of Christ*. Painted in 1508-11 for the carpenters' chapel in Antwerp Cathedral, it shows the dead Christ surrounded by mourners, flanked by panels showing the martyrdoms of St John the Baptist and St John the Evangelist. Metsys was particularly gifted as a portraitist, as we may see from the copy of his portrait of Pieter Gilles (pl. 22). Notice, too, Metsys' enchanting *Mary Magdalene with the Box of Spikenard*, reminiscent of Leonardo da Vinci, and his vibrant diptych of *The Saviour of the World and Mary at Prayer*. The diptych was once owned by Burgomaster Rockox, and can be seen to the right of the fireplace in the painting of the *Feast in the House of Burgomaster Rockox* (pl. 23).

In Gallery N, we come upon an unusual work by Hans Memling, *Christ as King of Heaven Surrounded by Angels*, which hung in a Benedictine convent in Spain until it was repatriated to Flanders. Four of the angels are copied from Memling's *St Ursula Shrine* in Bruges: the angel playing a psaltery (far left), the lutist (third from the left), the angel playing at a portable organ (third from the right) and the viol player (far right). Frans Floris' *Fall of the Rebel Angels*, which hangs in Gallery P, is an example of Antwerp Mannerism at its most tormented. Painted in 1554, this crowded composition anticipates somewhat the surging Baroque style of Rubens.

When we have explored the upper galleries, we can pause in the museum café at the foot of the back stairs. While we sit beneath a magnificent panorama of Antwerp harbour, let us read about some of the nineteenth-century and modern paintings in the collection.

Gallery 19 contains a collection of paintings by James Ensor, born in 1860 in Ostend. Ensor's father was a British expatriate and his mother

Flemish. *Afternoon at Ostend*, painted in 1881, reflects the solid Victorian milieu in which he grew up. Late in the 1880s, however, Ensor rebelled against this comfortable bourgeois world and his style of painting changed utterly, as is illustrated by *Skeletons Fighting for the Body of a Hanged Man*, painted just ten years after the languid *Afternoon at Ostend*. The dark browns and greys of his early palette are replaced by vivid reds and greens, and instead of solid Ostend citizens we see strange caricatures of people wearing carnival masks. Why Ensor should have changed his style so totally has never been satisfactorily resolved. It may have been that a visit in the 1880s to an exhibition of Turner paintings in London led Ensor in a new direction. This would explain the almost abstract style of *The Rebel Angels Struck Down*, painted in 1889. The gaudy masks that appear so frequently in Ensor's later works are more easily accounted for, as Ensor's uncle owned a novelty shop in Ostend crammed with carnival masks.

Ensor's later works caused a furore in the staid Belgian art world when they were first exhibited. Even *Les XX*, the independent group which introduced Impressionism to Belgium, refused to admit Ensor's work to the salons of 1889 and 1890. However, his reputation is now more firmly established; Ensor's greatest work, *The Entry of Christ into Brussels*, was recently sold to the voracious J. Paul Getty Museum in California. Painted in 1888, this large canvas was Ensor's favourite work and it hung in his house at Ostend until his death in 1949. Bought by Knokke Casino, it was then sold to an Antwerp banker, who in 1951 lent it to the Museum voor Schone Kunsten. It remained here until 1983, when it was put up for sale. The Belgian government could not be persuaded to buy the painting, and so *The Entry of Christ into Brussels* exited from Antwerp, one more masterpiece lost in the unending diaspora of Flemish art.

We find several attractive Impressionist works by Rik Wouters in Gallery 21. *Woman Ironing* is a tender domestic portrait of his wife Nel, painted in 1912. During World War I, Wouters was interned at Amsterdam, and he died there in 1916 after undergoing a series of operations for eye cancer. As we leave the museum, we will see two small cabinets in the Great Vestibule containing mementoes of Wouters.

Galleries 8-10 contain an engaging collection of eccentric works by Belgian surrealists. Hanging in room 10 is a melancholy early work by Paul Delvaux, *The Red Bow*, painted in 1937. The streets of a Classical city are strewn with black rocks and the walls of buildings are cracked, as if a volcano has recently erupted. Amidst this dark chaos, women wander naked, or with huge red bows over their breasts, their eyes filled with blank despair. In the same room stands René Magritte's impishly irreverent *Madame Récamier*. This sculptural work recalls the portrait by Jacques Louis David in the Louvre of Madame Récamier reclining on a chaise longue. In Magritte's work an L-shaped coffin has taken the place of Madame Récamier. With this haunting image to ponder, we are perhaps ready for a change of scene, so let us now explore the other two museums in this quarter, which are situated in warehouses in the old docklands.

To reach this area, which at the time of writing was in the throes of redevelopment, we should turn left outside the museum, then right down Verschansingsstraat. At the end of this street stands the **Waterpoort**, or Porta Regia as it was more grandly named in the seventeenth century. This city gate, the only one still standing in Antwerp, was designed by Hubert van den Eynde and adorned with a splendid sculpture of a river god by Artus Quellin the Elder. Erected in 1624 to commemorate the coronation of Philip IV of Spain, it of course has no business standing in this nineteenth-century quarter of Antwerp, where it was re-erected in 1937. But the gate does add a nice touch of grandeur to a somewhat desolate open square, which until recently was a dock.

Straight ahead is the **Museum voor Fotografie**, a museum of photography recently opened in a former warehouse at Waalse Kaai 47. It has a fascinating collection of historic photographs, including many studies of Old Antwerp. One which seems to me to sum up the spirit of Antwerp is Guy Vaes' *L'Avenir*, which shows a shabby café named L'Avenir (The Future) with a dilapidated railway track running alongside. The café in the photograph is, incidentally, just across the road from the museum, although its name has changed and the railway line that once ran down to the river has gone. The museum also contains antique cameras, a photographer's studio from the turn of the century, and several *camera obscura*. The most curious exhibit is a 1905 *Keizerspanorama* that was exhibited at the World Exhibition in Liège. The remarkable cylindrical device allowed 25 people simultaneously to view stereoscopic photographs.

From this museum, it is but a short walk along the Waalse Kaai, past various promising signs of urban regeneration, to the new **Museum van Hedendaagse Kunst Antwerpen** at Leuvenstraat 32. This museum of modern art occupies an Art Deco grain silo built in the 1920s. Expect to be amused, teased, tantalised, and bemused by the contemporary Belgian artists exhibited here, who have a delightful talent for assembling quirky surrealist constructions.

Continuing along the Waalse Kaai, we come upon the **Zuiderpershuis**, a severe Neo-Baroque building with massive rusticated stones, erected in the confident 1880s. This rugged building once housed enormous steam engines that were used to drive hydraulic cranes, operate sluices and even shunt goods trains within the port area. The solemn grandeur of the Zuiderpershuis is typical of the architectural style that developed at Antwerp in the heady years of the *Belle Epoque*. So, too, is an extraordinary monument that stands on Marnixplaats, on the site of the sixteenth-century Spanish citadel (reached by turning right down Scheldestraat at the end of Waalse Kaai). Adorned with glowering sea gods and severed chains, the monument was erected to commemorate the abolition in 1863 of the Dutch right to levy tolls on shipping on the Scheldt.

One last delight in this quarter is the curious dwelling house at **Schildersstraat 2**, which we reach by turning right down Zwijgerstraat. Its principal feature is a splendid balcony modelled exactly on the wooden prow of a sailing ship. This fanciful Art Nouveau house was designed in 1901 for an Antwerp shipbuilder by Frans Smet-Verhas, who has proudly signed his work in ornate lettering.

II. The Brouwershuis and the Waterfront

The **Brouwershuis** (Brewers' House), a sadly forgotten relic of Renaissance Antwerp, stands at Adriaan Brouwerstraat 20, near the Bonapartedok on the northern edge of the old city. The building was erected in 1553 by Gilbert van Schoonbeke, a founder of the girls' orphanage and promoter of the Friday Market. His most ambitious project was to create a new quarter, the Nieuwstad (New Town), to the north of the old city walls. The streets of the Nieuwstad were laid out according to Renaissance principles on a strict grid pattern. Van Schoonbeke planned to build some 24 breweries in this new quarter, of which only 16 were ever completed. All of the breweries were supplied with pure water from the Brouwershuis.

If we walk through to the back room on the ground floor, we can see the mechanism invented by Van Schoonbeke to fill reservoirs situated on the first floor of the Brouwershuis. This used a horse-drawn system of buckets to hoist water drawn from the city moat. The mechanism proved so effective that it was still being used to supply a few of Antwerp's breweries in the early years of this century.

After ascending the stairs, we walk along a corridor with walls that are disturbingly askew, to enter a seventeenth-century room where the guild held its meetings. Hung with gleaming gilt leather, this is one of the most beautiful rooms in Antwerp. It captivated the nineteenth-century artist Henri de Braekeleer, who painted several mellow studies of this room—one now hangs in Antwerp's Museum voor Schone Kunsten and another in Brussels' Musée d'Art Ancien.

On leaving this curious old house, we turn right and then left along a street that leads to the **Bonapartedok**. As its name suggests, this dock was constructed by Napoleon I. Turning left along the quayside, we come to the busy Tavenierkaai. Another left turn brings us to a flight of stairs leading up to the north promenade.

Walking along the Scheldt waterfront, we cannot help but wonder what lies on the opposite bank. If we are still feeling energetic, we can easily satisfy that nagging curiosity. A 10-minute walk through the St Annatunnel, a busy and bright pedestrian tunnel at the end of the south promenade, takes us across to the left bank of the Scheldt.

The left bank of the Scheldt once belonged to the Counts of Flanders, but it is now part of Antwerp. The main reason for crossing here is to enjoy the panoramic view of the city. Artists began coming here by boat in the sixteenth century to sketch what was then perhaps the most striking urban view in Europe. One of the first artists to do so was the anonymous Master who produced the 1515 woodcut (pl. 14). Anonymous he may be, but he is not invisible, for we see him quite clearly at the bottom left-hand corner of the sketch, sitting on the river bank with his sketch book. What better way to end our time in Antwerp than to stand on the same spot, almost half a millennium later, to admire the magnificent view?

Plate 24 The Waterfront at Antwerp

CHAPTER 4: MECHELEN

With its old houses and languid river, the beautiful Flemish town of Mechelen has something of the appeal of Bruges. Yet it remains virtually undiscovered by tourists, despite being favourably situated mid-way between Brussels and Antwerp. Mechelen is still a secret city where we can wander along quiet, cobbled streets overlooked by crumbling Renaissance houses and ancient Baroque convents built of mellow brick and soft white sandstone. Not that it is totally dead; there are elegant shops on Bruul and crowded cafés on Grote Markt, and the town is surrounded by factories mass-producing oak furniture of mediaeval proportions. But when we stray away from the centre, especially into the areas once occupied by the Begijnhofs and convents, we quickly become immersed in the peaceful mood of this old Catholic town.

Originally under the sway of the Prince-Bishop of Liège, Mechelen (Malines in French) passed in 1213 to the Berthoud family. In 1333 it was captured by Louis de Male, Count of Flanders, and so passed to the Dukes of Burgundy when Louis died in 1384. By the middle of the fifteenth century, the city was sufficiently prosperous to embark on the construction of a church spire that was planned to be the tallest in the world.

Mechelen assumed an important role in

mediaeval politics in 1473, when the Grote Raad, the supreme court of the Burgundian Netherlands, was established here by Charles the Bold. As a result, numerous lawyers, councillors and advisers settled in the city. When Charles the Bold died in 1477, his widow, Margaret of York, settled in Mechelen. Following the tragic death of her daughter in 1482, Margaret of York brought up her grandchildren here. One of them, Margaret of Austria, returned to Mechelen on being appointed Regent of the Netherlands in 1507. Her court became a centre of art and learning, drawing to Mechelen numerous northern Renaissance painters and scholars, such as Albrecht Dürer, Bernard van Orley and Erasmus.

When Margaret of Austria died in 1530, her successor Mary of Hungary moved the court back to Brussels. This proved as disastrous for Mechelen as the silting of the Zwin had been for Bruges. The decline of the city after 1530 can be gauged by the many sixteenth-century buildings left unfinished, such as the cathedral tower and the palace of the Grote Raad on Grote Markt.

In World War I Mechelen had the misfortune to be bombarded both by the retreating Belgians and by the advancing Germans. It also suffered badly in World War II, yet it has weathered these misfortunes and is today a very pleasing and picturesque city.

Mechelen can best be visited as a day excursion from Antwerp or Brussels. A fifteen-minute train journey, followed by a short walk, brings us into the heart of this historic old city. The two walks described in this chapter will pleasantly fill a complete day.

Mechelen

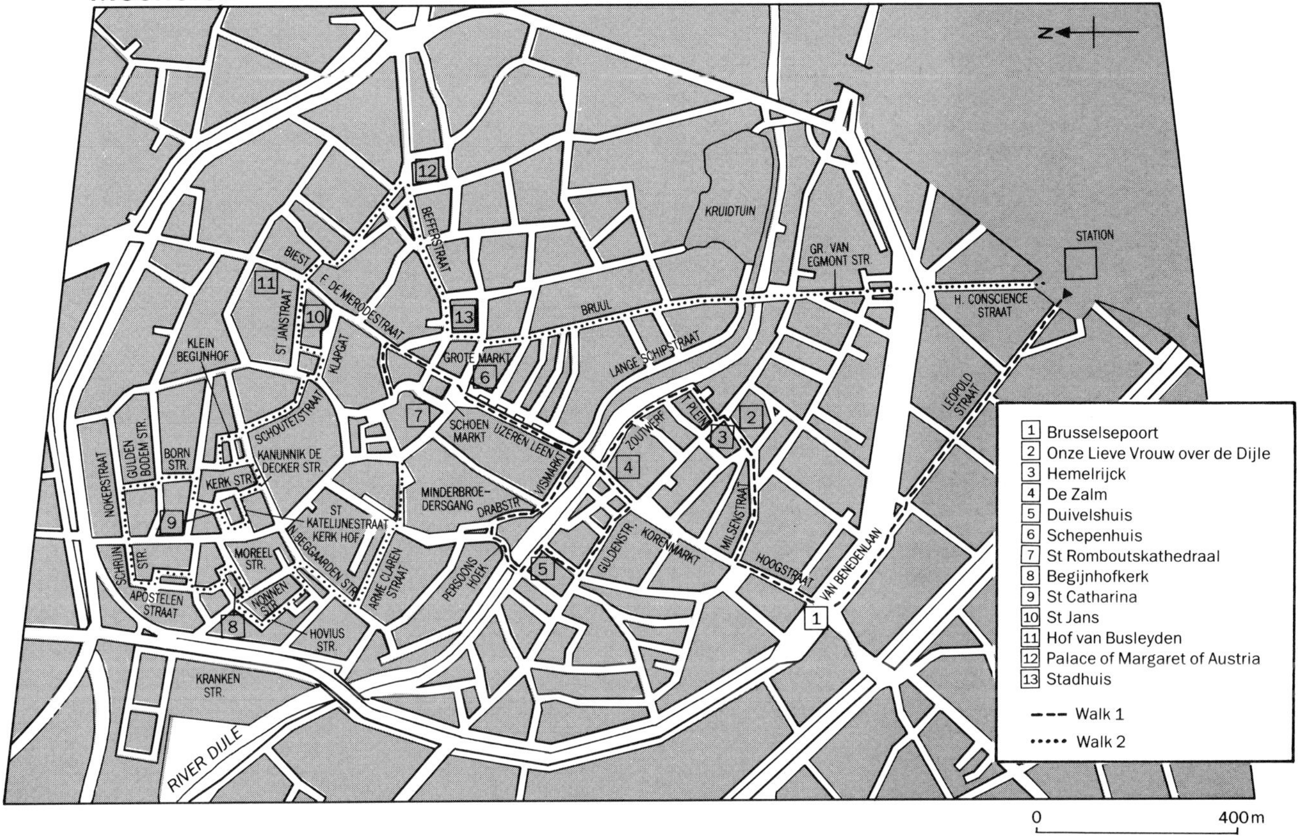

KRUIDTUIN
STATION
BIEST
BEFFERSTRAAT
F. DE MERODESTRAAT
ST JANSTRAAT
KLAPGAT
GR. VAN EGMONT STR.
BRUUL
H. CONSCIENCE STRAAT
GROTE MARKT
LANGE SCHIPSTRAAT
KLEIN BEGIJNHOF
SCHOUTETSTRAAT
SCHOEN MARKT
IJZEREN LEEN
LEOPOLD STRAAT
'T PLEIN
ZOUTWERF
GULDEN BODEM STR.
BORN STR.
KANUNNIK DE DECKER STR.
VISMARKT
NOKERSTRAAT
KERK STR.
MINDERBROEDERSGANG
DRABSTR.
ST KATELIJNESTRAAT KERK HOF
MILSENSTRAAT
SCHRIJN STR.
MOREEL STR.
IN BEGGAARDEN STR.
ARME CLAREN STRAAT
PERSOONS HOEK
GULDENSTR.
KORENMARKT
HOOGSTRAAT
VAN BENEDENLAAN
APOSTELEN STRAAT
NONNEN STR.
HOVIUS STR.
KRANKEN STR.
RIVER DIJLE
1 Brusselsepoort
2 Onze Lieve Vrouw over de Dijle
3 Hemelrijck
4 De Zalm
5 Duivelshuis
6 Schepenhuis
7 St Romboutskathedraal
8 Begijnhofkerk
9 St Catharina
10 St Jans
11 Hof van Busleyden
12 Palace of Margaret of Austria
13 Stadhuis
Walk 1
Walk 2
0
400m
N

Walk 1: Along the River Dijle

Standing before the mighty **Brusselsepoort** (which we reach from the station down Léopoldstraat, then left along Van Benedenlaan) provides us with a striking impression of Mechelen's mediaeval grandeur. The curious Baroque domes were added in the seventeenth century.

We now enter the old city and proceed down Hoogstraat, where we obtain our first beguiling glimpse of the cathedral tower. The busy street we are on leads straight into Grote Markt, the main square, but we take a less direct route there, since it is quite often in the quiet side streets of Flemish cities that we discover the most interesting and unusual details. So we turn right along Milsenstraat, soon to see the tower belonging to the church of **Onze-Lieve-Vrouw over de Dijle** (Our Lady Across the Dijle). Seen from Milsenstraat, this church appears as a harmonious Gothic edifice built of an attractive white sandstone, but from the rear it is a very much more complex composition. The north portal is a delicate Late Gothic addition designed by Rombout Keldermans the Younger, and the choir a Baroque embellishment added in the 1640s by Jacob Franckaert. If we are able to enter this church, which I have found generally to be locked, we will see a large work by Rubens called *The Miraculous Draught of Fishes*. He painted this in 1618 to hang in the guild house of the fishermen, a building we will shortly have an opportunity to explore.

At Onze-Lieve-Vrouwstraat 64, opposite the north portal of the church, stands a once handsome house, now rather mouldering, called **Hemelrijck** (The Kingdom of Heaven). A bas relief showing Adam and Eve in Paradise gives this house its name. Dating from about 1525, Hemelrijck is designed in a curious Transition style that combines elements of Late Gothic and Early Renaissance. Seen from afar it looks like a Gothic house, but examined in detail it proves to be decorated with Renaissance arabesques and the figures of griffins.

We now head down to the River Dijle by 't Plein, a narrow lane opposite this house. A quiet quay called **Zoutwerf** (Salt Quay), where salt for fish curing was once unloaded, leads along the waterfront. This used to be a bustling quay, but it is now

Plate 25 Mechelen: Prospect from the North

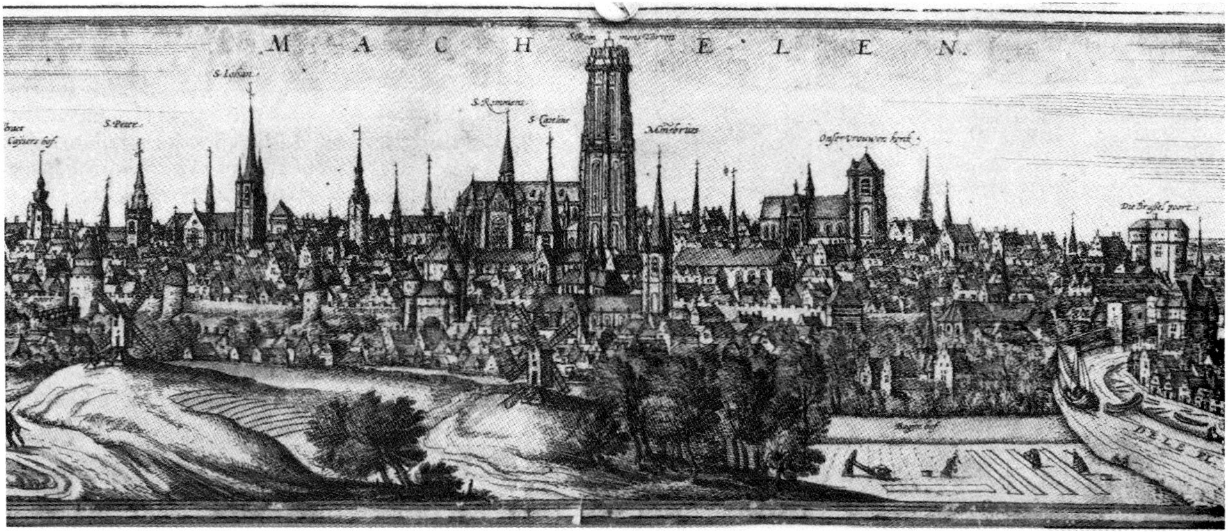

rare to see even a rowing boat on the Dijle. Some attractive quayside buildings have survived, however, including at numbers 7 and 8 two early sixteenth-century houses with jettied wooden façades. The magnificent guild house of the fishermen at number 5 dates from 1530-35. A beautiful gilded carving of a salmon above the entrance gives this house its name, **De Zalm** (The Salmon). One of the earliest and most beautiful Renaissance buildings in Flanders, its most striking feature is the superimposition of three architectural orders. This arrangement of columns is entirely in accordance with Italian theories of architecture, although the overcrowded decoration betrays the hand of a northern Renaissance architect. We also see a lingering attachment to the Gothic, for example in the tall, narrow gable. Once again we are looking at a Transition style of building, neither quite free of the Gothic, nor entirely at ease in the Renaissance style. De Zalm now contains a small museum devoted to local industries, such as lace-making, tapestry weaving and gilt leather manufacture.

On reaching the thirteenth-century Grootbrug, we turn left down Guldenstraat to enter **Korenmarkt**, the corn market. Number 8 was the home in the sixteenth century of a wine merchant, who gave it the enticing Late Gothic watchtower at the rear. In the seventeenth century the house was bought by the guild of crossbowmen, and a symbolic iron crossbow was added to the tower, together with gold-tipped arrows on the façade. The figure above the splendid Baroque portal is St George; he was, for no very obvious reason, the patron saint of the crossbowmen. Korenmarkt 6, a weather-beaten Baroque building, is nowadays occupied by a carillon manufacturer.

There is little else to occupy us on this square, so let us retrace our steps, then turn left down Adegemstraat, past a large brewery, and right down Hertshoornstraatje. Walking down this nondescript street, we obtain a splendid view of the glistening white sandstone tower of the cathedral. This brings us back to the River Dijle, here overlooked by a ragged fringe of decaying buildings. At the time of writing there were nevertheless some promising signs of renovation along the water's edge.

We want to look at three houses in particular that have survived in this quiet corner of Mechelen. They overlook the revolving iron bridge at the end of **Haverwerf** (Oats Quay). The house with the almost illegible number 23 is a most remarkable building called the **Duivelshuis** (Devil's House). It was constructed in 1519 in the curious Transition style that we have encountered already. Its jettied wooden façade, pierced by leaded glass windows, is unmistakably Gothic. But look now at the 12 wooden satyrs decorating the window mullions. Whoever carved these strange goat-like figures was obviously in touch with the ideas of the Renaissance. Originally this house was called the Prodigal Son after the scene decorating the wooden frieze on the door lintel. But later it became known as the Devil's House, which is indeed a far more fitting title for this dark and mysterious dwelling. The name also contrasts nicely with that of its neighbour to the right, which is called **Paradijs**. Now reduced to a rather sorry mosaic of brick and stone repairs, Paradijs is another example of Transition architecture from the 1520s. It takes its name from the two splendid, though much weathered, bas reliefs showing the Tree of Knowledge, and Adam and Eve in Paradise. This house is almost contemporary with Hemelrijck, which illustrated the same theme, clearly a popular notion then.

Our wanderings along the Dijle end here, and we now cross the iron bridge and turn right along Persoonshoek. Number 9, the former sixteenth-century refuge of the Cistercian abbey at Villers, was in a sad state of decay the last time I passed this way. Refuges—of which there are several in Mechelen—were built by rural abbeys and monasteries as safe havens for monks in troubled times.

Turning right along Drabstraat brings us to the **Vismarkt**, where fish is still very much in evidence. Ijzerenleen (Iron Avenue), upon which we emerge, derives its name from the double row of iron railings that once, centuries ago, enclosed a canal. We eventually turn left up this elegant street, but before doing so I recommend a short detour straight ahead down Lange Schipstraat to obtain a magnificent view of De Zalm on the opposite quay.

Back on Ijzerenleen, we will see an attractive Gothic building at the far end, formerly the **Schepenhuis** (Town Hall). Standing opposite the flight of stairs, we can distinguish the original thirteenth-century town hall to the left from the ornate fourteenth-century Brabant Gothic town hall added on at right angles. The Grote Raad met in this building from 1474 to 1618.

Standing where we are, we need only turn and look left to see a third town hall on the opposite side of Schoenmarkt, commenced in the fourteenth century but not completed until the sixteenth century. The present town hall—Mechelen's fourth—occupies a beautiful building on Grote Markt that we will look at later; its predecessor on Schoenmarkt is now the main post office.

Before entering the cathedral, which is our next concern, we might pause on a café terrace to prepare ourselves for the visit. To our right lies Grote Markt, where the most convivial cafés in Mechelen are situated. The café 't Voske at number 36 enjoys the best view of the cathedral, but any other would do just as well.

From Grote Markt, I suggest that we take a somewhat indirect route to the cathedral to obtain a succession of striking views of its majestic mediaeval architecture. Leaving Grote Markt on the north side along Frederik de Merodestraat, we turn left along Schoolstraat, passing the sixteenth-century **Koraalhuis**, once a school for choristers. Upon emerging on St Romboutskerkhof, formerly a cemetery, we head down the attractive lane at the back of the choir to enter the cathedral by the south portal.

Begun in the thirteenth century in Early Gothic style, **St Romboutskathedraal** was completed by the fourteenth century. However, a fire in 1342 destroyed the cathedral, and it was subsequently rebuilt in Brabant High Gothic style by Jan van Osy. Its west tower is one of the most beautiful works of Late Gothic architecture in Flanders. It was planned as the tallest spire in the world and, had it been completed, would have reached a height of 167 metres. However, the construction work came to a standstill in the 1520s, when the tower had attained a height of only 97 metres. Even in its unfinished state, some 26 metres lower than the cathedral tower at Antwerp, Mechelen's west tower is a magnificent architectural achievement, once praised by Vauban, Louis XIV's military architect, as the eighth wonder of the world. Its construction, which was funded by donations from pilgrims who flocked to the city to receive indulgences, was carried out by three successive generations of architects of the Keldermans family of Mechelen. Andries Keldermans the Elder began this great work in 1452, laying down a massive buttressed base to support the tower. Anthonis Keldermans took over from his father in 1481, and in 1488 was succeeded in turn by his son, Rombout Keldermans the Younger, who supervised the building work until about 1520, when the project was suddenly abandoned. The construction of the third tier of the tower had by then already commenced. The reason for the stoppage has never properly been understood; whether for lack of funds or some other reason, it must have struck the younger Rombout Keldermans as a bitter blow. The unused stone shipped to Mechelen remained in the masons' yard at the foot of the tower until 1583, when the troops of William of Orange carried it off for use in the construction of the new Dutch citadel town of Willemstad.

The interior of the cathedral is extraordinarily spacious and lofty, particularly the nave, which is built of a gleaming white sandstone. The intricate patterns of stonework in the clerestory of the choir are strikingly beautiful. There are, as always in Belgium, Baroque additions which we might prefer not to be there, but the spirit of the Counter-Reformation is fortunately restrained here. The pulpit, though, is an outrageously inappropriate Baroque intrusion brought here from a Norbertine monastery in Mechelen. The work of Michiel van der Voort, it illustrates St Norbert's dramatic conversion, with animals scuttling hither and thither as the lightning flashes.

The principal painting in the cathedral is a *Crucifixion* by Sir Anthony van Dyck. Painted in 1627, it hangs in the south transept on a large altar that partly conceals an intriguing Gothic fresco. Born in Antwerp in 1599, Van Dyck was a pupil in Rubens' atelier. Although he lived intermittently in Antwerp, Van Dyck worked mainly in England, where he painted numerous portraits of English monarchs and nobles, including a famous equestrian portrait of Charles I which hangs in London's National Gallery.

The interior of this great cathedral tells much about Mechelen's past. A chapel in the ambulatory, for example, contains a memorial to several local priests who died resisting the Germans during World War I. Another chapel in the north aisle commemorates the Malines Conversations organised by Cardinal Mercier in the 1920s in an attempt to reconcile the Church of England and the Catholic Church.

After exploring the cathedral, we will find numerous places in the neighbourhood for lunch. *Boerenbrood hesp*, a local speciality consisting of an open sandwich with ham and salad, is served in 't Voske and other cafés on Grote Markt. The farms around Mechelen grow most of Belgium's vegetables, including crisp, yellowish-white *witlof*, the Belgian version of endive, which features in local specialities such as *witlofsoep*, a herby cream of endive soup, and *prelaatshaantje*, chicken with endive. This delicacy was apparently discovered quite by accident during the Belgian Revolution in 1830. A farmer who had fled the country leaving some chicory roots in a dark cellar returned home after the fighting was over to discover that the chicory had sprouted shoots. As food was scarce, he fed these to his family. The countryside around Mechelen is also dotted with farms cultivating plump, white Belgian asparagus, which is briefly in season in May and June.

Walk 2: Late Gothic Architecture

Fortified by lunch, let us begin our afternoon walk by exploring the pleasant quarters to the west and north of the cathedral, where we come upon quiet cobbled streets and crumbling brick houses. Standing at the base of the cathedral tower, we will see an attractive little chapel opposite, the Heilig Geestkapel, dating from the end of the thirteenth century. From here a quiet cobbled lane, the Minderbroedersgang, takes us past a former Franciscan chapel. Continuing down Arme Clarenstraat, then right along Nieuwe Beggaardenstraat, we then turn left into Nonnenstraat. This street was once was closed off by one of the gateways of the **Groot Begijnhof**, a convent built in 1259. Though the walls of the Groot Begijnhof have gone, the streets once within its confines still preserve much of the atmosphere of a Begijnhof, with quaint bell-pulls, ancient iron lamp brackets, rose bushes trained up whitewashed walls and tiny statues of saints set in niches (such as a St Ursula smitten by an arrow in Twaalf Apostelenstraat).

If we turn left down Conventstraat, then right into Hoviusstraat, we come upon a particularly captivating street boasting several splendid Baroque portals, such as number 16 (pl. 26). At the end of the street, overshadowing a convent founded in 1620, the brewery Het Anker lends a distinctive smell of hops to the neighbourhood. Situated on the site of the Begijnhof infirmary, Het Anker has been brewing strong, dark Mechelen ales since 1421. Nowadays, it produces excellent traditional bottled beers such as *Gouden Carolus* and *Mechelschen Bruynen*, both of which can be sampled in the cafés on Grote Markt.

At the end of Krankenstraat we come upon the weathered Baroque frontage of the **Begijnhofkerk**, built by Jacob Franckaert from 1629-47. The majestic figure of God the Father at the top of the gable was carved by Luc Fayd'herbe. Following

Moreelstraat, which runs to the right of the church, then turning left behind the choir, we pass the romantic ruins of a monastery built in the fifteenth century by the Order of St Alexis, which cared for plague victims. We then walk along St Beggastraat, turn right on Cellebroedersgang and left into Acht Zalighedenstraat. This quiet Begijnhof lane named 'Eight Beatitudes Street' has much the same atmosphere as a Georgian mews. On emerging from it, we turn right along Twaalf Apostelenstraat and again right down Schrijnstraat, which leads out of the precincts of the Groot Begijnhof.

Thereafter we continue straight ahead down Nokerstraat, past a large Baroque monastery built by the Order of St Alexis after they had abandoned the mediaeval building behind the Begijnhofkerk. Turning right down Guldenbodemstraat, we pass an interesting enclave of modern architecture, then follow Bornstraatje, turn right on Heembeemd and left along Schuttevee. This leads to the **St Catharinakerk**, an attractive white sandstone

Plate 26 Baroque doorway in Mechelen

Gothic church with a simple wooden roof. There are several interesting details within, including seventeenth-century Baroque confessionals and a remarkable pulpit in the form of an overgrown Classical ruin. This was designed by Thomas Verhaegen in 1774 and cost, according to a small brass plaque attached, 1,554 guilders.

If, on leaving the church, we turn left along St Katelijnekerkhof, we come upon a lane called Kerkstraatje that leads us to Kanunnik de Deckerstraat. There we turn left, then again left at the Maria Magdalenakapel, to enter a little square. A small portal on the right leads into the **Klein Begijnhof**, an unexpected and delightful convent. But it is indeed *klein* (small) and we soon emerge once again on Kanunnik de Deckerstraat. Opposite is a handsome fifteenth-century building designed in Late Gothic style, with alternating courses of bricks and white sandstone. It was built as a refuge for monks from the Norbertine monastery of Tongerloo, which lies to the east of Mechelen. The building is now occupied by the Gaspard de Wit tapestry workshop, which can be visited on Saturdays at 10.30am.

Continuing down Schoutetstraat, we pass another refuge, built in the sixteenth century by the Benedictine abbey at St Truiden. We obtain a particularly striking view, rather like a Flemish Primitive painting, from a bridge a few steps to the right on Goswin de Stassartstraat. The ivy-clad brick walls overlook a stretch of stagnant water resembling thick pea soup, and called, not without reason, Groen Waterke (Green Water).

We now cross the road and turn down a narrow passage called Klapgat that leads to the **St Janskerk**. This simple white sandstone Gothic church contains a triptych painted by Rubens in 1616-19 of the *Adoration of the Magi*. Isabella Brant, Rubens' first wife, posed as the Virgin for this work.

On St Janskerkhof we turn right, soon to come upon an attractive garden overlooked by a splendid Late Gothic palace. If the weather is mild, we might enter the garden and sit on one of the benches in the corner on the right, there obtaining another glimpse of the beautiful cathedral tower.

When we leave the garden, we should turn left

into Frederik de Merodestraat. This takes us past the **Koninklijk Beiaardschool** (Royal Carillon School) on the corner. Sometimes a student can be glimpsed within practising on the carillon keyboard, which is operated by hammering the wooden keys with one's fists. The school has its own set of bells hung in a sixteenth-century octagonal watchtower.

Our next destination is the municipal museum at Frederik de Merodestraat 65. This is situated in the **Hof van Busleyden**, a Late Gothic town house begun in 1503 by Anthonis Keldermans the Elder and completed by his son Rombout the Younger in 1508. It was commissioned by Hieronymus van Busleyden, who trained as a lawyer at the universities of Leuven and Bologna, and moved to Mechelen after being appointed by Philip the Fair to serve on the Grote Raad. Van Busleyden was a leading Flemish humanist whose friends included Erasmus, Thomas More and Pieter Gilles. Thomas More, who stayed here in 1515, was so impressed that he wrote three poems in praise of the house and its collections of books and musical instruments. More's *Utopia*, first published in Leuven in 1516, begins with a dedication to Van Busleyden written by Pieter Gilles.

In 1517 Erasmus, who was a frequent guest here, persuaded Van Busleyden to provide in his will for the foundation of a *Collegium Trilingue* in Leuven, that would offer a humanistic education in Latin, Greek and Hebrew. In the same year, while on a diplomatic mission to Spain on behalf of Charles V, Van Busleyden fell ill in Bordeaux and, much to the distress of Erasmus, died there aged 47.

In 1620 the Hof van Busleyden was converted by Wenceslas Coeberger into a Mons Pietas, one of the charitable lending banks established in Flemish cities under the Archduchess Isabella. The quaintly named Berg van Barmhartigheid (Mountain of Charity) was still in operation in the early years of this century. After being badly damaged in World War I, it was rebuilt to house the municipal museum.

Fortunately, the delightful Renaissance dining room (number 12) has survived more or less intact. This lovely little room where Van Busleyden may have entertained Erasmus and More was decorated with Renaissance murals by Bernard van Orley and Michiel Coxie the Elder in 1507-17. Tragically, the murals were badly damaged by the bombardment, but copies made in 1916 give some impression of their strange beauty. One of the murals depicts Belshazzar's Feast, at which the king of Babylon, holding a lavish feast for his wives and nubile concubines, is suddenly terrified by a message written on the wall by a disembodied hand.

The collection of paintings, architectural fragments and furniture in this museum provides some interesting insights into Mechelen's history. A painting in room 5, for example, depicts a curious and perhaps apocryphal incident in which the townspeople mistook the moon shining through the tracery of the cathedral tower for a fire and promptly attempted to extinguish it. A seventeenth-century painting in the same room depicts the Groot Begijnhof, with 46 miniature scenes illustrating the Works of the Beguines, which ranged from lace-making to caring for the sick. In room 6 we see a set of six remarkable sixteenth-century consoles from the guild house of the swordsmen, and some interesting plans and views of Mechelen.

One of the highlights in the collection is the series of 16 panels of the *Legend of St Victor* painted by an anonymous master in 1510-20 for a convent in Mechelen. The scenes from the life of this minor saint of the second century are set amidst fantastic architecture, with beautiful costumes and expressive faces. The last painting of the series, in which angels receive the martyred body of St Victor, is particularly moving.

Room 11 is decorated with modern stained-glass windows depicting historical episodes, including Erasmus and Thomas More visiting the house. Notice also the fragments of gilt leather and the Renaissance fireplace rescued from the palace of Margaret of Austria. The upstairs rooms, though containing little of great importance, are nevertheless rather interesting to explore, like the attic of an old mansion in which miscellaneous curiosities have been stored.

After exploring the museum, we head down Biest, the street opposite the carillon school, to the **Veemarkt**. At number 3, next to the Baroque church of St Pieter en Paulus, stands the **Palace of Margaret of York**, or what is left of it. The palace was renovated in 1480 for Margaret of York, who retired to Mechelen after the death of her husband in 1477, and it was here that she raised Mary of Burgundy's children. Facing us is the sixteenth-century **Palace of Margaret of Austria**. If we now walk through to the second courtyard of this beautiful palace, we will find a bench in the delightful Late Gothic arcade where we can read about this palace.

Margaret of Austria was one of the children of Mary of Burgundy raised in Mechelen. Only two years old when her mother died in 1482, Margaret was immediately ensnared in the complex web of mediaeval politics. In 1483, under the terms of the Peace of Utrecht, this tiny toddler was married off by her father, Maximilian of Austria, to the future Charles VIII of France. Margaret spent the next eight years in the château of Amboise on the Loire, but when political allegiances altered the marriage was dissolved to permit Charles VIII to marry Anne of Brittany. Margaret was sent back to the Netherlands, and her father then married her off to Don Juan of Castile in the hope of combining the Austrian and Spanish Hapsburg territories. Margaret, then aged 17, was sent by ship to Spain for the wedding. But this scheme, too, failed when Don Juan died nine months later. Undeterred, Maximilian arranged a third marriage with Philibert the Handsome, the Duke of Savoy. Margaret, who had known Philibert since her childhood days at Amboise, spent three happy years at the château of Pont d'Ain in Burgundy. However, tragedy struck again in 1504 when Margaret's handsome husband, aged only 24, died of pleurisy. One year later, Margaret commissioned the Flemish architect Loys van Boghem to build a church in memory of Philibert at Brou, on the outskirts of Bourg-en-Bresse. It is one of the most delightful churches in France, built in a florid Late Gothic style with hints here and there of the Renaissance. Much could be said in praise of its choir stalls and its memorial effigies, but this is perhaps not the proper place to do so.

In 1506 Margaret was compelled to leave Brou and return to the Netherlands because of the death in Spain of her brother, Philip the Fair. Having inherited the Hapsburg territories upon the death of Maximilian in 1494, Philip had married Joanna of Castile two years later, thereby realising his father's ambition of uniting the Spanish and Austrian Hapsburg possessions. After his death, Margaret—who by that time had abandoned all hope of finding a faithful or robust husband—took charge of her nephews and nieces. In 1507 she was appointed Regent of the Netherlands on behalf of the eldest son of Philip the Fair, the future Emperor Charles V.

Margaret chose to establish her court at Mechelen, rather than Brussels, and moved into the palace of Margaret of York, where she had spent the first two years of her life. Four years later, she commissioned Rombout Keldermans the Younger to design a new palace in ornate Late Gothic style. However, only the rear wing, where we are now sitting, was built by Rombout Keldermans. It seems that Margaret became fascinated with Renaissance art and architecture in the second decade of the sixteenth century, and in 1515 she commissioned an outsider, Guyot de Beaugrant, to complete the palace in pure Renaissance style. It was one of the earliest Renaissance buildings in the Netherlands, and symbolised the end of the Keldermans' Late Gothic style.

Margaret's palace in Mechelen became a centre of northern Renaissance art and music, and here she was visited by many of the great Renaissance artists of the day, including Albrecht Dürer, Pieter Coecke van Aelst, Jan Gossaert, Jan Mostaert and Bernard van Orley, who painted the rather melancholy portrait of Margaret that now hangs in the Musée d'Art Ancien in Brussels.

Margaret died in 1530 of gangrene of the foot and her entrails were buried in Mechelen, while her heart was taken to a convent in Bruges. Two years later her body was carried to Brou to be buried in the exquisite chapel she had built in memory of Philibert. With the death of Margaret, Mechelen's brief period of splendour was over; the city became another Bruges, another dead city of Flanders. Philip II attempted to save Mechelen by elevating the city to an archbishopric in 1559. Antoine Perrenot, the first Archbishop, lived for the next two years in Margaret of Austria's palace, but was then recalled to Spain to assist Philip II in his campaign of religious terror and never returned to Mechelen. The palace was occupied by the Grote Raad from 1618 to 1794, and is now used as a court of law.

We can leave by the rear portal, turning right and again right to reach Keizerstraat, then returning to Grote Markt along Befferstraat. It is worth pausing in the long Gothic arcade on Befferstraat to obtain a marvellous view of the cathedral tower soaring above a cluster of Baroque gables.

It is now perhaps time for a coffee or a beer at one of the cafés on the square. We might select **In de Beer** (At the Bear) at number 32 for its historical associations. A tavern formerly stood here called 'At the Angel', which Charles V once visited to slake his thirst after a day in the saddle. The Emperor was so dirty, however, that the landlady of the tavern refused to admit him, until a passing soldier intervened on his behalf. Charles V decided that the tavern didn't deserve the name 'The Angel' and ordered the landlady to change it to 'The Bear'.

While sitting here, sipping perhaps a dark Mechelen beer, we can study the interesting range of buildings on the east side of the square. In the middle, we see the remains of a fourteenth-century cloth hall, modelled upon the Halle in Bruges. The building was gutted by a devastating fire in 1342 and the planned belfry abandoned, leaving a sad stump (pl. 28). The two octagonal corner turrets were added in the sixteenth century in an attempt to jolly up the appearance.

The florid building to the left of the belfry, whose arcade we have already walked down, is now the **Stadhuis** (Town Hall). It was originally commissioned by Charles V to serve as a splendid new palace for the Grote Raad, which at that time was still convening in the old town hall at the end of Ijzerenleen. Designed by Rombout Keldermans the Younger, it was begun in 1526 on the site of the north wing of the cloth hall, but work was suddenly halted in 1534 due to financial difficulties and the palace was left unfinished.

In 1551 the abandoned building was divided into shops, and by the end of the nineteenth century it had become a dilapidated ruin (pl. 27). In the early years of the twentieth century, however, an astonishing restoration was carried out using the

Plate 27 Palace of the Grote Raad before restoration

original architectural drawings of Rombout Keldermans. The ruin was replaced by a beautiful white sandstone edifice (pl. 28).

On leaving Grote Markt, we can make our way back to the station down Bruul, past the imposing Baroque frontage of **Onze-Lieve-Vrouw van Leliendaal**, a Norbertine convent designed by Luc Fayd'herbe in 1662-72. If there is time, we might stroll into the **Kruidtuin** (Botanical Gardens), once the site of a monastery belonging to the Order of Teutonic Knights. There are not many botanical specimens to be seen, but it is a pleasant spot by the River Dijle, with an interesting view of the Baroque church of **Onze-Lieve-Vrouw van Hanswijk** opposite. We then cross an attractive Neoclassical square and five minutes later are back at the station.

Plate 28 Palace of the Grote Raad after restoration

Brussels

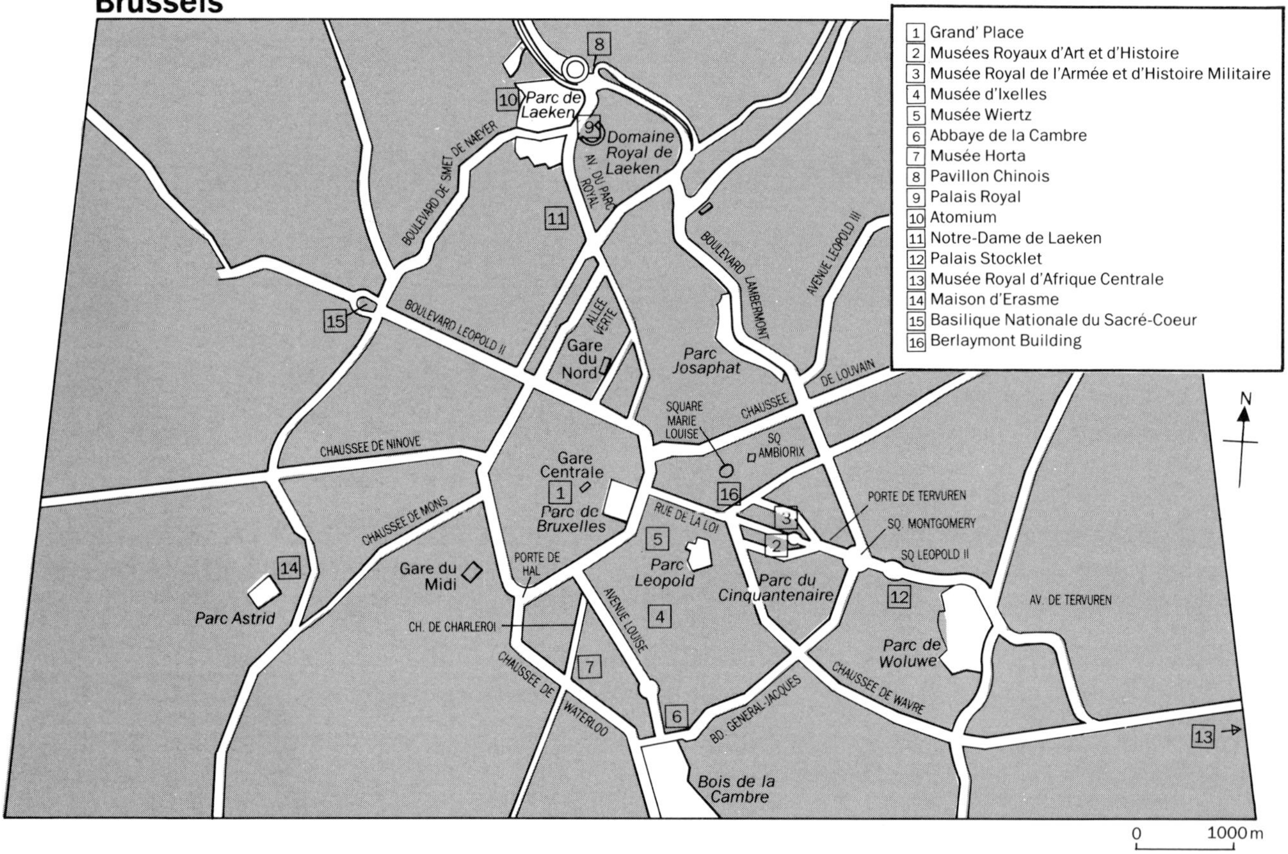

1 Grand' Place
2 Musées Royaux d'Art et d'Histoire
3 Musée Royal de l'Armée et d'Histoire Militaire
4 Musée d'Ixelles
5 Musée Wiertz
6 Abbaye de la Cambre
7 Musée Horta
8 Pavillon Chinois
9 Palais Royal
10 Atomium
11 Notre-Dame de Laeken
12 Palais Stocklet
13 Musée Royal d'Afrique Centrale
14 Maison d'Erasme
15 Basilique Nationale du Sacré-Coeur
16 Berlaymont Building
Parc de Laeken
Domaine Royal de Laeken
AV. DU PARC ROYAL
BOULEVARD DE SMET DE NAEYER
BOULEVARD LEOPOLD II
ALLEE VERTE
Gare du Nord
Parc Josaphat
BOULEVARD LAMBERMONT
AVENUE LEOPOLD III
CHAUSSEE DE LOUVAIN
SQUARE MARIE LOUISE
SQ AMBIORIX
CHAUSSEE DE NINOVE
Gare Centrale
Parc de Bruxelles
RUE DE LA LOI
PORTE DE TERVUREN
SQ. MONTGOMERY
SQ LEOPOLD II
CHAUSSEE DE MONS
Gare du Midi
PORTE DE HAL
Parc Leopold
Parc du Cinquantenaire
AV. DE TERVUREN
Parc Astrid
CH. DE CHARLEROI
AVENUE LOUISE
Parc de Woluwe
CHAUSSEE DE WATERLOO
BD. GENERAL-JACQUES
CHAUSSEE DE WAVRE
Bois de la Cambre
N
0 1000 m

CHAPTER 5: BRUSSELS

Of all the market squares in Flanders, none is more beautiful than Grand'Place in Brussels, with its splendid entourage of Baroque houses laden with gilded sculptures. Brussels also boasts numerous convivial Flemish restaurants warmed by blazing fires, where you can feast on hearty slabs of steak or overflowing pots of steaming mussels.

Yet Brussels is not at all a typical Flemish city. Nor is it truly French, despite the fact that most of the population are French-speaking. Brussels is a unique city, whose identity has been shaped by numerous European cultures: the Burgundians, who made Brussels a city of artistic excellence in the fifteenth century; the Spanish, who built many of its Baroque churches and guild houses in the seventeenth century; and the Austrians, who laid out elegant squares and parks in the eighteenth century. The confluence of so many cultures gives Brussels a fascinating diversity of buildings, parks, cafés and restaurants. Even in the most unpromising of streets, we will often encounter an unexpected delight, such as Cirio, a beautiful café reminiscent of Old Vienna in Rue de la Bourse, or the secret, nameless park below the Rue du Parme, with its strange mock-classical ruins.

As in the case of so many Flemish cities, the name Brussels has an etymology that refers to its watery origins. *Brucsella*, as the city was originally called, means 'dwelling on the marsh' in Old Dutch. According to popular legend, the city was founded in the sixth century by St Géry, a French missionary who built a chapel on an island in the River Senne. The 'dwelling on the marsh' prospered due to its favourable location on the important mediaeval trading route between the North Sea and the Rhine. This route, now followed by the E5 motorway and the Hans Memling Eurocity train, linked the northern European cities of Bruges, Ghent, Brussels, Leuven, Liège, Aachen and Cologne.

In the late tenth century Duke Charles of Lower Lorraine built a castle on the site of St Géry's chapel. The lands of Lower Lorraine later passed to the Counts of Leuven, who in the eleventh century erected a new castle on the heights to the south of the valley of the Senne. This move marked the beginning of the social division of Brussels: craftsmen and shopkeepers lived in the Lower Town, while the dukes and nobles inhabited the Upper Town.

Brussels became particularly important under the Dukes of Burgundy, whose possessions included the former lands of the Counts of Leuven. In 1430, Philip the Good decided to move the Burgundian court from Dijon to the Upper Town of Brussels. The knights and officials of his court were all French speaking, and so the Upper Town became an enclave of French culture and manners. But in the Lower Town, in the guild houses and markets around Grand'Place, Dutch continued to be spoken. The fatal frontier between Latin and Germanic cultures therefore cut straight through the city of Brussels, roughly along the line of the Boulevards de l'Empereur, de Berlaimont and Pacheo.

During the brief but spectacular period of Burgundian rule, the economy of the Lower Town was increasingly devoted to the production of luxury goods, as the Burgundians had an insatiable appetite for Flamboyant Gothic architecture, rich tapestries, exotic costumes and gargantuan feasts. Unfortunately not much Burgundian Gothic architecture has survived in Brussels; we have to go to Bruges for that. But the museums of Brussels contain some exquisite works of Burgundian

Gothic art, such as the paintings of Roger van der Weyden at the Musée d'Art Ancien and the sculpture in the Musée d'Art et d'Histoire.

Charles V's formal abdication in 1555 proved a decisive turning point in the history of the Low Countries. Philip II, Charles V's son, inherited his father's territories in Spain, the Netherlands, Italy and the New World. Austere and devout, he soon embarked on a pitiless policy of religious persecution in the Low Countries, which eventually sparked off the Dutch Revolt.

The prolonged war against Spain began in 1566 as a mild protest at the wedding in Brussels of Alexander Farnese, then Prince of Parma. Several hundred nobles soured the festivities somewhat by petitioning his mother, Margaret of Parma—Charles V's sister and the Governor of the Netherlands at the time—to adopt a more tolerant approach to the Protestants. This petition stung Philip II into ordering the execution of Counts Egmont and Hoorn in Grand'Place in 1568, and the Dutch Revolt erupted soon afterwards.

At first Brussels was held by the Protestant rebels led by William of Orange, known as 'the Silent', but in 1585 the city fell to the Spanish army led by Alexander Farnese. From then on Brussels was the capital of the Spanish Netherlands. However, it was in no sense a sparkling capital under Spanish rule, except for a brief period from 1596-1621 under the Archduke Albert and Archduchess Isabella.

The period of Spanish rule finally ended in 1706 in the War of the Spanish Succession, when the Duke of Marlborough captured Brussels. Under the terms of the Treaty of Utrecht of 1713, the former Spanish Netherlands passed to the Austrian Hapsburgs. The new governors were at first unpopular, and provoked an uprising in 1719. This was crushed, and Frans Anneessens, the leader of the guilds of Brussels, was beheaded on Grand'Place. A new era of prosperity began in 1744 when Charles, Duke of Lorraine, was appointed Governor by his sister-in-law, the Empress Maria Theresa. He embarked on an ambitious plan to restyle Brussels as a northern Vienna, and several elegant Neoclassical schemes were completed, such as the Place Royale and the Parc de Bruxelles in the Upper Town, and the square now known as the Place des Martyrs in the Lower Town.

In 1795 the French Republican army entered Brussels. All the street names were translated into French, although quite often erroneously. The French were driven out of Brussels in 1814, although one year later Napoleon I came close to recapturing the city. He was defeated by the combined forces of Wellington and Blücher at the Battle of Waterloo, some 12 miles south of the city. Under the terms of the treaties of Vienna and London, the Kingdom of the Netherlands was established under King William I. This led briefly to the reunification of the old Burgundian Netherlands, but the two Netherlands had developed quite differently since the sixteenth century and the match soon proved disastrous. The event that sparked off the Belgian Revolution was, somewhat surprisingly, a performance of the opera *La Muette de Portici* by Auber. As a duet about patriotism was being sung, some members of the audience stormed out of the Théâtre de la Monnaie and began to riot in the streets. It was a curious beginning to 'that little Biedermeier slapstick war', as the Dutch writer Jeroen Brouwers once described the Belgian Revolution.

Prince Léopold of Saxe-Coburg, the noble chosen to rule the new state of Belgium, was a German prince and a favourite uncle of Queen Victoria. In his efforts to create a prosperous Belgian state he looked particularly to Victorian Britain for inspiration. His achievements were widely approved by British visitors; a character in Thackeray's *Vanity Fair* praises Brussels as 'one of the gayest and most brilliant little capitals in Europe'.

Léopold I was succeeded by his son, the Duke of Brabant, who became Léopold II in 1865. He seems to have been an unpromising future king, judging from Madame de Metternich's description of his marriage to Marie-Henrietta of Austria as the union of 'a stable boy and a nun, and by nun I mean the Duke of Brabant'. Yet Léopold II proved to be an exceptionally vigorous, if not entirely virtuous ruler. He developed the Belgian Congo as a virtual private colony and used the profits from his ventures there to rebuild Brussels on a truly heroic scale. The great picture galleries and museums of

Brussels, the boulevards and arcades, the Palais de Justice and the Parc du Cinquantenaire, were all built during his 44-year-long reign. Most of these projects benefited the Upper Town, the aristocratic French quarter of the city. Indeed, it is quite likely that the old Flemish areas of Brussels would have vanished altogether had not Burgomaster Charles Buls campaigned strenuously for their preservation. Without these Flemish quarters the character of Brussels would now be quite different; it would be a rather dull and disappointing city of formal Neoclassical buildings, like the cities painted by Paul Delvaux.

Léopold's Brussels provided an attractive refuge for exiled French writers, as its boulevards, cafés and arcades gave it something of the allure of Paris. Many French exiles in Brussels were political refugees from Napoleon III, including Victor Hugo and Pierre-Joseph Proudhon. The revolutionary Neoclassical painter Louis David died in exile in Brussels, and his famous painting of Marat murdered in his bath now hangs in the Musée d'Art Ancien. Others fled here from France for less laudable reasons, such as Alexandre Dumas, who simply used Brussels as a convenient bolt hole from his creditors.

By the end of the nineteenth century Brussels had become one of the most scintillating cities in Europe, rivalling Paris and Vienna for glamorous cafés and dazzling Art Nouveau architecture. However, Brussels' *Belle Epoque* came to a sad and sudden end when the German army occupied the city in World War I. The Burgomaster of Brussels, Adolphe Max, was deported for stubbornly resisting the Germans, and in 1915 the courageous British nurse Edith Cavell was executed by the Germans for helping Allied soldiers to escape to the neutral Netherlands. The offices of the Belgian broadcasting organisation in Schaerbeek stand on the site of the military firing range where Edith Cavell was shot.

Brussels regained some of its cosmopolitan sparkle in the 1920s and 1930s, when many apartment blocks in Art Deco style were built on the grand boulevards. The most imposing of these was the **Residence Palace** at 155 Rue de la Loi, a luxury apartment complex built in 1926, complete with a restaurant, swimming pool and theatre. After

World War II, however, Brussels was again in the doldrums. The 1958 World Fair gave a boost to the economy, and one year later Brussels became the capital of the recently founded European Economic Community. It is now the seat of the European Communities, an organisation created in 1967 by the fusion of the European Economic Community, the European Coal and Steel Community and Euratom. The **Berlaymont Building**, overlooking Rond Point Schuman, houses the offices of the European Commission, while the European Parliament has its Brussels base nearby in the Rue Belliard. Brussels is thus virtually the capital of Europe, a fitting role for a cosmopolitan city whose identity has been shaped by so many different European cultures.

Walk 1: Grand'Place and its Neighbourhood

For our first glimpse of this convivial and likeable city, I propose that we stroll to **Grand'Place**. The finest approach to this square is, I think, down Rue des Harengs (next to the tourist office at 61 Rue du Marché aux Herbes), then right along Rue du Poivre, and left into Rue Chair et Pain. The advantage of this convoluted and secret route is the thrilling view it offers of the mediaeval spire of the town hall framed by the tall buildings on Rue Chair et Pain.

We will cross Grand'Place several times during our peregrinations in Brussels for, just as Brussels is (as it boasts) the crossroads of Europe, so Grand'Place is the crossroads of Brussels. The square is a source of inexhaustible pleasure, its character changing at different hours and in different seasons. Grand'Place is particularly enchanting at twilight on a crisp winter's evening, when the last rays of the sun touch the gilded details of the gables, and the cafés lure us inside with their

Brussels

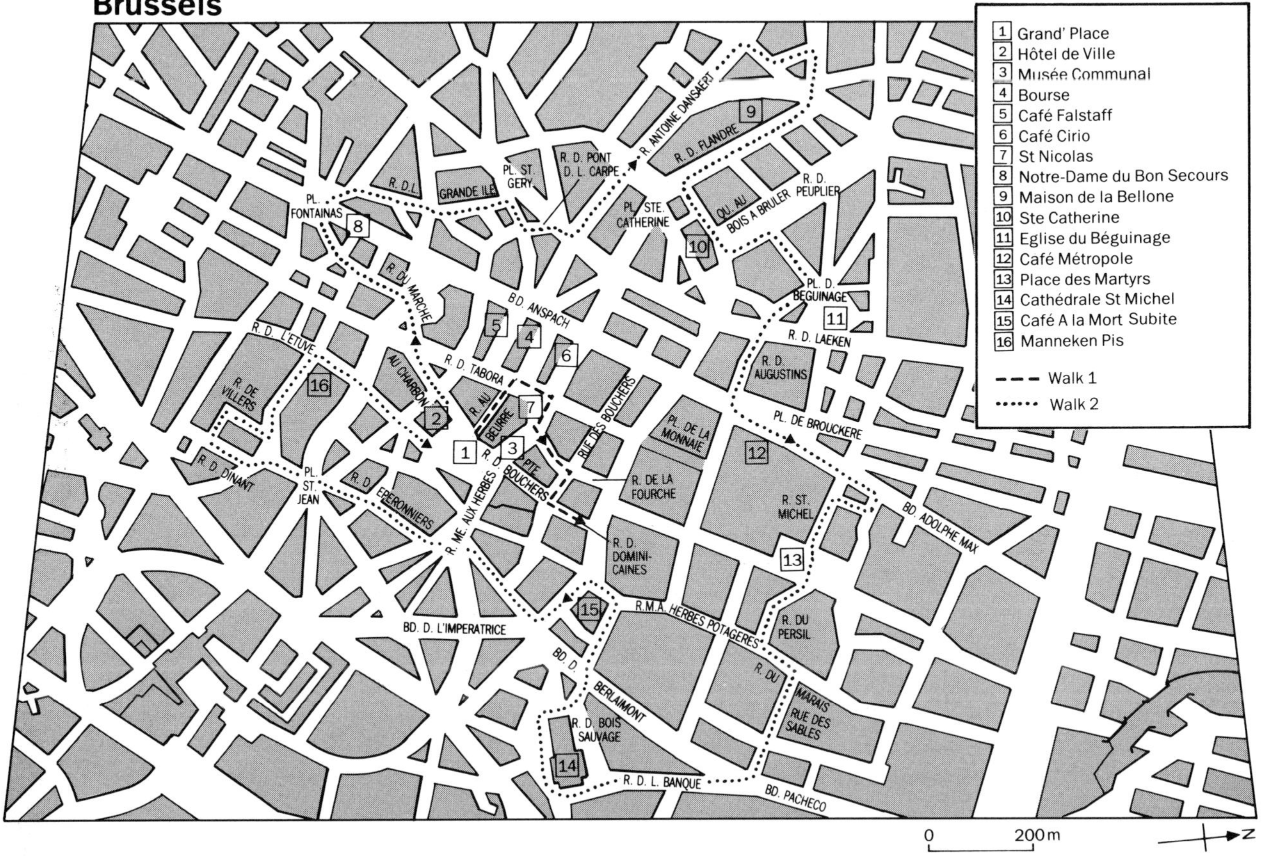

1 Grand' Place
2 Hôtel de Ville
3 Musée Communal
4 Bourse
5 Café Falstaff
6 Café Cirio
7 St Nicolas
8 Notre-Dame du Bon Secours
9 Maison de la Bellone
10 Ste Catherine
11 Eglise du Béguinage
12 Café Métropole
13 Place des Martyrs
14 Cathédrale St Michel
15 Café A la Mort Subite
16 Manneken Pis
Walk 1
Walk 2
R. ANTOINE DANSAERT
R. D. FLANDRE
R. D. PONT D. L. CARPE
PL. ST. GERY
GRANDE ILE
R. D. L.
PL. FONTAINAS
PL. STE. CATHERINE
QU. AU BOIS A BRULER
R. D. PEUPLIER
PL. D. BEGUINAGE
R. D. LAEKEN
R. D. AUGUSTINS
PL. DE BROUCKERE
R. DU MARCHE
BD. ANSPACH
R. D. L'ETUVE
R. D. TABORA
AU CHARBON
R. AU BEURRE
RUE DES BOUCHERS
PL. DE LA MONNAIE
R. DE VILLERS
R. D. BOUCHERS
PTE
R. DE LA FOURCHE
R. ST. MICHEL
BD. ADOLPHE MAX
R. D. DINANT
PL. ST. JEAN
R. D. EPERONNIERS
R. ME. AUX HERBES
R. D. DOMINICAINES
R.M.A. HERBES POTAGERES
R. DU PERSIL
BD. D. L'IMPERATRICE
BD. D. BERLAIMONT
R. DU MARAIS
RUE DES SABLES
R. D. BOIS SAUVAGE
R. D. L. BANQUE
BD. PACHECO
0
200 m
N

ATQUE

blazing fires, gleaming brass fittings and rich red cherry-flavoured *kriek* beers. Once darkness has fallen, floodlights transform the square into a magnificent theatre. Here, according to John Motley, the nineteenth-century American historian of the Dutch Revolt, 'so many tragedies, so many scenes of violence have been played out'. On Sunday mornings, a bird market is held on Grand'Place, giving the square a more local flavour.

The magnificent architecture of Grand'Place is the proud creation of the guilds of Brussels. The majority of the houses on the square were rebuilt soon after 1695, when much of the Lower Town was devastated by Louis XIV's artillery, commanded by Marshal De Villeroi. Some 3,630 houses and 16 churches in the Lower Town were destroyed in this attack. The drawing (pl. 29) shows the sorry state of Grand'Place after the bombardment. To the left is the Hôtel de Ville, which miraculously survived the attack, while opposite is the side wall of the badly damaged Maison du Roi.

Plate 29 Ruins of Grand'Place in 1695

The guild houses were rapidly rebuilt in a vivacious Italo-Flemish Baroque style, somewhat reminiscent of the buildings in Antwerp designed by Rubens in the early seventeenth century. But the buildings on Grand'Place are even more ostentatious, flashing with gilded details, and bristling with pinnacles and statues.

The best place to begin an exploration of Grand-'Place is the **Hôtel de Ville** (Town Hall), which is some three centuries older than the guild houses. In 1402 Duke Wenceslas of Luxembourg laid the first stone of the wing to the left of the belfry, designed by Jacob van Thienen and Jan Bornoy in an ornate Brabant Gothic style. The wing to the right of the belfry was not originally planned and the constraints of the site meant that it had to be somewhat shorter than its counterpart. Charles the Bold, Duke of Burgundy, laid the first stone in 1444 and it was completed a mere four years later. In 1455 the town hall was embellished with a slender and delightful belfry designed by Jan van Ruysbroeck. Victor Hugo, who had the enviable good fortune to lodge in a hotel at 27 Grand'Place, praised the belfry in 1837 as 'a jewel comparable to the spire of Chartres'.

The town hall is encrusted with effigies of dukes and duchesses, and the upper tier is trimmed with a delicate border of masonry. The effect, especially at night, is like a lace screen; so fragile is the appearance that we might imagine a puff of wind blowing away the entire edifice. Yet we know from a 1695 drawing (pl. 29) that the building survived the French bombardment, and so it cannot be as flimsy as it appears.

The arcade to the right of the belfry is particularly delightful to investigate; the fifteenth-century masons have decorated the capitals with amusing little scenes, the most enigmatic of which shows people busily shovelling three-legged stools. The preliminary drawing for the capital—probably produced in Roger van der Weyden's studio in about 1450—is now owned by New York's Metropolitan Museum of Art (pl. 30). The curious scene is probably a whimsical play on the name of a local building, De Scupstoel, which literally means 'the shovel chair'. Another building known as De Papenkelder (The Pope's Cellar) is treated to a similar gentle mockery.

Let us now walk around the square in a clockwise direction, beginning with the row of six houses on the north side of the Hôtel de Ville. Plate 31 shows these six guild houses in the

Plate 30 Men Shovelling Chairs

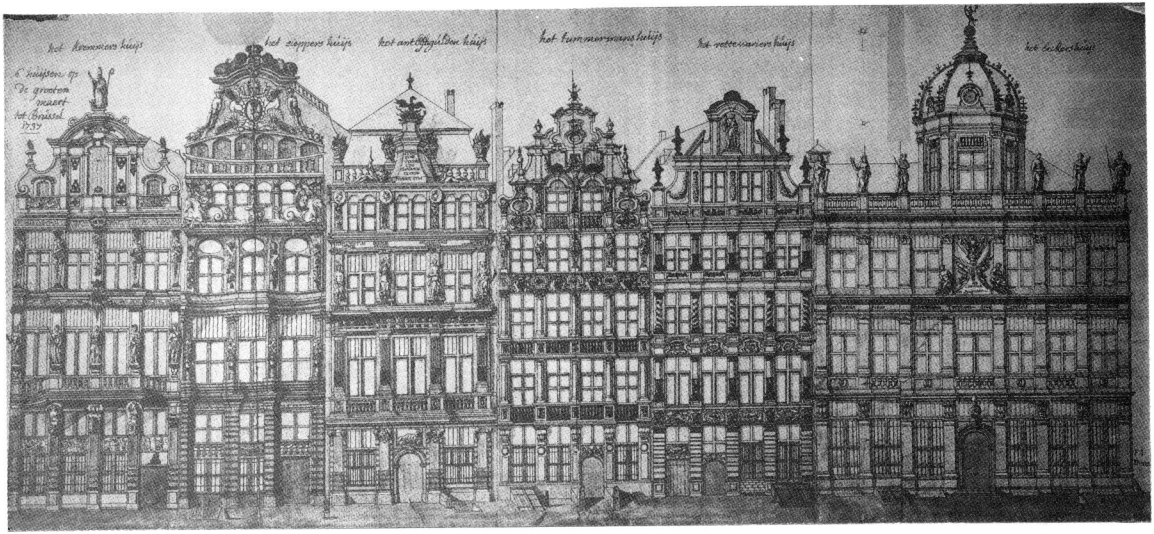

Plate 31 Grand'Place numbers 1 to 7

eighteenth century, and little has changed since then. The house on the far left (number 7), known as **La Maison du Renard** (The House of the Fox), was designed in 1699 for the guild of haberdashers and pedlars, whose patron, St Christopher, is perched atop the gable. The trading activities of this guild are amusingly illustrated by the cherubs in the four bas reliefs on the ground floor, while their far-flung travels are alluded to by four caryatids on the second floor. They represent the continents then known to exist; Africa is shown carrying ebony and ivory, Asia bears incense and ivory, America is symbolised by gold, while the figure of Europe is laden with a cornucopia of riches. The fifth figure represents Justice.

A certain furniture-maker named Antoon Pastorana designed two of the most remarkable buildings on Grand'Place, at numbers 4 and 6. A bas relief above the doorway of number 4 gives **La Maison du Sac** (The House of the Sack) its name. This building, third from the right on Plate 31, was commissioned by the guild of joiners and coopers in 1696. Its most striking feature is a decorative top which somewhat resembles an ornate Baroque cabinet. The following year, Pastorana designed the eccentric **Maison du Cornet** (House of the Horn) at number 6 for the guild of boatmen. If we turn to the drawing (pl. 31), we can see that the building, which is second from the left, is surmounted by an elaborate confection resembling the stern of a seventeenth-century ship. A bust commemorates the sickly Charles II of Spain, who was ruler of the Spanish Netherlands at this time. Seahorses and lions add further animation to this extraordinary building.

La Maison de la Louve (The House of the She-wolf) at number 5, third from the left on Plate 31, belonged to the guild of archers. Its name derives from the bas relief above the entrance showing Romulus and Remus being suckled by a she-wolf. Four Baroque caryatids on the second floor represent the opposites of Truth and Falsehood, Peace and Disorder. The pediment is surmounted by a phoenix rising from the flames, which recalls the repeated rebuilding of this house in the seventeenth century. It was twice destroyed by fire, but the third building, designed by Pieter Herbosch in 1691, proved sufficiently robust to survive the French artillery bombardment four years later; we can see its four-floor frontage standing amidst the ruins in the 1695 drawing (pl. 29).

La Brouette (The Wheelbarrow) at number 3, second from the right on Plate 31, is the simplest in this row of six houses. Rebuilt in 1697 by Jan Cosyns, it was once the guild house of the tallow merchants, who traded in candles and oil. The wheelbarrow above the entrance gives the building its name, while on top of the gable is a statue of St Giles, patron saint of the tallow merchants.

La Maison du Roi d'Espagne (The House of the

King of Spain) at numbers 1–2, on the far right of Plate 31, was also rebuilt by Jan Cosyns in 1697. Commissioned by the guild of bakers, it is a particularly palatial building surmounted by a dashing cupola on which the figure of Fame is delicately perched. Six figures on the balustrade represent Energy, Grain, Wind, Fire, Water and Prudence, while above the door is a bust of St Aubert, the patron saint of bakers. The relief in the upper floor honours Charles II of Spain, who is flanked by Turkish flags and chained prisoners. This magnificent building now houses Brussels' largest café, Le Roi d'Espagne. In contrast to the splendid Baroque exterior, the café is convivial and cluttered, with a blazing fire, solid wooden tables and a curious, rather moth-eaten, stuffed horse. If we decide to visit Le Roi d'Espagne—a favourite with Brussels students and, indeed, almost everyone—we should try to obtain a window table on the mezzanine to enjoy a very attractive view of Grand'Place through the tiny barred windows.

The side of Grand'Place facing the Hôtel de Ville is dominated by the **Maison du Roi** in which the delightful Musée Communal is situated. The museum, devoted to Brussels' art and history, occupies a building known in Flemish as the Broodhuis (Bread House), but in French by the rather grander title of the Maison du Roi (King's House). The Flemish name is the more accurate, as this site was once occupied by the guild house of the bakers, whereas it was never a royal residence. Early in the reign of Charles V, it was rebuilt in Late Gothic style, probably by the Antwerp architects Rombout Keldermans and Domien de Waghemakere, assisted by Hendrik van Pede and Lodewijk van Bodeghem. After being badly damaged in 1695 by the French bombardment, the Maison du Roi was hurriedly rebuilt by Jan Cosyns. By the nineteenth century the building had fallen into such disrepair that the city authorities resolved to rebuild it. Using historical sources supplemented, where necessary, by conjecture and imagination, Victor Jamaer erected the present building in 1873-95.

The **Musée Communal**—established in the rebuilt Maison du Roi in 1887—is a marvellous place to while away a rainy afternoon. The ground-floor rooms contain a fine collection of Brussels' paintings, tapestries, altarpieces, sculpture, furniture and porcelain. The most charming painting is Pieter Bruegel the Elder's *Marriage Procession*, which portrays the group of guests attending a country wedding, with an ashen-faced father at the head of the procession glancing back rather ruefully to his beaming daughter.

The first floor is devoted to a fascinating collection of scale models, maps, topographical paintings and photographs of Brussels, which enable us to grasp something of its complex development. Brussels' history is rather dominated by destruction, unfortunately, as is vividly illustrated by the series of engravings showing the sorry state of the Lower Town after the bombardment in 1695. We also see a nostalgic series of watercolours of the River Senne threading its way through the old town, before it was buried below the streets like a sewer. Another series of paintings shows the Ducal Palace on the heights of Coudenberg, which burned down in 1731, while a watercolour depicts the beautifully named Rue Nuit et Jour, which has also vanished. We also glimpse Brussels as it might have been in an Art Nouveau drawing illustrating a bold scheme to build an elevated arcade between Boulevard Anspach and Rue Royale. Notice, too, the amusing series of satirical sketches from *Charivari* magazine ridiculing the grandiose schemes of Léopold II. One delightfully irreverent drawing represents the Palais des Beaux-Arts by a group of artists working in an empty space.

If all this conveys a rather negative impression of destruction and planning disaster, we can immediately restore our faith in Brussels by glancing out of the first-floor windows of the Maison du Roi to see, through a veil of Neo-Gothic tracery, the rich architecture of Grand'Place. After we have visited the top floor of the museum to look at the costumes worn by the Manneken Pis, the famous bronze statuette of a urinating boy which stands in the Rue de l'Etuve, we can sit down on the worn stone bench outside the Maison du Roi to admire, as many generations have done, the exquisite spire of the Hôtel de Ville.

Plate 32 Grand'Place numbers 20 to 28

al de huijssen van aen
den hoeck van de
heerinck straet, tot
aen den hoeck van de
keijserstraet, op de
groote meet,
16
97

Continuing a clockwise tour of Grand'Place, we come next to the row of six houses illustrated in the eighteenth-century drawing by De Rons (pl. 32). **La Chaloupe d'Or** (The Golden Caravel) at numbers 24–25, third from the left on Plate 32, was designed in 1695 for the guild of tailors by Willem de Bruyn, architect of several houses on Grand'Place. It is built in a marvellously heavy and unabashedly opulent Baroque style which is thrilling to behold on even the greyest of Belgian days. The figure poised on the gable top represents St Bonifacius holding aloft a pair of tailor's scissors, while the guild's patroness, St Barbara, occupies a bull's-eye window above the entrance. A pleasant café named La Chaloupe d'Or now occupies this building. I suggest that we settle ourselves in this café to read the remainder of this chapter. Should we be fortunate enough to secure a table by a window, we may admire the remaining houses on Grand'Place as we sip our coffee.

Two doors down from this café is a **Godiva chocolate shop** (at numbers 21–22, second house from the right on Plate 32). The Godiva Company, founded by Joseph Draps in the 1920s, has recently become an international success, opening glamorous shops in capital cities of the world, where Belgian chocolates are displayed amidst silk and lace as if they were precious gems. About one-third of Godiva's chocolates are still hand-made, and many are flavoured with a generous dash of alcohol.

The adjacent side of Grand'Place is dominated by the **Maison des Ducs de Brabant** (House of the Dukes of Brabant), designed by Willem de Bruyn in 1695. Named after the busts decorating the façade, this magnificent building creates an illusion of grandeur by concealing six guild houses, each three bays wide, behind a monumental Baroque frontage. Tucked away in a corner to the right of this house is a tiny building known as 'Fame'. Appropriately, the figure of Fame blowing a trumpet, which gives this house its name, now adorns the entrance to the Brussels Jazz Club.

Maison des Brasseurs is boldly emblazoned in gold letters on the frieze of the brewers' guild house at number 10. It can be seen in the drawing by De Rons (pl. 33), forming the centrepiece of a row of five houses. This portly Baroque pile, also designed by Willem de Bruyn, is a masterpiece of Baroque gusto, crowned with a staggering weight of ornamentation, including a dashing equestrian statue of Charles of Lorraine hoisted up there in 1752. If we consult the drawing (pl. 33), which dates from 1737, we will see that the building was then surmounted by a different figure, that of Maximilian Emanuel II of Bavaria, who was Governor of the Spanish Netherlands from 1692-1711. Maximilian Emanuel II contributed to the diaspora of Flemish painting by acquiring numerous works by Rubens, which now form one of the highlights of the collection at the Alte Pinakothek in Munich.

La Maison du Cygne (The House of the Swan) at number 9, to the right of the Maison des Brasseurs, was once the guild house of the butchers. Built in 1698 as a private house in French Baroque style, in 1720 the guild of butchers bought the building and added a bulbous mansard roof above the pediment, creating a most unsettling effect. Karl Marx frequented a tavern located in this building during his three years of exile in Brussels, which ended with his expulsion from Belgium in 1848.

The little house at number 8 named **L'Etoile** (The Star) on the far right on Plate 33, surmounted by a star, was once occupied by the city magistrates. We will see that its former ground floor has been replaced by an open arcade. This represents an elegant solution to a pressing problem that arose in the nineteenth century, when the lane between this house and the town hall became so thronged with traffic that L'Etoile had to be demolished in 1852. But a few years later Burgomaster Charles Buls proposed this ingenious reconstruction, thereby appeasing both the hawks of progress and the doves of conservation.

The arcade contains some curious memorials, including an elaborate monument to Everard 't Serclaes designed in 1902 by Julien Dillens. Three bas reliefs illustrate a famous episode in the fourteenth century during the Brabant War of Succession. In the uppermost tablet, Everard and his men are scaling the city walls to expel Count Louis de Male, who had staked his claim to Brussels and installed himself in the magistrates' house on Grand'Place. The second scene shows the citizens of Brussels welcoming Duke

Plate 33 Grand'Place numbers 8 to 12

Wenceslas of Luxembourg, while the bottom tablet illustrates the assassination of Everard some thirty years later by hirelings of the Lord of Gaasbeek. Some six centuries have passed since Everard died, yet he is still revered as a saintly martyr. According to a local legend, it brings luck to touch the right arm of the recumbent figure of Everard, which explains the highly polished lustre to his arm. Not everyone, apparently, follows this tradition to the letter, for we can also see a very shiny dog, a gleaming cherub and even a glowing mouse concealed in a garland.

Having looked at Grand'Place, we might now explore the streets in the neighbourhood in search of a restaurant or café. One of the most delightful restaurants in Brussels is Chez Jean, just off Grand'Place at 6 Rue des Chapeliers. Chez Jean has been serving steaks drenched in butter, accompanied by enormous servings of *frites*, since 1931.

The tangle of mediaeval lanes to the east of Grand'Place known as the **Quartier de l'Ilot Sacré** (The Holy Isle Quarter) is the liveliest area of Brussels after nightfall. It is also the most European quarter of the city, for here there are restaurants, cafés and bars from virtually every member state of the European Communities (apart, I think, from Luxembourg). This is an area so exclusively devoted to food that (paraphrasing Emile Zola's description of Les Halles in Paris as *Le Ventre de Paris*) it might be called 'the Belly of Europe'. Even the street names in this old quarter of Brussels make a direct appeal to the stomach; there is a Rue au Beurre (Butter Street), Rue des Harengs (Herring Street), Rue des Bouchers (Butchers' Street) and Rue Chair et Pain (Meat and Bread Street).

Many of the restaurants in the old quarter of Brussels tend to be traditional Flemish establishments where the emphasis is placed on simple, substantial cooking at a moderate price. Brussels restaurants have long been renowned for their generous portions; the 1905 Baedeker guide warned travellers that, 'A single portion of soup or beefsteak or *filet de boeuf* is enough for two persons, and a single portion of any of the other dishes is enough for three.' The most popular dishes in these restaurants are *steak-frites* (steak with french fries) or overflowing pots of *moules* (mussels). To add to their appeal in winter, many of these restaurants have blazing open fires.

Following Rue au Beurre from the Roi d'Espagne, we pass **Dandoy** at number 31, an attractive old shop specialising in *spekulaus*, a spicy biscuit cut in the shape of human figures using moulds of seventeenth-century design. Straight ahead is the Bourse (Stock Exchange), which is surrounded by attractive cafés, such as Le Falstaff (described on page 251) and Cirio (described on page 260). Turning right along Rue de Tabora, we pass the **Eglise St Nicolas**, a church now so hemmed in by houses that it is almost hidden from sight. Nor does it now have a tower to give it prominence; the first one collapsed in 1367, a second tower was destroyed in the bombardment of 1695, while the third collapsed in 1714. Once the parish church of Brussels' merchants, St Nicolas is dedicated to their patron saint, Nicolas of Myra.

Several attractive nineteenth-century taverns are hidden in the narrow alleys of this old quarter. Opposite St Nicolas, a neon sign at 11 Rue de Tabora points down an alley to **La Bécasse** (The Woodcock), an inn dating from 1877. When crowded, the upstairs room of La Bécasse becomes particularly Bruegelian and merry.

On turning right up Rue Marché aux Herbes, we pass two more taverns tucked away in narrow lanes. The Impasse St Nicolas at number 12 leads down to **Au Bon Vieux Temps**, and the Impasse des Cadeaux at number 6 descends to **A l'Imaige Nostre Dame**. Although these *estaminets* bear French names, they have much of the atmosphere of a seventeenth-century Flemish tavern. My favourite is A l'Imaige Nostre Dame, a rustic Old Flemish interior of uncertain age.

Rue de la Fourche, the first street on the left, takes us into the heart of the Ilot Sacré. Strains of zither music spill out of the many Greek restaurants on this street. To add to the Mediterranean atmosphere, tables are set out in the street even on days when a light dusting of snow covers the tablecloths. A passage on the right leads through to Petite Rue des Bouchers, past Actor's Studio, a small cinema with an interesting programme of international films. Turning left brings us to Rue des Bouchers. Aux Armes de Bruxelles at number 13 is an elegant and reliable old Brussels restaurant, while directly opposite, at number 18, stands Chez Léon, where enormous potfuls of steaming mussels are served with *frites* and beer. Chez Léon began in 1905 as a tiny restaurant named after its founder Léon Vanlancker. The restaurant has now expanded to occupy a row of eight old houses which can accommodate about 500 patrons at one time. The kitchen is open from midday to midnight throughout the year, and on an average day will serve some 1,000 kilograms of Zeeland mussels. Chez Vincent, just around the corner at 8 Rue des Dominicains, was established in the same year as Chez Léon. Again the emphasis is on solid, substantial cooking. If not deterred by the giant slabs of butter piled high in Vincent's window, we enter this restaurant through the kitchen, which is decorated with a gleaming tile tableau depicting a herd of grazing cattle. The rear room is decorated with another painting on tiles of a small Flemish fishing boat battling against the North Sea, while the adjoining room is furnished in an attractive Old Flemish style with shiny brass cooking utensils strung from the ceiling.

We may be amused to note, not far from Vincent's, a narrow alley with a curious name. Situated opposite 28 Rue des Bouchers, the alley is so narrow that we might easily pass by without noticing it. Its name is the Rue d'une Personne (One Person Street), for the obvious reason that no more than one person may walk down it at a time. Indeed, after a hearty meal in Brussels, even one person may find Rue d'une Personne a tight squeeze.

Walk 2: The Lower Town

On our second walk in Brussels we venture into the old Flemish quarter of the city, following streets that W.H. Auden described as 'tangled like old string'. In this interesting area visited only by the most adventurous of tourists, we will come upon a rich diversity of architectural styles bearing witness to the complex evolution of Brussels. Old Flemish houses stand next to elegant French arcades, gleaming skyscrapers overlook weather-beaten Baroque churches, and secret squares are concealed behind modern office blocks. Nowhere else in Brussels do we receive such a vivid impression of the many conflicting forces that have shaped and shaken this city, be they Flemish, Spanish, Austrian, French, British or American. Admittedly, the contemplation of this clash of cultures is not always an agreeable experience, but it offers, I believe, a fascinating insight into the tumultuous history of which Europe is made.

We begin this walk (*see page 197 for map*) on **Grand'Place**, and enter the courtyard of the **Hôtel de Ville** through the portal below the belfry. The vaulting in the portal is decorated with eight prophets' heads, copies of originals, dating from about 1405, which are now safely protected from the elements in the Musée Communal opposite. In the courtyard beyond are two eighteenth-century fountains picturesquely overgrown with ivy. They are adorned with reclining figures representing the river gods of the Scheldt and the Meuse, the two principal rivers of Belgium.

We leave the courtyard by a gateway on Rue de l'Amigo and turn right. The building opposite stands on the site of the old town jail, known as the Amigo—an obsolete Southern Netherlands word for a prison. History has taken an ironical turn here, for the Amigo is now a very luxurious hotel. We now turn left along the Rue du Marché au Charbon, a winding street lined with interesting, though sadly dilapidated old shops. Hints of nineteenth-century Brussels remain, such as the shop front of Au Soleil at number 86, which cries out for restoration. An unconventional shop opposite (number 87) displays a large selection of brushes in one window and a comprehensive range of candied sugar in the other. Just beyond this mecca for sweet-toothed decorators, we come to the Baroque façade of **Notre-Dame du Bon Secours**, designed by Willem de Bruyn, the architect of La Chaloupe d'Or and the Maison des Brasseurs on Grand'Place. Its pleasingly compact and harmonious interior is the work of Jan Cortvriendt.

On reaching Place Fontainas, we take Rue de la Grande Ile, which begins on the far side of Boulevard Anspach and swings off to the right. Romantic though it sounds, we will find no trace of any Grande Ile (Great Island) here any more. The island vanished when the River Senne was ignominiously buried under the streets in the nineteenth century. The river now disappears into a tunnel near Ruisbroek and emerges some 10 miles to the north-east, not far from the Gare de Schaerbeek, following the line of boulevards running from Gare du Midi to Gare du Nord. At the unveiling of this momentous urban project in 1871, Burgomaster Anspach boasted that he had 'replaced the dangerous and dreary river with the most important and arguably the most beautiful boulevards in our city'. Baudelaire, however, grumbled of 'the sadness of a city without a river'.

Rue de la Grande Ile takes us from here past the **Eglise Notre-Dame aux Riches Claires**, designed by Luc Fayd'herbe in 1665. The choir of the convent church is a highly unusual composition with numerous tiny apses surmounted by scrolled gables and picturesque turrets. This curious architectural ensemble can be seen in the background of the drawing of Place St Géry (Pl. 34).

Soon we come to the nineteenth-century meat hall on **Place St Géry**, once the heart of the Grande Ile. It was on this site, according to legend, that St Géry, Bishop of Cambrai, established a sixth-century church. Not a whisper of the church remains. It was demolished by the French when they occupied the country in the eighteenth century. Although Brussels, like Paris, began as a settlement on a river island, it has developed quite differently: the two islands in the Seine in Paris have flourished, whereas those once in the Senne in Brussels have been left to decay. As we look at the crumbling houses in this historic neighbourhood, we may find ourselves for once nodding in agreement with G.K. Chesterton, who grumbled that: 'Except for some fine works of art, which seem to be there by accident, the City of Brussels is like a bad Paris, a Paris with everything noble cut out, and everything nasty left in.'

A drawing (pl. 34) shows Place St Géry as it was in the eighteenth century. Notice the small carriage being drawn by dogs, a curious form of transport which John Evelyn commented upon when he visited the Flemish cities in 1641. Travelling from Brussels to Ghent, he noted 'divers little wagons prettily contrived and full of pedling merchandises, drawne by mastive-dogs, harnessed compleately like so many coach horses, in some 4, in others 6, as in Brussels itselfe I had observed. In Antwerp I saw, as I remember, 4 dogs draw 5 lusty children in a charriot: the master commands them whither he pleases, crying his wares about the streetes.'

Another interesting detail in this drawing is the curious Renaissance fountain standing in the middle of the square. When the Marché St Géry was erected here in 1881, a proposal was put forward to save the fountain by placing it inside the market. As a result of this pleasing conservation measure, the obelisk-shaped fountain now dominates the central aisle of the former meat hall.

At the time of writing, the Marché St Géry was being restored to create a small-scale version of London's Covent Garden, containing shops restaurants and cafés. Opposite, some old Flemish brick houses have been attractively restored and, to the delight of local historians, a short stretch of the River Senne has been uncovered in the courtyard beyond (reached through an archway). If enthusiasm does not wane, as it sometimes does in Brussels, this old quarter should become increasingly animated as time goes by.

We now wander down Rue du Pont de la Carpe; the street name sounds promising but proves

Plate 34 Place St Géry

doubly disappointing for we will see neither a bridge nor any carp. Before the Senne was tidied away below the streets of Brussels, there was at least a *pont* here, but it seems very unlikely that *carpe* ever flourished in the murky river. We then cross the busy Rue Van Artevelde and continue down Rue Antoine Dansaert. L'Archiduc, at number 6, is a chic Art Deco jazz bar dating from the 1920s; the liveliest sessions do not really begin until well after most of Brussels has retired to bed. We also find some fashionable boutiques in Rue Dansaert, with striking interiors designed by young Belgian architects. Just beyond the Place du Nouveau Marché au Grain we turn right along Rue du Rempart des Moines. Apart from a curious name, the only interesting feature of this street is the sandstone portal on the left, which leads us into a beguiling old cobbled lane called Rue de la Cigogne.

At the end of the lane we turn right along Rue de Flandre, also a nondescript street apart from one remarkable building hidden down a long passage at number 46. Overlooking a secret courtyard is the splendidly ornate **Maison de la Bellone**, designed in Italo-Flemish style by Jan Cosyns in 1697. Military accoutrements decorate the façade of this house, which was built soon after the bombardment of Brussels, and named after Bellona, the Roman goddess of war. The Maison du Spectacle now uses the building for interesting exhibitions on French theatre in Brussels.

We now carry on to **Place Ste Catherine**, once the site of the fish market and still the best place in town for seafood. There is usually a stall in the square where we can eat mussels or oysters, when in season, washed down with a glass of Muscadet. Or we can visit one of the many excellent fish restaurants in this neighbourhood, such as La Belle Maraîchère at 11 Place Ste Catherine, a comfortable, traditional Brussels restaurant where the emphasis is rightly placed on cooking and service, rather than frills.

The weather-beaten **Eglise Ste Catherine** looks as if it has been looming over the old fish market for several centuries, but it is in fact something of a parvenu, for it was designed in 1854 by Joseph Poelaert, the architect of the Palais de Justice. The mysterious Baroque tower standing nearby once had a small chapel to justify its existence, but this was demolished in the nineteenth century. There was even talk in the 1950s of demolishing the Eglise Ste Catherine, but it has fortunately so far been spared.

We now walk down the **Quai aux Bois à Brûler**, formerly a quay overlooking a bustling harbour on the River Senne. But the harbour has been filled in to create a rather bleak and windswept square. Turning right off this square down Rue du Peuplier, we come upon the beautiful, billowy **Eglise du Béguinage**. Its seventeenth-century Baroque façade is divided into three bays, each topped with a curlicued Flemish scroll gable, giving the church the appearance of a row of three houses. The secluded religious community of Béguines was shattered some seven years after this map was published, when a Protestant mob broke into the church and plundered its treasures. The Béguinage was dealt a further blow in the nineteenth century when most of the 60 or so houses belonging to the sisterhood were demolished.

Let us leave this somewhat sad corner of the old city along Rue des Augustins, which brings us to the animated **Place de Brouckère**. We can pause for coffee in the magnificent Café Métropole (described on page 241), or we can turn left down Boulevard Adolphe Max to reach the curious **Café Vossegat**, at number 54. Vossegat's air of tattered elegance reminds me somewhat of the *chansons* of the Belgian singer Jacques Brel, whose 1960s songs perfectly captured the sad moods of Brussels, Liège and the flat Flemish landscape. Vossegat opened its doors in 1884, not long after the boulevard was created. A *vossegat* in Dutch is a fox-hole, and the café is crammed with dusty glass cabinets displaying stuffed foxes posed to illustrate scenes from La Fontaine's fables.

To reach our next destination, Place des Martyrs, we cross Boulevard Adolphe Max and turn down Rue du Finistère, past a tempting shop which does a brisk trade in Leonidas chocolates. Rue Neuve, the shopping street to which the narrow lane leads, is not particularly interesting. It was once a street of aristocratic allure, to which the Marquis of Spinola moved in 1675, but modern shops have put an end to its pretensions of grandeur. However, we should not overlook the Baroque church on the corner, **Notre-Dame de Finistère**, which is particularly pleasing because it manages, amidst the glittering distractions of Rue Neuve, to retain an atmosphere of piety. Perhaps it succeeds because it is itself crammed with glittering distractions, including grey stucco, Baroque paintings and ornately carved confessionals. It also boasts a splendid carved pulpit decorated with cherubs struggling to secure a canopy using a complicated system of ropes and pulleys. In the small chapel on the right there is a sixteenth-century statue of Notre-Dame de Bon Succès, apparently shipped to Brussels in 1625 from Aberdeen.

On leaving the church we return briefly to the crush of Rue Neuve and turn right, then left down Rue St Michel, one of the narrow streets leading into the **Place des Martyrs**. Even without its martyrs' monument, Place des Martyrs would be a rather ghostly square. It was designed in the 1770s by Claude Fisco in the harmonious Neoclassical style imposed on Brussels by its Hapsburg rulers, but the cool symmetry obviously does not appeal to the Brabant temperament of Brussels, for the buildings are now sadly derelict and empty. I suspect the only reason the square has been spared is that it contains a subterranean shrine to the 445 rebels who died in the Belgian Revolution in 1830.

We leave the square on the opposite side along Rue du Persil, a winding mediaeval lane lined with disconcerting futuristic buildings. Turning left and then right, we climb Rue des Sables, where there are some attractive early twentieth-century buildings, including **Magasins Waucquez** at number 20, designed by Victor Horta in 1903 for an Art Nouveau jeweller. This is the only surviving department store designed by Horta, and at the time of writing it was being restored to house a museum of Belgian comic strips. I rather look forward to the day when this wonderfully eccentric plan is realised.

We now ascend a flight of steps and cross the busy Boulevard Pachéco. Perched on the hill above is the **Colonne de Congrès**, designed in 1850 by Joseph Poelaert to commemorate the drafting of the Belgian constitution in 1831 by the National Congress. It stands on a square offering an interesting view of the Lower Town, but it is a rather windswept and bleak site, besides which it is rather difficult to reach from here, so let us leave it until another day and proceed now up Rue de la Banque to reach the street enchantingly named **Rue du Bois Sauvage** (Wild Wood Street). The origin of this name may serve as a cautionary tale to the large community of translators now working in Brussels. Originally it bore the Dutch name, Wout de Wildestraat, after a certain Wolter de Wilde, but during the French occupation, when the Napoleonic administrators altered all the street names from Dutch to French, the translator mistook Wout for *woud* (a wood) and so gave the street its beguiling, but quite erroneous name. Curiously, the Dutch name for this street is now Wildewoudstraat, which is a straight translation of the French! Number 14 in this lane is an attractive Late Gothic town house with a slender turret. Photographers tend artfully to conceal the fact that this house has lost half of its step gable to number 13, but I rather think that the juxtaposing of these two different styles creates an interesting curiosity. Let us now enter the cathedral by the south portal and sit down to read a little about the building.

The **Cathédrale St Michel**, now rather forgotten, has been the scene of many momentous events, including the spectacular chivalric ceremonies of the Order of the Golden Fleece held in the fifteenth century by Philip the Good and Charles the Bold. Among the many tombs we come across here are those of Duke John II of Brabant and his wife Margaret of York, daughter of Edward I of England, who are buried in the mausoleum of the Dukes of Brabant behind the high altar. The Late Gothic chapel attached to the north side of the choir contains the tombs of the Archduke Albert and Archduchess Isabella, and Charles of Lorraine. Roger van der Weyden, City Painter of Brussels, is also buried somewhere in St Michel, though the only indication of this is a rather mildewed reproduction of *St Luke Painting the Virgin*. This marvellous work by Van der Weyden is now in Boston, but a very good copy hangs in the Groeningemuseum in Bruges.

The oldest part of the cathedral is the choir, an early thirteenth-century Gothic structure, to which the nave and transepts were added in the fourteenth century, probably to designs by Jan van Ruysbroeck and Jacob van Thienen. The west front of the church was then splendidly terminated by twin towers, which were completed in 1451 and 1475. The beautiful Late Gothic Chapelle du St Sacrement de Miracle, appended to the north side of the choir in 1534-9, commemorates an unpleasant anti-Semitic legend of the fourteenth century. The story relates how a consecrated Host allegedly stolen by a Jew miraculously spurted blood after being stabbed by the congregation in a synagogue. The Host was subsequently venerated as a holy relic in St Michel.

At the time of writing, the nave of the cathedral was undergoing a major restoration and only the choir was accessible. The atmosphere here was marvellously mysterious and melancholy, with dusty Pre-Raphaelite statues and curious Neo-Gothic chapels eerily illuminated by dim pools of light cast by cobwebbed lamps. Let us hope that restoration does not entirely eradicate the antiquated charm of Brussels' Cathedral.

From here we head back down the slope and into the Lower Town along Rue d'Assaut. Turning left along the curiously named Rue Montagne aux Herbes Potagères brings us to the delightful **Café A la Mort Subite** at number 7. The café takes its name, which means literally 'sudden death', from a dice game once played by its regulars that involved reckless drinking bouts. Designed in 1910 by Paul Hamesse, this marvellous Neoclassical café has been in the hands of the same family since the 1920s. The owners have preserved the interior intact and virtually the only sign of progress is a gleaming chrome espresso machine. The café specialises in family-brewed Mort Subite beers. These are traditional ales from the Pajottenland, a rural area to the west of Brussels where Bruegel found inspiration in the sixteenth century for many of his scenes of peasant weddings and village fêtes.

Our walk is now almost over, but we have one important sight still to visit: the Manneken Pis fountain, which we must see if our visit to Brussels is to be considered complete. From Mort Subite, we turn left up Rue d'Arenberg, then right along Rue de la Montagne. After passing a statue of

Charles Buls, Burgomaster of Brussels from 1881-99, we proceed down Rue des Eperonniers, where we can buy nostalgic old tin toys at La Trottinette (number 4), art and architecture books at Post-scriptum (number 37) and attractive art and architecture postcards at Plaizir (number 50). We then cross Place St Jean to reach Place de la Vieille Halle aux Blés. Still continuing straight ahead, we follow Rue de Dinant (or what is left of it), then turn right into Rue de Villers. To our left is a fragment of Brussels' oldest fortifications, which enclosed the city from 1267 to 1357. Other sections of this wall crop up in unexpected locations: a tower and a length of wall at the foot of the picturesque Rue de Rollebeek, and another tower, saved by Charles Buls from demolition, just off Place Ste Catherine. Brussels' second city wall was more efficiently disposed of in the nineteenth century and all that now remains is the stalwart Porte de Hal at the end of Rue Haute.

But we are forgetting our purpose; once we have looked at this ancient stone wall, we should continue to the end of Rue de Villers, then turn left down Rue du Chêne to reach the **Manneken Pis**. Baedeker's 1905 guide warned travellers that this statue of a boy urinating was 'a great favourite with the lower classes', but conceded that 'the figure is not without considerable artistic excellence'. The present statue, which replaced an older version, was cast in bronze in 1619 by the sculptor Jerome Duquesnoy.

From the Manneken Pis we can return to Grand-'Place along Rue de l'Etuve, a narrow street with the well-trodden look of a pilgrimage route. The shops along this street have given up selling bread or cheese and have dedicated themselves with alarming single-mindedness to the sale of Manneken corkscrews, Manneken beer-dispensers and the like.

Walk 3: The Upper Town

Let us now explore the heights of the Upper Town, where the dukes and nobles of Burgundy erected their splendid Gothic palaces in the fifteenth century. Sadly, little now remains of this chivalric court apart from a solitary town house and a tiny chapel. The elegant architecture of the Upper Town now mainly dates from the eighteenth century, when impressive Neoclassical houses were built around parks and squares. Nineteenth-century boulevards and twentieth-century shopping arcades add further allure to the Upper Town, yet the main attractions of this walk are the two magnificent collections of paintings housed in the Musée d'Art Ancien and the Musée d'Art Moderne, collectively known as the **Musées Royaux des Beaux-Arts**. We should set aside an entire day for this walk if we are not to be rushed, avoiding Mondays when both museums are closed.

To plan our peregrinations in the Upper Town, I suggest that we familiarise ourselves with the route over coffee in Mokafé, a well-preserved 1930s café at 9 Galerie du Roi. This introduces us to the **Galeries St Hubert**, a magnificent glass-covered shopping arcade situated off Rue du Marché aux Herbes. Designed by Jean Pierre Cluysenaer in 1847, the Neoclassical arcade comprises three intersecting wings with the appropriately grandiose names of Galerie du Roi, Galerie de la Reine and Galerie des Princes.

The Galeries St Hubert proved particularly popular in the nineteenth century with the exiled French community in Brussels. During his stay in Brussels in 1864, Baudelaire sullenly paced the arcade every day as he worked on *Pauvre Belgique*, a bitter diatribe against Belgium. Another French habitué of the arcade was Verlaine, who obtained the pistol with which he shot his friend Rimbaud in a shop here.

The arcade has scarcely changed since its

Brussels

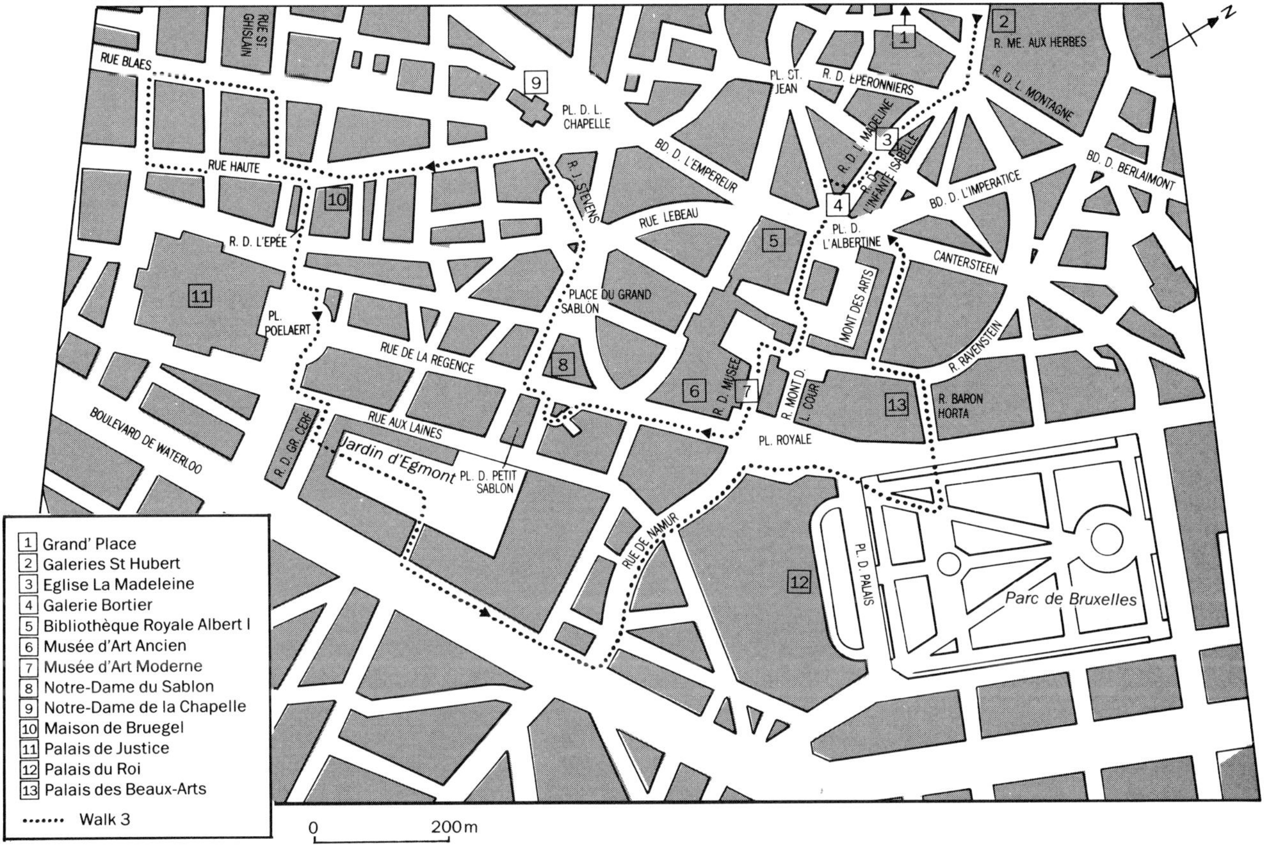

RUE ST GHISLAIN
RUE BLAES
PL. D. L. CHAPELLE
RUE HAUTE
R. J. STEVENS
BD. D. L'EMPEREUR
RUE LEBEAU
PL. ST. JEAN
R. D. EPERONNIERS
R. ME. AUX HERBES
R. D. L. MONTAGNE
R. D. L. MADELINE
R. D. L'INFANTE ISABELLE
BD. D. L'IMPERATICE
BD. D. BERLAIMONT
PL. D. L'ALBERTINE
CANTERSTEEN
MONT DES ARTS
R. RAVENSTEIN
R. BARON HORTA
R. D. L'EPÉE
PLACE DU GRAND SABLON
PL. POELAERT
RUE DE LA REGENCE
R. D. MUSEE
R. MONT D.
L. COUR
PL. ROYALE
RUE AUX LAINES
BOULEVARD DE WATERLOO
R. D. GR. CERF
Jardin d'Egmont
PL. D. PETIT SABLON
RUE DE NAMUR
PL. D. PALAIS
Parc de Bruxelles
N
1 Grand' Place
2 Galeries St Hubert
3 Eglise La Madeleine
4 Galerie Bortier
5 Bibliothèque Royale Albert I
6 Musée d'Art Ancien
7 Musée d'Art Moderne
8 Notre-Dame du Sablon
9 Notre-Dame de la Chapelle
10 Maison de Bruegel
11 Palais de Justice
12 Palais du Roi
13 Palais des Beaux-Arts
Walk 3
0
200 m

construction, and it still has old wrought-iron lamps, marble pilasters and lithe statues set in little niches. We may while away an hour or two here on a rainy afternoon, looking at the elegant shops, of which the best-preserved is Neuhaus at 25 Galerie de la Reine, whose chocolates have been tempting the Belgian sweet tooth since 1857. Another attractive shop to browse in is the Librairie des Galeries at 2 Galerie du Roi, which stocks sumptuous art books, including thick tomes on Burgundian art and elegant little guides to the architecture of Brussels. The attractively modernised Neo-Renaissance interior of the French bookshop Tropismes at 11 Galerie des Princes is also worth a glance.

We can explore another less famous arcade designed by the same architect when we ascend to the Upper Town by Rue de la Madeleine. On the way there we pass the attractive fifteenth-century **Eglise La Madeleine**, which was carefully transplanted during the construction of Gare Centrale to a site some 50 yards from its original location. The houses that once surrounded this church did not receive such charitable treatment and have all vanished, leaving La Madeleine looking somewhat isolated.

Entered by a Neoclassical portal at 23-5 Rue de la Madeleine, **Galerie Bortier** was erected by Cluysenaer very soon after the Galeries St Hubert, but seems never to have enjoyed the same fashionable allure. A short passage leads into a curving glass-roofed arcade with shops on one side and the back of an old market opposite. Bookshops specialising in second-hand French paperbacks now occupy this rather sad arcade.

From the entrance on Rue St Jean we turn left to reach the windswept Boulevard de l'Empereur, which marks the broad swathe cut by the railway tunnel linking Gare du Nord with Gare du Midi. Begun in 1911, this scheme was finally completed in 1952 with the opening of Gare Centrale, designed by Victor Horta in Art Deco style. The tunnel, which runs from the botanical gardens to a lovely Baroque chapel dedicated to St Bridget, has left Brussels permanently scarred.

As we wait for a pause in the traffic, we can look across to the **Mont des Arts** opposite. This series of stepped terraces was created in the 1950s to link the Lower and Upper Towns. There are several interesting features of this complex, including a modern glockenspiel programmed to chime Flemish and Walloon folk tunes alternately. Hidden on the rear wall of the building bridging the road to our left, the glockenspiel plays every 15 minutes, though seldom to an audience.

Our route to the summit proceeds straight ahead up a flight of steps leading to the **Bibliothèque Royale Albert I**, the national library. Built in a sober Neoclassical style in 1954-69, it houses many beautiful illuminated manuscripts from the Burgundian court. The manuscripts are sometimes exhibited in the **Nassau chapel**, an exquisite Late Gothic chapel buried in the fabric of the new library building. The outside wall of the chapel is visible from the upper arcade, just beyond the library entrance. The chapel—the most curious Burgundian memento in Brussels—once formed part of the Nassau palace. It was built in the late fifteenth century for Engelbert of Nassau, who served as Governor of the Netherlands under Philip the Fair, Duke of Burgundy. William the Silent later inherited the palace, but it was confiscated by the municipal authorities when he sided with the Dutch rebels. When the palace of the Dukes of Burgundy was destroyed by a fire in 1731, Governor Maria-Elisabeth took up residence in the Nassau palace. A later Governor of the Austrian Netherlands, Charles of Lorraine, rebuilt it in eighteenth-century Neoclassical style, but fortunately spared the fifteenth-century Nassau chapel. Nor, miraculously, did it perish in the 1950s, when much of Charles of Lorraine's Neoclassical palace was demolished to make way for the royal library. So it still stands today, an intriguing relic of Burgundian Brussels and the perfect setting for exhibitions of rare manuscripts.

Let us now climb up to the breezy terrace situated on the flanks of the aptly named **Coudenberg** (Cold Hill). From here we obtain a panoramic view of the guild houses and spires of the Lower Town. Ignoring one or two unfortunate modern intrusions, this is very much the view of Brussels which the Burgundian nobles would have enjoyed from the Gothic windows of their palaces. From this vantage point, Brussels seems a remote and rather unreal city, very like those distant clusters of city gates and spires that we see in the backgrounds of fifteenth-century Flemish paintings.

Behind us is the **Rue Montagne de la Cour** (Mountain of the Court Street), one of the streets whose names intrigued Gérard de Nerval on a visit to Brussels in the 1840s. 'Imagine in the middle of the flattest country on earth,' he wrote in a letter, 'a city consisting almost entirely of mountains: Montagne du Parc (Mountain of the Park), Montagne de la Cour (Mountain of the Court), Montagnes des Larmes (Mountain of Tears), Montagne aux Herbes Potagères (Mountain of Vegetables); horses and dogs are exhausted after a ten-minute trot, and anyone on foot soon runs out of breath.'

We now ascend Rue Montagne de la Cour. To our left, the Delacre chemist at 64 Rue Montagne de la Cour is an imaginative revival of Burgundian Gothic architecture designed by Paul Saintenoy in 1897. The tile tableau at the top is particularly attractive, reminiscent of a scene from an old illuminated manuscript. Two years later Paul Saintenoy switched to Art Nouveau style when he designed the beautiful **Old England** department store perched on the slope at number 94.

A flight of steps on the right-hand side of the street leads into the former courtyard of the Nassau palace. The **Ancien Cour**, a striking Neoclassical building on our right, is one of the last vestiges of a palace built in the 1760s for Charles of Lorraine, Governor of the Austrian Netherlands. The most astonishing feature of the quiet Neoclassical square is the subterranean court of the Musée d'Art Moderne, which a too hasty tourist might easily overlook. We spy the semicircular gallery through small oval windows in the parapet surrounding the court. Before visiting this gallery, let us look first at the Flemish Masters in the **Musée d'Art Ancien**, which we reach up Rue du Musée, then right along Rue de la Régence, entering by a giant portico flanked by massive columns of Scots granite.

It is fitting that this museum should be situated on the heights of Coudenberg, for it contains many paintings linked to the Burgundian court that once flourished here. As City Painter of Brussels from 1436-64, Roger van der Weyden provides many clues as to the characters and customs of the vanished court of the Dukes of Burgundy. He vividly portrays the sharply chiselled features of the *Man with an Arrow* (room 11), who is depicted wearing the collar of the Order of the Golden Fleece and carrying an arrow. Also by Van der Weyden is the attractive portrait of Laurent Froimont. About the life of Laurent Froimont we know nothing, but we may assume that he was a member of the aristocracy, as his motto, *Raison l'ensaigne* (reason giveth knowledge), is written in French rather than Dutch. We may also surmise that he was a devout Christian, as this painting was originally part of a diptych; the portrait of the Virgin which once accompanied it now hangs in a museum in Caen.

There are several fifteenth-century portraits from Bruges in the museum. Two by Memling show Burgomaster Willem Moreel and his wife (room 14), painted some six years before the other triptych by Memling featuring this couple, now in the Groeningemuseum in Bruges. In the tiny triptych by the Master of 1473, we see Jan van de Witte, Burgomaster of Bruges, and his second wife Maria Hoose. According to the Latin inscription at the base of the frame, this painting was completed in 1473 and shows the Burgomaster aged 30, with his 16-year-old bride. Behind the child bride is a small white dog, the familiar Flemish symbol of marital fidelity.

Dirk Bout's *The Justice of the Emperor Otto* (room 13) was commissioned in 1468 by the councillors of Leuven to hang in the courtroom of the beautiful Gothic town hall. It illustrates the cautionary tale of a young noble unjustly accused by the Emperor's wife. In the panel to the left, we see the arrest of the young man and his execution, observed by the Emperor and his wife from behind a wall. In the second panel, the wife of the executed nobleman, shown carrying her husband's head, is subjected to an ordeal by fire before the Emperor. Having thereby proved the nobleman's innocence, the Emperor Otto orders the Empress to be burned at the stake; we see the sentence being carried out on a distant hill. A curious feature of this diptych is the tracery at the top of the wooden frame, which matches the pattern of tracery in the doorway in the right-hand painting, a technique that adds to the illusion of depth.

Hieronymus Bosch's *Christ on the Cross* (room 17) illustrates the artist's eccentric religious imagination. The summery blue sky and the gaily striped trousers worn by one of the onlookers seem rather incongruous in the context of the Crucifixion. The walled city in the background has been identified as Bosch's home town of 's-Hertogenbosch.

The paintings by Bernard van Orley portray Flemish figures of the early sixteenth century, such as thrice-widowed Margaret of Austria (room 26), and Dr Georges de Zelle, a young doctor who lived close to Bernard van Orley in the Place St Géry. The pattern of crossed hands on the hanging behind Dr Zelle probably indicates that the artist and his sitter were close friends, but the meaning of the interlocked letters remains mysterious. We will also see here Van Orley's dramatic *Triptych of the Virtue of Patience*, commissioned by Margaret of Austria to give to a friend. The work illustrates a poem written by the thrice-widowed Margaret on the sufferings of Job. It is often arguable whether a painting was executed by Van Orley or his workshop, but here there can be no doubt, for the artist has added his name twice—once on the edge of the step at the bottom of the painting, and again in a tiny inscription on the pillar to the left. If we peer closely, as we are so often required to do by Flemish artists, we will also see on the pillar the motto *'Elx syne tyt'* ('A time for everything'). The painting's date—1521—can also be read here.

Portrait of a Man by Jan Mostaert (room 24) is another delightful painting tempting us into scholarly speculations. Its subject is a bony-faced, somewhat anxious man—perhaps a scholar—who is resolutely facing away from a scene of bizarre architecture and strange events. A group of people are gazing up at the sky, where a Madonna floats mysteriously in the clouds, surrounded by angels. The chained ape sitting on a ledge suggests that the painting may be an allegory of folly.

Quinten Metsys' *Triptych of the Life of St Anne* (room 22) also repays close scrutiny. Painted in 1509 for the St Pieterskerk in Leuven, it treats the lives of Joachim and Anne in a pleasingly unorthodox manner. In the left-hand panel we see Joachim being told by the angel that Anne is to bear a child, the future mother of Christ. A miniature scene in the background shows a shepherd tending his flock—an allusion to the legend that Joachim was living with shepherds in the desert when the angel appeared. The beautiful figure of Anne holding the Virgin Mary reveals Metsys' skill as a portraitist. Notice, too, the little child seated at the bottom left-hand corner of the centre panel solemnly reading a book upside down.

One of the most appealing paintings in the collection is Gerard David's *Virgin and Child* (room 21). Also known by the intriguing title of *The Madonna of the Porridge Spoon*, this miniature painting shows the Virgin feeding porridge to the Christ Child with a wooden spoon. The setting and the sentiment are typically Flemish, and the quiet domesticity anticipates seventeenth-century Dutch Masters such as Vermeer. Another painting of great tenderness is *Child with a Dead Bird* (room 22), painted by an anonymous artist.

The Musée d'Art Ancien is particularly proud of its collection of paintings by Pieter Bruegel the Elder, which includes the famous *Fall of Icarus*, painted in the 1550s when Bruegel was still resident in Antwerp. In the beautiful poem *Musée des Beaux-Arts*, Auden dwells on this painting as an illustration of the way that suffering 'takes place/While someone else is eating or opening a window or just walking dully along'. At first, we do not see Icarus at all; our eye falls first on the figure of a daydreaming ploughman in the foreground, and then on a sailing ship. Only upon examining the painting closely do we see a tiny splash in the water and a leg about to disappear below the waves. Auden suggests that Icarus is ignored because 'the expensive delicate ship that must have seen/Something amazing, a boy falling out of the sky,/Had somewhere to get to and sailed calmly on'.

In Bruegel's *Census at Bethlehem*, painted in 1566 after he had moved to Brussels, the main characters are again difficult to find. The scene is a Flemish village of the Pajottenland on a crisp winter's day. Looking at this work, one's attention constantly shifts, from the charming scenes of children playing on the ice to the construction of a house, and from the dilapidated village to the red ball of the setting sun. The Census is just one more detail in this bustling scene, as are the figures of Mary, seated on a mule, and Joseph.

The other important work here by Bruegel, *The Fall of the Rebel Angels*, was painted at about the same time as *Dulle Griet* in Antwerp, and it is an equally disturbing work, crowded as it is with bloated fish and winged monsters. Yet I think that *The Census at Bethlehem* has an underlying horror which is far more powerful, for it tricks us into smiling at the happy children engaged in various games, until the terrible thought occurs to us that the census which is quietly taking place in a corner of the scene will be followed all too soon by the massacre of the innocents. Bruegel's *Massacre of the Innocents* is now in Vienna's Kunsthistorisches Museum; the Musée d'Art Ancien has a copy made by Pieter Bruegel the Younger.

Once we have seen the Bruegels, we should look at the Rubens collection one floor higher. Interestingly, this includes a sketch of the *Fall of Icarus* which, unlike Bruegel's, captures the full drama of the tragedy. The sketch is one of a series of mythological scenes ordered by Philip IV of Spain in 1636 to decorate the Torre de la Parada, a royal hunting lodge near Madrid.

Of the nineteenth-century paintings in the museum, the most famous is Louis David's *L'an Deux* (room 71), painted in 1793. It depicts the murder of the revolutionary Jacobin leader Marat. He was sitting in his bath writing when Charlotte Corday, a beautiful young woman from Normandy, burst in and stabbed him to death. Marat is shown holding a letter dated 13 July 1793 written by his assailant. In the next room (number 70) we see David's *Mars Disarmed by Venus*, a late work painted in Brussels the year before he died. Louis David had fled to Brussels from France in 1816, and died there in 1825.

Room 69 contains the preliminary study by Antoine Wiertz of *The Apotheosis of the Queen*. This painting, commissioned to commemorate the Belgian Silver Jubilee in 1856, was to have been 150 feet high! Had it been executed, it would have been taller than the Colonne de Congrès on Rue Royale. Also in this room is Gustave Wapper's painting *Day in September 1830*, showing Belgian rebels hoisting the flag at Grand'Place during the 1830 revolution. A small room opposite is devoted to Henri Leys, whose nineteenth-century paintings nostalgically evoke Flemish cities under the Burgundians and Hapsburgs.

Many of the most interesting nineteenth-century paintings in the Musée d'Art Ancien are hidden away in rooms 72-91. As an antidote to Leys' Flemish patriotism, we should search out the drawings by Ensor displayed on the mezzanine level above room 83. Dating from 1891, his drawing of *The Battle of the Golden Spurs* is a marvellously irreverent depiction of the fourteenth-century conflict between the French knights and the Flemish workers. In room 80 we see the rich, heavy Renaissance interiors of Antwerp in paintings by Henri de Braekeleer. The interior of the Brouwershuis, with its glowing gilt leather walls, particularly attracted this quiet, nostalgic artist. Notice also in room 88 the works by Henri Evenpoel, including some attractive portraits of children and a marvellous still life titled *White Dress*.

The **Musée d'Art Moderne** can be entered directly from the Musée d'Art Ancien, or from 1 Place Royale, an eighteenth-century town house where Alexandre Dumas wrote much of an almost forgotten novel called *La Comtesse de Charny*. A fascinating collection of modern art is displayed in a striking subterranean gallery sunk eight floors below the level of the Place Royale. At level -2, Saul Steinberg's whimsical mural *The Americans—The Road, South and West* celebrates the glorious ugliness of America's traffic jams and trailer parks. Notice also the cubicle containing Luc Peires' awesomely vertiginous construction of mirrors, *Environment—1966*. Descending to level -3 we come upon Vic Gentils' *Rua de Amor*, a macabre wooden sculpture depicting two unattractive women and a male client in a seedy Spanish brothel.

The next level down contains many works by the eccentric Ostend artist James Ensor, who is discussed in the chapter on Antwerp (see page 163). A portrait of his father, an English resident of Ostend, illustrates Ensor's early Impressionism, which used the same melancholy brown and grey tones as the Dutch Impressionists. His style then changed dramatically in the 1880s, as we see from the explosive, luminous *Carnival on the Beach*, painted in 1887.

On the same floor is Rik Wouters' affectionate portrait of his wife Nel as *The Woman in the Red Necklace*, and his Cézanne-like *Flautist*, painted shortly before the outbreak of World War I. The felicitous pre-war period of Belgian history is reflected, too, in Louis Thevenet's alluring paintings such as *Honeymoon*. Thevenet seems to have retained his optimistic outlook throughout the war years, or so his 1917 painting *Hat-stand* seems to suggest.

Eight floors below Place Royale, we come upon an eerie collection of surrealist paintings. The works by Paul Delvaux date mainly from his melancholy middle years in Brussels; they are chilling paintings depicting skeletons, night trains, empty trams and statuesque nude women. Occasionally we detect the echo of a famous Old Master, as in *Vox Populi* painted in 1957. Set in a melancholy street of Brussels' Upper Town, it shows a group of strait-laced ladies, widows perhaps, gazing sternly at a reclining nude in the style of Titian. Another work reinterprets the story of Pygmalion, the King of Cyprus who fell in love with a statue that was then brought to life by the goddess Venus. Delvaux alters the roles so that the statue is male and the lover female. There is also a strange study by Delvaux of the *Crucifixion* painted in 1951 in which all the human figures are replaced by skeletons.

In the paintings by René Magritte, to whom a room is devoted, we see unexpected images depicted with the objectivity of photographs. In one, *Empire of Light*, a clear blue sky is juxtaposed with a benighted suburban street illuminated by a solitary lamp. In another painting the body of a nude female on a beach has become partially blue, the colour of the sea.

On leaving the museum we should cross Place Royale and turn right along Rue de la Régence. Soon we turn off this busy street into the surprising Rue des Six Jeunes Hommes, where we discover a nook of attractive old houses which have tenaciously survived the redevelopment of this quarter. The lane emerges on **Place du Petit Sablon**, an intimate square created in 1890. Weather permitting, we can sit on a bench here to read about the 60 or so statues that surround us. The main figures are Counts Egmont and Hoorn, proudly placed on a lofty pedestal. These two nobles were executed by order of the Duke of Alva in 1568 for alleged treason. The statue of the two friends on their way to the scaffold originally stood on Grand'Place, where the execution took place, following their imprisonment in the Maison du Roi. The statues are surrounded by a miscellany of sixteenth-century Flemish figures, including William the Silent, Bernard van Orley, and the geographers Mercator and Ortelius. A hedge has been clipped to create niches for these statues; at night when the figures are floodlit the effect is particularly romantic. A further set of 48 bronze figures representing Brussels' sixteenth-century guilds stand atop the Neo-Gothic columns surrounding this park, ensuring that statues far outnumber people in this quaint retreat.

The park overlooks the attractive **Eglise Notre-Dame du Sablon**, founded in 1304 by the guild of crossbowmen. Pilgrims flocked to this church in the Middle Ages after a statue of the Virgin, brought here by boat from Antwerp in 1348, proved to have miraculous qualities. A tapestry in the Musée Communal depicts this legend. The miracle was later celebrated in the annual Ommegang procession, which culminated in a competition to shoot a wooden bird from the roof of the Sablon church. When the Archduchess Isabella won this competition in 1615, the event was meticulously recorded by Antoon Sallaert in a painting now hanging on the main staircase of the Musée d'Art Ancien.

To cope with the huge influx of pilgrims, this church was rebuilt in the fifteenth and sixteenth centuries in Brabant Late Gothic style. Its most ornate feature is a small sacrarium appended to the outside of the choir on the north side. Built in 1549, it eventually fell into decay (as Late Gothic architecture is wont to do). The architect who restored it at the turn of the century added an ornate upper tier of his own invention, where once had been a small cupola.

It is worth venturing into the church to enjoy a harmonious Late Gothic interior without the customary clutter of second-rate Baroque sculpture. What Baroque there is tends to be first-rate, particularly the twin chapels flanking the choir, erected by the Von Thurn und Taxis family, who founded Europe's first postal system in the late fifteenth century. Von Thurn und Taxis was one of many aristocratic families residing in this quarter of Brussels, but of their palace nothing now remains.

As its name suggests, the **Place du Grand Sablon** was originally a sandy hill. Several inns were established on the square in the Middle Ages to serve the needs of pilgrims. Now there are numerous cafés and restaurants here and in the quiet side streets nearby, such as Rue Ste Anne, Rue des Pigeons and Rue de Rollebeek. Whatever buildings are not devoted to restaurants tend to be occupied by exclusive antique shops, some of which are situated in attractive arcades opened up in the courtyards behind the houses. A Sunday morning in Brussels can be enlivened by a visit to the antique and book market held here.

We now descend from the aristocratic heights of the Sablon quarter to explore the curious streets and narrow alleys of the Marolles. Rue Joseph Stevens plunges down to the Marolles from the bottom of Place du Grand Sablon, cutting across Place Emile van der Velde, where Victor Horta's Maison du Peuple was erected in the 1890s. A banal office block has replaced Horta's Art Nouveau masterpiece, much to the dismay of enthusiasts of architecture.

At the foot of the hill we come upon one of the most unusual churches in Brussels. The **Eglise Notre-Dame de la Chapelle** presents us with a baffling diversity of styles to unravel. Its transepts are Romanesque, the choir dates from the Early Gothic period, and its nave and aisles were rebuilt in Late Gothic style following a fire. The tower is a curious Baroque embellishment, replacing a slender spire which the French bombardment brought down in 1695. It was designed by Antoon Pastorana, the architect of the bizarre guild house of the boatmen at 6 Grand'Place.

It was in this church, in 1563, that Pieter Bruegel the Elder married Maria Coecke, the daughter of Pieter Coecke van Aelst, a leading Flemish artist of the day. Bruegel, who died in his early forties, only six years after the marriage, was probably buried here, although no grave survives.

The only hard evidence is a memorial in the church erected in honour of his father by Jan Bruegel in 1625. It once incorporated a painting by Rubens of *Christ Handing the Keys of Heaven to St Peter*, which he presented as a token of his admiration for Bruegel. Unfortunately the church authorities sold this painting to a private collector in the eighteenth century, replacing it with a copy.

Bruegel probably lived in the house now known as the **Maison de Bruegel** at 132 Rue Haute, which we reach by taking the street that ascends from the church. The attractive step-gabled building was certainly owned by the artist's grand-daughter Anne Bruegel, who bequeathed it to her son, David Teniers III. However, the assumption that Anne inherited it from her father, Jan Bruegel, and he in turn from Pieter Bruegel the Elder, is not proven. The house now contains a museum devoted to Pieter Bruegel the Elder, but I suspect that more pleasure is to be gained from looking at the five paintings in the Musée d'Art Ancien, two of them—*The Census at Bethlehem* and the tiny portrait *Yawning Man*—executed in Brussels, the others in Antwerp.

Bruegel's house stands in the heart of the **Marolles**, a quarter settled by weavers in the Middle Ages. The weavers of Brussels, like those of Ghent, were a notoriously unruly crowd, giving the Marolles its enduring reputation for lawlessness; even Baedeker felt it necessary to warn his readers in 1905 that the streets of the Marolles 'exhibit many drastic scenes of popular life'. Nowadays we rather relish scenes of popular life, as long as they are not too drastic, and the Marolles as a result has experienced a certain revival of interest. It is the only quarter left in Brussels where we might, on a rare moment, come upon a scene evoking a painting of children's games by Bruegel. Eating out in a restaurant in the Marolles may likewise recall the convivial mood of Bruegel's paintings of wedding feasts. One of the most atmospheric bistros in this quarter is La Grande Porte at 9 Rue Notre Seigneur. Situated near the attractive Baroque chapel of a vanished convent, this bustling restaurant has a festive mood, with hanging lanterns and memorabilia of the 1950s. We can enjoy La Grande Porte's traditional dishes up to 1.30am, or 3.30am at weekends.

We now continue along Rue Haute, past a curious old-fashioned hatter's shop at number 158, and turn right down Rue St Gisleins. The kindergarten at number 40 was designed in 1895-9 by Victor Horta. Examining the façade closely we can discern numerous delightful details such as the tiny leaf-like decoration at the tops of the windows and the eccentric little turret. Notice, too, to the left of the name 'Jardin d'Enfants', Horta's ingenious treatment of a horizontal gutter's intersection with a vertical shaft, the effect rather like ivy entwined around a post.

To continue our exploration of the Marolles, we must retrace our steps a short distance to Rue Blaes, where we turn right to reach the **Place du Jeu de Balle**. Named after a ball game traditionally played here, the square is now the scene of a popular daily flea market. Even if we are too late to catch the market, which peters out in the early afternoon, the curio shops on Rue Blaes provide us with an equally entertaining variety of bizarre bric-à-brac. We may also glimpse an example of the humour for which the Marolles is famed; the lobby of a modest *frites* shop at 2 Place du Jeu de Balle has been decorated as a *Hommage à Magritte*. Customers sheltering from the wind as they eat *frites* can enjoy a parody of Magritte's famous surreal painting *Ceci n'est pas un pipe* titled *Ceci n'est pas une frite*. Or they can look at a strange landscape with ketchup bottle while indulging their passion.

Having now perhaps discovered something of the fascination of the Marolles, let us return to the aristocratic heights of the Upper Town. From Place du Jeu de Balle, we should ascend Rue des Renards, turn left along Rue Haute and then right up Rue de l'Epée.

Looming above us now is the monstrous **Palais de Justice**, on the construction of which the architect Joseph Poelaert toiled from 1866 until his death, from exhaustion, in 1879. Finally completed in 1883, the building is one of the most potent symbols of the reign of Léopold II, who once declared his ambition to be 'to make Belgium greater, stronger and more beautiful'. Poelaert helped Léopold to achieve the first two of these aims, though perhaps not the third, by modelling the Palais de Justice on the massive monumental temples of Egypt and Assyria. The elevated site on Galgenberg (Gallows' Hill) was deliberately chosen to strike terror into the lawless folk of the Marolles.

We ascend to the main entrance of the Palais de Justice by a series of ramps reminiscent of the temples of the Nile. As we enter the building between colossal statues of Cicero, Demosthenes, Lycurgus and Domitius Ulpian, we may espy a ghostly floodlit head of a Sphinx gazing down from a window above. I suggest that we do no more than glance into the cavernous and echoing *Salle des Pas Perdus* (Waiting Room), for it is a rather chilling place, which I think does not really belong in this country of miniature paintings, intimate interiors and eccentric details.

From the terrace in front of the Palais de Justice we obtain another panoramic view of northern Brussels, this time too crowded with modern architecture to recall the paintings of the Flemish Primitives. Northern Brussels is dominated by two gigantic eccentricities. The nearer one is the **Basilique Nationale du Sacré-Coeur**, situated in the *commune* of Koekelberg. Léopold II laid the first stone of a planned Neo-Gothic church on this site in 1905, but the project was abandoned in 1914 with nothing more than the foundations sunk. In the 1920s, however, an Art Deco church designed by Albert van Huffel was begun. Work was halted by World War II, but it was later resumed and the church finally completed in 1970. The other bizarre structure looming in the distance is the Atomium, a 120-metre-high building representing the nine atoms of an iron crystal (described on page 252).

We can retreat into the secluded **Jardin d'Egmont** by crossing Place Poelaert, turning left along Rue aux Laines and then right into Rue du Grand Cerf; the park is down a lane on the left. The 27-floor Hilton Hotel, which overlooks this park, proves to be a useful aid to navigation in this quarter of the Upper Town.

The Jardin d'Egmont is named after the eighteenth-century palace overlooking the park. The Late Gothic precursor of this palace was built by the mother of the executed Count Egmont in 1548. Delving into the mysterious park, we discover a lovely fifteenth-century well which stood on the flank of Coudenberg until redevelopment necessitated its removal to this leafy spot. Leaving by a cobbled lane on the far side brings us to the Boulevard de Waterloo, a busy thoroughfare following the course of the second city wall. All that remains of the fortifications is the massive Porte de Hal, a grim and gloomy fourteenth-century city gate at the end of Rue Haute; at the time of writing it was being restored to accommodate a museum of folklore.

We now turn right along the boulevard, past the Hilton doorman and the Hermès boutique, to reach two attractive old cafés highlighted by a gaudy assortment of neon signs. Both are tempting places to pause; Waterloo is the more formal, its waiters dressed like luxury liner stewards; Le Nemrod next door is owned by the same family as Le Métropole, La Chaloupe d'Or and La Brouette, and possesses the same distinctions as these Lower Town cafés. Le Nemrod's blazing fire will certainly tilt the balance in its favour on a chilly winter's day. After coffee, we may wish to explore the elegant shops along Avenue Louise and in the contiguous arcades. Once shopping has been done and the services of a guide are again required, I suggest that we head along the Avenue de la Toison d'Or to the Porte de Namur. The steep Rue de Namur descends thence to **Place Royale**, an elegant Neoclassical square designed by Barnabé Guimard in the eighteenth century. Guimard's original plan achieved a pleasing intimacy by linking the individual aristocratic residences by Neoclassical arches, but Rue de Namur is the only street to retain this unusual feature.

Turning right at Place Royale we cross the road to the **Parc de Bruxelles**. 'The trees offer us shade,' states an antiquated iron sign at the park entrance. 'Along with the plants and the flowers, they are the joy and the beauty of the countryside. Anyone who damages the trees and the plants causes damage to himself.' Mindful of this stern warning, let us sit on a bench to read about the park.

Despite the sign we have just read, the trees offer us very little shade, for they have been ruthlessly trained on trellises. Indeed this park may well strike us as an object lesson in geometry rather than botany. Designed in 1787 by the Austrian landscape gardener Joachim Zinner, the avenues of the Parc de Bruxelles are laid out in the form of a compass—a masonic conceit which can best be appreciated by studying a map.

The park is dotted with a curious miscellany of statues, including Roman emperors, Venus, Diana and Narcissus. There is also a statue of Peter the Great, who visited Brussels in 1717. Wandering down the straight alleys of the Parc in 1844, Thackeray complained that: 'Numbers of statues decorate the place, the very worst I ever saw. These cupids must have been erected in the time of the Dutch dynasty, as I judge from the immense posterior developments.' Robert Louis Stevenson was a more enthusiastic visitor, lyrically describing the pleasures of the park at night in a letter to his mother penned in 1872. 'If any person wants to be happy I should advise the Parc. You sit drinking iced drinks and smoking penny cigars under great old trees. The band place, covered walks, etc., are all lit up. And you can't fancy how beautiful was the contrast of the great masses of lamplit foliage and the dark sapphire night sky, with just one blue star set overhead in the middle of the largest patch. In the dark walks, too, there are crowds of people whose faces you cannot see, and here and there a colossal white statue at the corner of an alley that gives the place a nice *artificial*, eighteenth century sentiment.'

Before being prettified by Zinner, these woods were a ducal hunting estate dating back to the fourteenth century. In the sixteenth century, Charles V converted part of the woods into a tilting yard. It can be seen in the foreground of the painting reproduced on the cover of this book. Behind it is the Late Gothic palace of the Dukes of Burgundy, which was gutted by fire in 1731. It was within this palace that Margaret of Parma received a petition in 1566 calling for the abolition of the inquisitorial courts. During this historic audience, Count Berlaymont whispered to Margaret, 'Madam, it is nothing but a gang of beggars.' The following day, when several hundred nobles met in Count Kuilemburg's palace on Rue des Petits-Carmes to toast their success, they proudly declared themselves *Gueux* (beggars). Berlaymont's casual insult later prompted the rebels to dub themselves Sea Beggars and to equip themselves with a symbolic beggar's bowl.

The quarter around the park is now very definitely Viennese, rather than Burgundian, in tone. Barnabé Guimard, the creator of the Place Royale and Rue Royale, designed the Neoclassical **Palais de la Nation** which attractively encloses the northern end of the park. Originally the seat of the Council of Brabant, this building has been home to the Belgian Parliament since 1831. The **Palais du Roi** which faces it across the formal parterres was erected on the site of the old Palais du Coudenberg in the early twentieth century to provide Léopold II with a suitably grandiose town residence.

To return to Grand'Place, I recommend a somewhat indirect descent by two little-used flights of steps. The first leads down from Rue Royale to Rue Baron Horta, and permits us to glance at the programme of the **Musée du Cinéma** at 9 Rue Baron Horta, where three different international films are screened daily, together with two classic silent films with piano accompaniment. The cinema museum is tucked away in a corner of the **Palais des Beaux-Arts**, built by Victor Horta on a tricky sloping site in the 1920s. By then, his Art Nouveau adventure was ended and he had fallen in line with the international Art Deco style. We can enter at 23 Rue Ravenstein to pick up a programme and perhaps visit the pleasant café there.

The Palais des Beaux-Arts occupies the site of the garden of the Pensionnat Héger, where Charlotte and Emily Brontë stayed as students in 1842. It was quite common for wealthy British families to send their daughters to a finishing school in Brussels during the reign of the Anglophile Belgian monarch Léopold I. Charlotte returned alone the following year to teach here, and based *Villette* on her experiences as a single woman in Brussels. An evocative passage in the novel describes the lonely heroine wandering through the garden at sunset listening to the bells of the Eglise du Béguinage 'peal out with their sweet, soft, exalted sound'.

Left along Rue Ravenstein brings us to the **Hôtel Ravenstein** at number 1. Built in the fifteenth century for Count Adolphe Cleve, it was restored in 1899 by Paul Saintenoy, the architect of the Delacre chemist and the Old England department store on the nearby Rue Montagne de la Cour. The

Hôtel Ravenstein is now the sole surviving aristocratic town house in Brussels from the Burgundian period. An ancient flight of steps in front of the residence known as the Jodentrap, or Jews' Stairs, once linked the Lower and Upper Towns through the former Jewish quarter. When the Jews were driven out of this quarter in the fourteenth century, many fashionable new town houses such as the Hôtel Ravenstein were built here.

Let us now descend the steps to Rue Terarken, a dark alley overshadowed by this enormous town house. If we look right at the bottom we will see two splendid Late Gothic bay windows projecting from the blackened stone walls. A tunnel below Rue Ravenstein leads to Rue des Sols, past a European Communities office identifying itself in nine languages. On reaching Cantersteen, we are back on familiar ground and should have no difficulty making our way back to Grand'Place.

Brussels Explored Further

If you still have time to spare in Brussels, an enjoyable day or two can be spent exploring the suburbs of the city by tram and metro. The **Café Métropole** at 31 Place de Brouckère is a convenient place in which to plan an excursion, as it is close to De Brouckère metro station. The Hôtel Métropole was designed in 1894 by a French architect, Alban Chambon, who had made his reputation in the previous decade by designing numerous Victorian theatres in London, Brussels and Amsterdam. The Métropole, too, is designed in a rather theatrical spirit, with gleaming brass, large mirrors and chandeliers. Its old-fashioned charm is enhanced by waiters in long white aprons, excellent coffee served on a silver tray with a small chocolate, and a terrace on the bustling boulevard. So let us sink into a plump sofa in the Métropole to study the six excursions suggested below.

I. Museums in the Parc du Cinquantenaire

To commemorate the 50th anniversary of the foundation of the Belgian state, Léopold II created the Parc du Cinquantenaire in 1880. The park—reached by taking the metro to Mérode—contains two large exhibition halls built by Gédéon Bordiau, who also designed the lovely Square Marie-Louise nearby. The south hall was destroyed by fire and rebuilt in a sober late Art Deco style, but the north hall has survived intact. The huge triumphal arch linking these two buildings was designed during the 75th anniversary celebrations in 1905 by Charles Girault, the French architect responsible for the Congo Museum in Tervuren.

The rarely visited **Musées Royaux d'Art et d'Histoire** (Royal Museums of Art and History) share the south hall of the Cinquantenaire palace with a museum of motor cars. On any given day rather less than half of the rooms of the Musées Royaux d'Art et d'Histoire are open, and it is worth being diligent and checking the calendar carefully, as the rooms that are most interesting are only open on days with an odd-numbered date. If we turn up on an even date, we will be confined to the collection of Roman, Greek and Classical antiquities.

The rooms that are open on odd-numbered days contain an extraordinary collection of Flemish and Walloon decorative art. Nowhere else in Belgium will we see such marvellous tapestries, altarpieces, tombs, silverware, globes, porcelain and locks.

Room 8a, perhaps the best place to begin, contains some beautiful examples of Mosan art. With its extraordinary detail and liveliness, this early mediaeval art of the Meuse valley prefigures the miniature perfection of the Flemish Primitives. One of the most fascinating works is the *Portable Altar of Stavelot*, which a twelfth-century traveller carried on his journeys. Notice the delightful seated figures of the Four Evangelists that form the feet of the altar, each of them holding a book in which the opening words of his gospel are inscribed.

An oval hall (room 18) contains a number of luminous Byzantine objects beautifully bathed in a mellow golden light. Another little room contains two magnificent seventeenth-century globes. In an airy Neo-Renaissance room (number 9) we come upon a delightful bronze font resting on six lions. This was cast in 1149 for the church of St Germain in Tienen, and is decorated around the rim with 14 Biblical scenes. If the reader of this book is more fortunate than the writer ever was, he or she will be able to enter the side room off this gallery to look at the reconstructed Art Nouveau shop interior designed by Victor Horta for Magasins Waucquez. Art Nouveau jewellery and other objects are apparently also displayed in this room.

A large hall in the depths of the museum contains a magnificent series of eight Flemish Renaissance tapestries. Flemish tapestries were highly prized in the courts of Renaissance Europe, which is why today the best examples are found in such far-flung places as Prague and the Vatican. The eight tapestries here, together with another two which have been lost, were sold to Cardinal Lorenzo Cambeggi, who shipped them to his palace at Bologna. The series was recently repatriated and restored at the De Wit tapestry workshop in Mechelen.

Based on cartoons by Bernard van Orley, the tapestries were woven by Willem de Kempeneer in the 1530s. The letters B.B. in the margin signify that they were produced in Brussels, in the province of Brabant. The series illustrates the story of Jacob, who deceived his father into bestowing his fortune upon him rather than his brother Esau. As was customary in sixteenth-century art, the various scenes from Jacob's life are set in Flemish interiors. If we look at the tapestry illustrating Jacob's vision of a ladder ascending to heaven, we can see that the floor tiles are decorated with the Hapsburg double eagle.

The Neo-Gothic cloisters beyond the hall of tapestries contain several interesting tombs of mediaeval knights and abbesses. There are also curious fragments of stained glass from Brussels Cathedral, showing human faces and angels. The rooms beyond contain several large retables, such as the *St Joristafel* from Leuven, which depicts an unpleasant catalogue of cruelties, and the more appealing *Retable of Claude de Villa and Gentine Solaro*, dating from 1470.

The **Musée Royal de l'Armée et d'Histoire Militaire** (Royal Army and Military History Museum), which shares the 1880 north wing with a museum of space exploration, is another interesting and somewhat forgotten museum. I suggest that we begin in the Salle des Provinces Réunies, an attractively modernised wing filled with the arms and armour borne by the many armies to have marched across Belgium. We see the curious cannon that pounded Flemish cities in the fifteenth century, as well as dented Spanish armour of the sixteenth century and stained coats worn during the Thirty Years War. We can also admire the horses, now carefully preserved, on which the Archduke Albert and Archduchess Isabella made a triumphal entry into Brussels in 1599.

The other departments of this museum, though antiquated and unbelievably cluttered, are fascinating to explore. Some cabinets in the entrance hall contain objects found on the battlefield of Waterloo, including rusted horseshoes, Prussian sabres, coins, buttons, guns and a portrait of an unidentified soldier. Perhaps the most interesting relic is Napoleon's satchel, or at least what remained of it after a fire in Madame Tussaud's in London, where it was on display. The satchel was discovered by Prussian soldiers in Napoleon's carriage, along with his hat and sword. Another interesting memento of the battle is a fragment of shrapnel that served Victor Hugo as a macabre paperweight.

The one-day Battle of Waterloo in 1815, at which some 40,000 soldiers died, seized the imagination of all Europe. To novelists, the battle provided an irresistible backdrop, with episodes of heroism and tragedy to satisfy the most demanding of romantic readers. In 1816, when the battlefield was still littered with boots, buttons and bullets, Lord Byron was taken there by Major Lockhart Gordon. After casting an approving eye over the scene, Byron 'galloped across the fields of Waterloo', the Major recalled, 'cloak flying out behind, eyes fixed ahead.' On returning to his lodgings at 51 Rue Ducale, opposite the Parc de Bruxelles, Byron drafted several stanzas on the battle to incorporate into *Childe Harold*. His poem *The Eve of Waterloo* vividly captures the excitment in Brussels: 'There was a sound of revelry by night,/And Belgium's Capital had gathered then/Her beauty and her Chivalry.' The novelist Thackeray also penned a marvellous description of the battle in *Vanity Fair*, based on a military description of the battle. Waterloo also features in several French classics such as Victor Hugo's *Les Misérables*, part of which he wrote while staying at the Hôtel des Colonnes in the village of Mont St Jean, the site of the British field hospital. Stendhal's *Charterhouse of Parma* also includes a Waterloo episode, which magnificently captures the confusion of battle.

The romantic obsession with Waterloo was not confined to novelists, for Britain is dotted with obelisks and other miscellaneous monuments to the battle. A peculiar practice of the day was for landowners to lay out plantations of trees to represent the formation of their regiment on the eve of the battle. There is one at Peniel Heugh in Roxburghshire and another near Hadnall in Shropshire.

Unfortunately, the battlefield itself has lost much of its romance. Surrounded now by souvenir shops and coaches, we are very unlikely to sense 'horror breathing from the silent ground', as Wordsworth did on his pilgrimage there in 1820. It is perhaps better therefore to give the battlefield a miss, and to let the relics here evoke the events of that decisive day in European history.

After passing through a long gallery crammed with nineteenth-century uniforms, medals and other military memorabilia, including Léopold II's tricycle, we enter the largest room in the museum, devoted to World War I. No attempt has been made here either to glorify or to condemn this horrendous war; the museum has merely assembled an extraordinary diversity of exhibits, including machine guns, howitzers, tanks, uniforms, torn stretchers, first aid kits, maps, fragments of crashed aircraft, wreckage from sunken ships, and innumerable other relics of the war. Were these objects displayed in a modern museum with well-lit display cabinets and informative labelling, we would feel securely distant from the war, I think, but the nonchalant disarray we see here creates a vivid immediacy, as if all these things were only recently dredged from the mud of Flanders.

The vast L-shaped hall is divided into a German wing and an Allied wing, so that we obtain a unique impression of the war from both sides of the front. We see, for example, a touching photograph of a German brass band playing in some empty field in deep snow, a British recruiting poster that asks 'Are you fond of horses? Then join the cavalry,' and an Italian gun with the name *Gigolette* painted on the barrel. We also obtain an impression of the war from the angle of occupied Belgium. In one photograph a peasant family has been stopped at a German frontier post somewhere near the front; in another some German bakers are posing outside a Belgian shop, where a sign inscribed 'Deutsche Feinbäckerei' partly covers the word 'Pâtisserie'. All these relics have quite a different impact, I think, from the souvenirs dug up in the fields around Waterloo; the sabres and pistols wielded in 1815 have a decidedly romantic aura, whereas the gas masks and machine guns of a century later possess a grim and haunting realism. It seems most unlikely that any aristocrat in 1918 would have thought of planting a row of trees on his estate to mark the position of his regiment on the eve of the First Battle of Ypres.

After exploring this museum, we leave the park on the south side and turn left along the Avenue des Nerviens, pausing at Rue des Francs to admire the **Maison Cauchie** at number 5, built by Paul Cauchie in 1904 as his home and studio. The business sign by the door gave callers an indication of Cauchie's skills, as did the sgraffito murals, which are designed in a willowy Pre-Raphaelite style. The oval studio window which pierces this Art Nouveau composition looks as if it may have been inspired by the marvellous Maison de Saint-Cyr at 11 Square Ambiorix, but the rest of the façade seems more like early Art Deco.

If we continue along the Avenue des Gaulois, we reach the busy Porte de Tervuren. The most cosmopolitan café hereabouts is La Terrace at 11 Avenue de Tervuren, where we can settle into fabulously plump sofas in Art Nouveau partitioned compartments. Alternatively, we might stroll down Avenue de Tervuren to the elegant tea room adjoining René Marchal's pâtisserie at number 107.

II. Museums in Ixelles

The *commune* of Ixelles contains two curious and captivating museums that are worth exploring if we find ourselves with an afternoon to spare. The **Musée d'Ixelles** at 71 Rue Jean van Volsem, founded in 1892, boasts a splendid and varied collection of paintings and sculpture, from a sixteenth-century drawing by Dürer to various contemporary Belgian works. Several rooms contain paintings by French Impressionists, including an extensive collection of Toulouse Lautrec posters. The emphasis is mainly on modern Belgian paintings, however, and there are marvellous surrealist works by Magritte and Delvaux. *The Dialogue*, painted by Delvaux in 1974, illustrates the serene style of his later years; it shows two nude women in a mysterious setting that suggests an unbuilt classical city. One of the most enjoyable works in the collection is Philippe Vindal's piece *The Brothel* in room 11, a precisely detailed model of a derelict house used as a brothel, crammed with an extraordinary miscellany of domestic rubbish.

Ixelles' other museum is the secluded **Musée Wiertz** where, as an art student, Delvaux discovered the strange nude studies of Antoine Wiertz such as *La Belle Rosine*, a voluptuous Rubensian woman confronting her own skeleton. The Ostend painter James Ensor was also drawn to this haunting art collection at 62 Rue Vautier.

In a leafy setting at the top of a hill, the Musée Wiertz looks almost like an artist's villa in Rome.

This is quite fitting, for Antoine Wiertz, like his hero Rubens, had spent some years in Rome, and retained a fond attachment to Italy and its art. Three small rooms of the house contain numerous delightful little studies by Wiertz of festive Italian scenes. But the paintings that prompted Thomas Hardy to write in *Tess of the d'Urbervilles* of 'the staring and ghastly attitudes of a Wiertz Museum' are found in the huge atelier adjoining the house. On the back of the atelier door is written a definition of modesty as 'a mask that flatters the vanity of others to draw praise to oneself'. Antoine Wiertz certainly could not be accused of modesty, for his works are among the largest ever painted. The *Revolt of Heaven Against Hell*, the largest work in the museum, is 11.5 metres high and 7.9 metres wide! The canvas has been tilted forward to improve visibility, and the cleaning staff, somewhat irreverently, have used the space behind to store their mops and brooms.

The Musée Wiertz is perhaps not a museum for a dark winter's day, for many of the paintings are deeply pessimistic, such as *The Suicide*, which captures the terrible moment when a man, with a book named *Matérialisme* lying on the table, blows out his brains. Another gruesome work titled *Premature Burial* depicts a man's blind panic as he tries to escape from a coffin.

Now considered only a minor artist, Antoine Wiertz was immensely popular in mid-nineteenth-century Belgium. He even managed to solve the obviously difficult problem of storing and selling his giant works by concluding an agreement with the government of Belgium in 1850. The government agreed to build this house and studio for Wiertz on condition that the building became a state museum when he died. Under the terms of this peculiar agreement, all the paintings that he completed after 1850 became the property of the state. The house has changed very little since then, and the studio is still lit by natural light. One intriguing feature described in Baedeker's 1905 guide has unfortunately disappeared: 'In the corners of the room are wooden screens, through peep-holes in which paintings hung behind them are seen. The effect is curiously realistic.'

Not far from the Musée Wiertz is the **Parc Léopold**, a romantic nineteenth-century retreat dotted with interesting old buildings. Another more extensive park in Ixelles is the **Bois de la Cambre**. 'The alleys of this park are thronged with fashionable equipages,' Karl Baedeker informed his readers in 1905. Now they are thronged with fancy dogs and red-faced joggers, but it is still a very pleasant place for wandering on a Sunday afternoon. Once part of the Forêt de Soignes, the Bois de la Cambre was imaginatively landscaped in the nineteenth century. Its most beguiling feature is an artificial lake with an island, which can be reached by rowing boat or by a quaint mechanical ferry. The restaurant Chalet Robinson is, as its name betrays, situated on the island, and on summer days its tables are invitingly spread out beneath the trees.

Lying in a hollow to the north of the Bois de la Cambre is the attractive **Abbaye de la Cambre**, a Cistercian abbey founded in the twelfth century in what was then an idyllic river valley in the Forêt de Soignes. Most of the abbey was rebuilt in the eighteenth century in Baroque style, but the attractive fourteenth-century church still survives.

III. Art Nouveau architecture

The nervous and flowing style of Art Nouveau, inspired by the sinuous lines of flowers and trees, originated in Britain in the 1880s, but it flourished particularly in the great Continental cities of Paris, Vienna, Brussels and Barcelona. The finest Art Nouveau buildings in Brussels were built at the turn of the nineteenth century by Victor Horta, who once confessed that 'the warmth of stone has made my happiness'. Tragically, many of his buildings have been demolished, but one has been preserved as a museum: the **Musée Horta** at 23-5 Rue Américaine, which can be reached by taking tram 18, 81 or 92 to Place Janson. The house, which was Horta's home and studio from 1898 to 1919, contains a wealth of delightful Art Nouveau details, such as the magnificent staircase which ascends through the interior like an exotic tropical plant, with its polished wooden banisters tightly intertwined like creepers. In the attic, an extraordinary illusion of infinite space is created by means of mirrors. Notice also the radiator cleverly concealed behind a sofa on the staircase.

Despite exuding a warmth and exhilarating beauty, the Horta family home was not entirely harmonious, for Madame Horta was uninterested in Art Nouveau and treated Horta's architectural associates coldly. In 1919 Horta sold the house and atelier because he needed more space to work on the large-scale projects that were then coming his way. The departure from this house effectively marked the end of Art Nouveau and a shift to a rather chilling Art Deco style, as evidenced by Brussels' Gare Centrale and Palais des Beaux-Arts.

There are a number of attractive Art Nouveau houses in the neighbourhood, including one, the **Hôtel Hannon** at 1 Avenue de la Jonction, which is now occupied by the Contretype photography gallery. It was designed in 1903 by Jules Brunfaut, a student of Victor Horta, for Edouard Hannon. He was employed as an engineer by the Belgian industrialist Ernest Solvay, for whom Horta designed a house at 224 Avenue Louise. As well as holding temporary exhibitions of contemporary photography, the gallery houses a small collection of early twentieth-century photographs taken by Hannon on his travels.

A house at 85 Rue Faider has splendid, if faded, frescoes featuring languid Pre-Raphaelite women. It faces down Rue Paul Emile Janson, where Horta built his first Art Nouveau house—the Hôtel Tassel—in 1893. At 48 Rue Defacqz is another attractive Art Nouveau house built in 1897 by Paul Hankar for the symbolist painter Albert Ciamberlani. Its decorated frieze is sadly too far gone for us to make out what it is about.

The big round windows of Ciamberlani's studio face down Rue Veydt, where an Art Nouveau building at number 13 is occupied by a delightfully whimsical café-restaurant, Amadeus. After passing through a courtyard painted deep blue and decorated with a miscellany of sculptural fragments, we penetrate the café's dark interior. Surrounded on all sides by curious details such as Classical sculptures and a mysterious illuminated row of miniature houses, we can sample delicious coffee, served with a *spekulaus* biscuit and a small chocolate.

Perhaps the most spectacular Art Nouveau restaurant in Brussels is **De Ultieme Hallucinatie** (The Ultimate Hallucination), concealed behind a rather drab nineteenth-century façade at 316 Rue Royale (reached by taking tram 92, 93, 94 or 62 to Ste Marie). Paul Hamesse—a pupil of Paul Hankar—remodelled the interior of this mid-nineteenth-century town house in 1904. The Dutch name of the restaurant alludes to the dream-like mood of the interior, with its painstakingly restored murals and gleaming brass fittings. Perched upon third-class Belgian railway carriage seats in a winter garden filled with ferns and statuary, we can eat a simple omelette or a *plat du jour*. Alternatively, we can eat a full dinner in the beautiful former dining room.

On the same street, the **Maison Isabelle de Backer** at 13 Rue Royale is a beautiful Art Nouveau florist's shop designed by Paul Hankar in 1899. Its carved mahogany frontage seems as delicate as the tendrils of the exotic orchids displayed within.

Situated in the Lower Town opposite the Bourse, **Le Falstaff**, at 17-23 Rue Henri Maus, is a beautiful Art Nouveau café designed in 1903 by E. Houbion, one of the architects who worked in Victor Horta's studio. Its large round windows are a familiar motif of Belgian Art Nouveau, although some of the other features such as the signs outside seem more in the geometrical style of Art Deco, and the woodwork and stained-glass windows inside look rather more like lingering Victorian eclecticism. What makes Falstaff Brussels' most popular café is not merely its interior design, however, but also its excellent menu, good selection of beers and virtual 24-hour service.

IV. Laeken

To the north of Brussels, on the heights of Laeken, we find a curious ensemble of buildings from the reign of Léopold II. Taking tram 52 from De Brouckère to the stop named Araucaria, we see a remarkable **Japanese pagoda** looming above the trees. We then ascend by the road to look more closely at this intriguing and exotic building, purchased by Léopold II at the 1900 Paris Exhibition. Now situated in the grounds of the royal park, it is sadly not open to the public. We can, however, enter the beautiful **Pavillon Chinois**, a short walk up the hill. Richly decorated with exquisite carved details, this magnificent building was also acquired by Léopold at the Paris Exhibition, and its Rococo interior now provides a dazzling setting for a large collection of Chinese porcelain.

The Chinese pavilion is now unfortunately surrounded by a tangle of busy roads. Watching the international trucks rumble by, we can meditate on the disadvantages which stem from being 'the crossroads of Europe', as Brussels is often dubbed. The ornate fountain marooned on a traffic island is a copy of a famous sixteenth-century fountain in Bologna's Piazza del Nettuno, which was designed by the Flemish sculptor Jan van Bologna. On reaching the far side of the road, we turn right and skirt the edge of the **Park de Laeken** to reach the entrance. Once in the park, we will see, crowning a summit on the left, a Neo-Gothic monument erected to Léopold I in 1881. From there we can look down upon the eighteenth-century **Palais Royal**, where Napoleon signed the fateful order in 1812 that sent his armies into Russia.

No directions are needed to reach our next destination, the **Atomium**, whose ghostly aluminium spheres loom above the trees. This strange memento of the 1958 World Fair is very much a creation of the 1950s, standing in the middle of a traffic roundabout like a space craft in a boys' comic. Representing the nine atoms of an iron crystal, the Atomium rises to a height of 120 metres and dominates the northern skyline of Brussels, especially at night when its nine spheres are picked out with lights. A high-speed lift takes us up to the topmost sphere, where we can enjoy a panoramic view of Brussels, although skyscrapers tend to blot out the older and more interesting buildings. We then descend through various other spheres by very long escalators, or staircases located in the tubular arms linking the spheres. It may sound exciting, but in fact the building is rather decrepit and cold, while the exhibitions (dealing with subjects such as atomic energy) seem very dated. Like much futuristic architecture, the Atomium has rapidly become old-fashioned, so that a visit here now tells us more about our past than our future. I should perhaps add that at the time of writing plans were announced to restore and revitalise the building, so that it may soon be this book, rather than the Atomium, that is out of date.

The main building we see from the observation deck of the Atomium is the Art Deco **Palais du Centenaire**, built in 1930 for the centenary celebrations of the founding of the Belgian state, and now part of a sprawling exhibition centre. To the left is the Bruparck, which was still unfinished at the time of writing. It will eventually include a sophisticated swimming pool, a 23-screen cinema complex, and a park laid out with several hundred scale models of European buildings. There will also be various restaurants, cafés and taverns situated in mock old Flemish houses, similar to those built for the 1958 World Fair.

The metro takes us straight back to the centre, but if we still have time to spare we might visit one more curiosity. Taking tram 81 to Royauté, then turning left along Rue du Champ de l'Eglise, we come upon a huge Neo-Gothic church bristling pinnacles, **Notre-Dame de Laeken**, where the Belgian kings and queens are buried. We should not worry too much if the church is closed, as it is the exterior which is striking, especially when seen from the cemetery behind.

The cemetery contains an extraordinary collection of nineteenth-century tombs of eminent Belgians. As well as Neo-Gothic and Neoclassical monuments, there are several eccentric monuments here, including a mosque, an Egyptian temple and the tomb of a general symbolically decorated with a shattered cannon. The most famous Belgian buried here is the architect Joseph Poelaert, who designed Notre-Dame de Laeken in 1870. His face betrays the exhaustion he suffered from as he struggled to complete the Palais de Justice. Tucked away in a corner of the cemetery is a fragment from a thirteenth-century church built of an attractive honey-coloured stone. Old Baedeker guides also refer to underground catacombs, but these I am unable to locate. Once we have explored this fascinating cemetery, we take tram 81 back to Bourse.

V. Tervuren and the Forêt de Soignes

One of the most beguiling excursions from Brussels is by tram 44 to the Flemish village of Tervuren. We can easily do this trip in a half day, but if the weather is pleasant then it is worth devoting a whole day to the expedition. We can then have lunch in one of the restaurants in Tervuren and spend the afternoon walking in the beautiful woods nearby.

We first take the metro to Montgomery station, where tram 44 begins its 20-minute journey to Tervuren. The tram returns to street level on the elegant Avenue de Tervuren, which Léopold II built to connect the Parc du Cinquantenaire with the village of Tervuren. Just beyond the stop Père Damien, look out on the right for the splendid **Palais Stocklet**, designed by the Austrian architect Josef Hoffman in 1905 for the rich Belgian industrialist Mons Stocklet. The pure geometric lines of this building illustrate the principles of the Wiener Werkstätte, which Hoffman founded with Koloman Moser in 1903. The battle-cry of this movement clearly implied a rejection of Art Nouveau aesthetics. 'We will use ornament where appropriate,' they declared, 'but without compulsion and not just for its own sake.' As we can see in the photograph (pl. 35), even the trees in front of the Palais Stocklet have been trimmed into neat geometric shapes. The interior contains some murals by Gustav Klimt but, to the chagrin of enthusiasts of the Vienna style, the house remains firmly closed to the public.

Tram 44 then rumbles on past the gently rolling **Parc de Woluwe**. If we are tempted to stretch our legs in this attractive park, we should leave at a stop curiously named Chien Vert. However, Tervuren offers even better walks, so perhaps we should leave Woluwe's park to another day.

Soon we leave the city behind and plunge into the **Forêt de Soignes**, a wonderfully wild forest of oak and beech which stretches in a wide sweep around the southern edge of Brussels from Tervuren to Waterloo. One of the delights of Brussels, especially on a crisp autumn day, is to head

Plate 35 Palais Stocklet

off into the wilderness of the Forêt de Soignes, all that remains of the great forest which once covered most of present-day Belgium. Known to the Romans as the Sylva Carbonaria, the Charcoal Forest, it still contains a few charcoal kilns which the Romans worked.

The forest was dotted with monasteries in the Middle Ages, with some seven religious orders seeking solitude in the depths of these woods. At **Groenendael**, to the south of Brussels, the fourteenth-century mystic Jan van Ruysbroeck founded an Augustinian abbey, where he wrote most of his religious works. Cloître Rouge, also in the forest, was the priory into which the painter Hugo van der Goes retreated in about 1475. Here he completed several major works, including the *Death of the Virgin*, now in the Groeninge museum in Bruges. In the sixteenth century, the forest was a favourite hunting ground of Charles V; many Flemish tapestries of the period, including one in Brussels' Musée Communal, depicted hunting scenes in the Forêt de Soignes.

On arriving at Tervuren's delightfully rural station, where the tram terminates, we simply walk straight ahead down Leuvensteenweg (the street names here revert to Flemish, for we have left the bilingual enclave of Brussels). Our destination is the **Musée Royal d'Afrique Centrale** (Royal Museum of Central Africa) on the right-hand side of the road.

The quiet village of Tervuren seems an unlikely setting for this museum, which was erected on the site of the Château de Tervuren. The old castle was destroyed by fire in 1879, at which time it was the home of Léopold II's sister, the unfortunate Charlotte. She had moved here in 1867, following the execution of her husband, the Emperor Maximilian of Mexico, whose death is movingly depicted in the famous painting by Manet in the Städtische Kunsthalle in Mannheim. The loss of her husband left Charlotte deranged for the rest of her life.

After moving his unhappy sister to another royal castle, Léopold used what remained of the Château de Tervuren to house a collection of booty brought back from his private colony in the Congo. The present building was begun in 1904 by Charles Girault, the architect of the Petit Palais in

Paris, but it was not completed until after Léopold's death.

Léopold stressed that his interest in the Congo was purely philanthropic, but many saw the venture as a brutal quest for profit. In an unusually vicious outburst, Mark Twain wrote that 'In fourteen years, Léopold has deliberately destroyed more lives than have suffered death in all the battlefields of this planet for the past thousand years.' And if this was not indictment enough, Joseph Conrad's chilling novel *Heart of Darkness* was based on his experiences in the course of a horrifying journey through the Congo in 1890.

The museum contains a rich and exotic collection of masks and sculpture, together with plants, animals and even insects brought back from Central Africa. Yet I think the most interesting rooms are those devoted to European explorers in Central Africa. There are several relics of the American journalist, Henry Morton Stanley, who was employed by Léopold to explore the Congo. Look out for the battered old suitcase taken by Stanley on his African journeys, which still has a label attached to it by his wife Dolly, declaring imperiously, 'This Portmanteau belonged to H.M. Stanley. It was carried across Africa. It must never be removed from my Room and *never* on any account be used.' Equally unexpected are the objects connected with Dr Livingstone. We see the metal travelling case which the Scottish explorer took on his final, sad journey, and also a handful of dry leaves plucked by a devoted admirer from the tree beneath which his heart was buried. Another traveller removed part of the tree's trunk and preserved it like the relic of a mediaeval saint, prompting one to wonder what, if anything, remains of the mpundu tree in Chitambo, Zambia, where Dr Livingstone's heart was laid to rest in 1873.

This room also contains several marvellous old maps of Central Africa, including one from Ortelius' *Theatrum orbis terrarum*, published in 1612. It is interesting to compare this with a British map published by John Cary in 1821, which marks a large blank area in the centre of Africa as 'Unknown Parts', even though these had been charted in great detail by Ortelius over two centuries earlier.

VI. Anderlecht

Our final trip takes us west to Anderlecht, a former village which was swallowed up by the expansion of Brussels in the nineteenth century. Anderlecht has an interesting Late Gothic church and a small Begijnhof, but the main reason for visiting this *commune* is the **Maison d'Erasme** at 31 Rue du Chapitre. To reach this house (which is closed on Tuesdays and Fridays) we should take metro line 1A to St Guidon, then make for the spire of the church, near which is the house we are looking for.

Maison d'Erasme is a somewhat misleading name, for it was in fact the chapter house of the nearby Eglise St Guidon. Erasmus stayed here for a mere five months in the summer of 1521 as the guest of his friend Pieter Wychman, a canon in St Guidon. Yet the house has become something of a shrine to Erasmus, prompted by a visit here in 1691 by William III, the Stadholder-King of the Netherlands, accompanied by the Dutch diplomat Constantijn Huygens. In 1930 the house was purchased by the local council and opened as a museum.

Most of the building dates from 1515, as the four iron numerals attached to a wall reveal, although we enter by a small building erected in the fifteenth century. Tastefully restored in the style of the early sixteenth century, the Erasmus House is furnished with heavy oak chests, apothecaries' vases and paintings in that strange, somewhat disturbing style of the Antwerp Mannerists. There is also an *Adoration of the Magi* painted in about 1485 by Hieronymus Bosch (number 236), which once hung in St Guidon.

The museum displays an extensive collection of portraits of Erasmus; many are facsimile copies of sixteenth-century works by artists such as Holbein and Metsys, but there are also less well-known paintings by nineteenth-century romantics, and twentieth-century ephemera, such as banknotes, theatre posters and caricatures featuring Erasmus. His portrait even appears on an L.N.E.R. poster advertising railway excursions to Cambridge, where Erasmus spent some unhappy months teaching theology and Greek. More surprising still, we see the figure of Erasmus at the far right of a painting of *The Judgement of Solomon* by Frans Francken the Younger (number 258).

Erasmus relished having his portrait painted by the great artists of the day, and was clearly piqued when Albrecht Dürer abandoned a portrait begun in 1520. 'I would like to have my portrait painted by Dürer,' he wrote to Willibald Pirckheimer in 1525, 'for who would not wish to be painted by such a great artist . . . He began by making a charcoal sketch in Brussels, but he claims to have lost it long ago.' Dürer and Erasmus met several times in Brussels and Antwerp in 1520 and 1521, but their opposing attitudes to the vexing question of Luther appear to have soured their relationship. Dürer's diary entry of 17 May 1521 included a hysterical outburst against Erasmus: 'O Erasmus of Rotterdam, where do you wish to stand?' he asked in strongly Lutheran language. 'Hark, ye knight of Christ, ride off with Christ our Lord at your side, defend the truth, grasp the martyr's palm.' Erasmus, however, remained rather more level-headed about the claims of Lutheranism, writing in a letter to Ulrich von Hutten: 'If Christ were to grant me the strength, then I would elect to be a martyr, but I would not want to be a martyr for Luther.'

Despite their differences, Dürer eventually produced a portrait of Erasmus in 1526, apparently using the sketch which he once claimed to have lost. The woodcut portrait (number 123 in the collection) now hangs in the study—a fastidious reconstruction of the room depicted by Dürer. The woodcut shows Erasmus sitting at his desk in winter, wearing three coats on top of one another, a hat pulled down over his ears, and an ink bottle held in his left hand to prevent the contents from freezing. Dürer seems to have had some misgivings about this portrait, for he included an apologetic inscription in Greek: 'His works provide a better impression.' He also added—this time in Latin—the untruthful assertion: 'Painted from nature'. Erasmus, too, was unimpressed with the final result, commenting laconically, 'Resemblance: none'. In a letter to Pirckheimer, he grumbled, 'It is hardly surprising that the portrait is not a better likeness, since I am not the same person that I was five years ago.'

After exploring the garden, in which are a few fragments of local architecture, we have seen almost all that Anderlecht has to offer. The cafés hereabouts are disappointing; despite its name, the Darts Club Erasme opposite the museum does not look as if it seriously intends to tempt passing Erasmians within. Signposts behind the church may persuade us to explore Anderlecht's **Béguinage**, but this, too, is rather disappointing, apart from the striking view from its courtyard of the nineteenth-century spire of St Guidon. As for the church, its main attraction would appear to be the eleventh-century tomb of St Guidon, who is revered locally as the patron saint of horses and cattle. Unfortunately, the church, which is sadly dilapidated, is seldom open, so we have little prospect of examining the tomb of St Guidon, or the fifteenth-century murals depicting the deeds for which he earned his renown.

The perfect café to conclude a visit to Brussels is situated opposite the Bourse. **Café Cirio** at 18 Rue de la Bourse opened its doors in 1886, four years before the explorer Henry Morton Stanley made a rousing speech in the Bourse in praise of Léopold II's development of the Congo. Cirio's interior rather recalls Georges Simenon's description of a Brussels café: 'It was as restful as a warm bath, this huge room hazy with smoke, full of the fumes of coffee and beer, where the chink of plates and glasses blended with the languorous strains of a Viennese waltz.' My favourite corner in Cirio is the back room, with its gleaming brass and its ancient glass cabinets filled with faded family photographs. It seems far removed from the world outside, as do the elderly ladies who quietly tipple Cirio's Italian white wine in the afternoon. The only complaint one might have is that the antiquated coin-operated eau-de-cologne dispensers in the toilets have long since ceased to function.

Appendix I: Choosing a Hotel

Bruges

Bruges is undoubtedly the most attractive Flemish city in which to base ourselves, and there is no shortage of delightful hotels, many of which are situated in old brick Gothic houses with attractive canal views. All the sights are within walking distance of the hotels, making it quite unnecessary ever to use a car or public transport. The hotels close to the centre tend to be rather more expensive and luxurious. Perhaps the most splendid of these is the **Orangerie** (telephone 050-341649), at Kartuizerinnestraat 10, situated in a restored sixteenth-century house just behind the belfry, with views of a pretty canal. **Die Swaene** (telephone 050-342798), at Steenhouwersdijk 1, is another elegant and tasteful hotel near the Burg, occupying a historic canalside house dating from the fifteenth century, with Romanesque cellars that go back to the twelfth century. The nearby **Pand Hotel** (telephone 050-340666), at Pandreitje 16, which is slightly less expensive, is a friendly and attractively furnished hotel.

Many cheaper, but still attractive hotels are situated in the interesting former mercantile quarter to the north of Markt. **Ter Brughe** (telephone 050-340324), at Oost-Gisthelhof 2, is a friendly hotel beautifully situated in two typical fifteenth-century Gothic brick houses overlooking a wistful canal. The **Europ** (telephone 050-337975), at Augustijnenrei 18, is another comfortable hotel on this same lovely canal. Three reliable and inexpensive hotels overlook the quiet St Gilliskerk: **De Pauw** (telephone 050-337118), at St Gilliskerkhof 8, **Jacobs** (telephone 050-339831), at Baliestraat 1, and **Fevery** (telephone 050-331269), at Collaert Mansionstraat 3. The small hotel **Egmond** (telephone 050-341445), at Minnewater 15, is picturesquely located in a leafy setting close to the Begijnhof, and is conveniently close to the railway station.

Ghent

Ghent's most interesting hotel is the **St Jorishof** (telephone 091-242424), at Botermarkt 2, which claims to be the oldest hotel in Europe. Situated in a historic fifteenth-century building, it is ideally situated for exploring the sights of Ghent. The **Gravensteen** (telephone 091-251150) is an elegant hotel occupying a nineteenth-century town house close to Ghent's castle. **Novotel** (telephone 091-242230), at Goudenleeuwplein 5, and **Ibis** (telephone 091-330000), at Limburgstraat 2, are attractively designed modern hotels, well situated near the cathedral.

Antwerp

Antwerp, rather surprisingly, has few hotels of any character. None of the grand *Belle Epoque* hotels listed in Baedeker's 1905 guide have survived. My only recommendation is the **Waldorf** (telephone 03-2309950) at Belgielei 36, an attractive modern hotel on a broad boulevard near the Stadspark.

Brussels

Brussels has a good selection of hotels in all price categories. The **Métropole** (telephone 02-2172300), at 31 Place de Brouckère, is a grand nineteenth-century hotel designed by Alban Chambon, ideally located for exploring the Lower Town. The **Astoria** (telephone 02-2176290), at 103 Rue Royale, is also splendid, but not so well situated. Less expensive, but still elegant, the **Palace** (telephone 02-2176200), at 3 Rue Gineste, was designed in 1910 by Alban Chambon in a dazzling Art Deco style. **De Boeck's** (telephone 02-5374033), at 40 Rue Veydt, is a friendly, inexpensive hotel, with tastefully furnished rooms. Situated just off Avenue Louise, it is ideal for visiting the Musée Horta and exploring the Art Nouveau architecture of southern Brussels.

Appendix II: Opening Times of Museums and Art Galleries

Bruges

Heilig Bloed Basiliek: October-March, Thursday-Tuesday 10am-noon and 2pm-4pm, April-September, 9.30am-noon and 2pm-6pm.

Stadhuis: October-March, daily 9.20am-noon and 2pm-5pm, April-September, daily 9.30-noon and 2pm-6pm.

Museum van het Brugse Vrije: April-September, Tuesday-Sunday 10am-noon and 1.30pm-5pm, October-March, Saturday and Sunday 2pm-4pm.

Groeningemuseum: April-September, daily 9.30am-6pm, October-March, Wednesday-Monday 9.30am-noon and 2pm-5pm.

Memlingmuseum: April-September, daily 9am-12.30 and 2pm-6pm, October-March, Thursday-Tuesday 10am-noon and 2pm-5pm.

Gruuthusemuseum, **Brangwynmuseum**: April-September, 9.30am-noon and 2pm-6pm, October-March, Wednesday-Monday 9.30am-noon and 2pm-5 pm.

Onze-Lieve-Vrouwekerk mausoleums: April-September Monday-Saturday 10am-11.30am and 2.30pm-5pm, Sunday 2.30pm-5pm, October-March Monday-Saturday 10am-11.30am and 3pm-4.30pm, Sunday 2.30pm-4.30pm.

St Salvatorskathedraal Museum: Monday, Tuesday, Thursday, Friday, Saturday 2pm-5pm; in July and August Monday, Tuesday, Thursday, Friday 10am-11.30am and Sunday 2pm-5pm.

Belfry: April-September, daily 9.30-12.30pm and 1.30pm-6pm, October-March, daily 9.30am-12.30pm and 2pm-5pm; carillon concerts at the belfry: mid-June-mid-September, Monday, Wednesday and Saturday 9pm-10pm, Sunday 2.15-3pm, mid-September-mid-June, Sunday, Wednesday and Saturday 2.15-3pm.

Ghent

Museum voor Schone Kunsten, **Bijlokemuseum**, **Museum voor Sierkunst**, **Museum voor Stenen Voorwerpen**: Tuesday-Sunday 9am-12.15pm and 1.30pm-5.15pm.

St Baafskathedraal: April-September, Monday-Saturday 9am-noon and 1.30pm-5pm, Sunday 1.30pm-5pm, October-March, Monday-Saturday 10.30am-noon and 2.30pm-4pm, Sunday 2pm-5pm.

's-Gravensteen: daily 9am-5.15pm.

Museum voor Volkskunde: April-October, 9am-12.30pm and 1.30pm-5.30pm, November-March, Tuesday-Sunday 10am-noon and 1.30pm-5pm.

St Nicolaaskerk: Monday-Friday 2pm-5pm, Saturday and Sunday 10am-noon and 2pm-6pm.

Antwerp

Rubenshuis, **Museum Plantin-Moretus**, **Nationaal Scheepvaartmuseum**, **International Cultural Centre**: daily, 10am-5pm.

Museum Mayer van den Bergh, **Koninklijke Museum voor Schone Kunsten**, **Museum voor Fotografie**, **Museum van Hedendaagse Kunst Antwerpen**, **Vleeshuis**, **Rockoxhuis**, **Hessenhuis**, **Brouwershuis**: Tuesday-Sunday 10am-5pm.

Onze-Lieve-Vrouwekathedraal: Monday-Friday noon-5pm, Saturday noon-3pm, Sunday 1pm-4pm; carillon concerts: every Friday at 11.30am-12.30am, also mid-June-mid-September, Mondays at 9pm-10pm.

St Jacobskerk: Monday-Saturday 10am-noon and 2pm-5pm.

St Carolus Borromeuskerk: guided tours on Wednesday at 2pm and 3pm and Friday at 5pm.

Bourgondische Kapel: Tuesday, Thursday and Saturday 2pm-4pm.

Mechelen

Hof van Busleyden: Tuesday-Saturday 10am-5pm;

Museum 'De Zalm': Saturday-Thursday 10am-noon and 2pm-5pm.

Brussels

Musée Communal: Monday-Friday 10am-5pm (October-March closes one hour earlier), Saturday and Sunday 10am-noon.

Musées Royaux des Beaux-Arts (comprising Musée d'Art Ancien & Musée d'Art Moderne), **Musée de la Maison de la Bellone**: Tuesday-Sunday 10am-noon and 2pm-5pm.

Musées Royaux d'Art et d'Histoire: Monday-Friday 9.30am-12.30pm and 1.30pm-4.45pm, Saturday and Sunday 10am-4.45pm (Departments of Ancient Egypt, Classical Greece & Rome open only on days with even dates; Departments of Islamic Art, Decorative Arts open only on days with odd dates).

Musée Horta: Tuesday-Sunday: 2pm-5.30pm.

Musée d'Ixelles: Tuesday-Friday 1pm-5pm, Saturday and Sunday 10am-5pm.

Musée Wiertz: Tuesday-Friday 10am-5pm (November-March closes one hour earlier).

Musée Royal de l'Armée et d'Histoire Militaire: Tuesday-Sunday 9am-noon and 1pm-4.45pm (closes one hour earlier in winter months).

Pavillon Chinois: Tuesday-Sunday 9.30am-noon and 1.30pm-4.50pm.

Atomium: daily 9.30am-6pm (mid-April-September panorama level open 6pm-10pm).

Maison d'Erasme: Saturday, Sunday, Monday, Wednesday and Thursday 10am-noon and 2pm-5pm.

Public Holidays

Museums and galleries are liable to close on 1 January, 1 May, 1 November, 11 November and 25 December.

Index

Main entries in italics